CORE CONCEPTS
IN
HEROISM SCIENCE

VOLUME TWO

First published 2020
by Palsgrove

Library of Congress Cataloging in Publication Data
Name: Allison, Scott T., Editor

Title: Core Concepts in Heroism Science, Volume 2
Edited by Scott T. Allison

Description: 1 Edition | Richmond: Palsgrove, 2020 | Includes bibliographical references
Identifiers: ISBN-9798650178880

ISBN: 9798650178880

COVER IMAGE: Illustration by Jamie Katz. Design by Dylan Vavra

P_G Palsgrove

CORE CONCEPTS

IN

HEROISM SCIENCE

VOLUME TWO

EDITED BY

SCOTT T. ALLISON
UNIVERSITY OF RICHMOND

PRAISE FOR CORE CONCEPTS IN HEROISM SCIENCE

"Meticulously researched, and a lively read, this book is a brilliant example of the meaningful and collaborative scholarship that emerges from the partnership between gifted students and their faculty mentors."

-- Dr. Ronald A. Crutcher, President, University of Richmond

"This book represents the ideal integration of teaching and scholarly work that is an exemplar of a University of Richmond education."

-- Dr. Jacquelyn S. Fetrow, Provost and Vice President of Academic Affairs, University of Richmond

"A extraordinary collection of readings that illuminate the origins of heroic action. Reading *Core Concepts in Heroism Science* gave me a fresh, bold appreciation of heroism science."

-- Dr. James K. Beggan, Professor of Sociology, University of Louisville

"*Core Concepts in Heroism Science* is an inspiring book about inspiring people. Heroes teach by the example of their lives and those lives are explored here in both personal detail and broad perspective. We are fortunate to have such a book."

-- Dr. Edward Ayers, Tucker-Boatwright Professor in the Humanities, President Emeritus, University of Richmond

"Scott Allison has succeeded in gathering an all-star team of student scholars who provide a masterful analysis of the central concepts of heroism. This is an inspired volume that forges new ground in enhancing our understanding of the best of human nature."

-- Dr. Robert A. Giacalone, Professor of Management, John Carroll University

CONTENTS

Acknowledgements

This book is the fifth in the Palsgrove series of student-authored books that my team and I have edited over the past several years. It was made possible by many sources of support from a number of generous individuals. Foremost, I thank my student-authors for their enthusiastic participation in this enterprise. These gifted young people have taught me much about heroism and they give me such nourishing hope for the future of humanity and for our planet.

This volume could not have been produced without the encouragement and support from several University of Richmond sources. My heartfelt thanks go out to Ronald Crutcher, President of the University of Richmond; Patrice Rankine, Dean of Arts & Sciences; and Cindy Bukach, Chair of the Psychology Department. These extraordinary individuals have provided the inspiration to continue this series of student-authored books on heroism.

I am also grateful to Greg Smith, my friend and colleague for the past 15 years. Greg's help with the technical aspects of publishing these books has been invaluable. Additional thanks go to Karyn Kuhn, one of the best academic administrators in the history of the University of Richmond. Whenever I need any kind of assistance, Karyn is always there with the perfect answer, always delivered with kindness and wisdom.

Perhaps the one person most responsible for my interest in heroism is my dear friend and colleague, Al Goethals. Al and I have been buddies and research collaborators since 1985. For almost 40 years, the two of us have enjoyed innumerable lunches and conversations about leadership and heroism. These chats are always a delight and have served as the genesis of our many co-authored books and articles. I owe a huge debt of gratitude to Al for his generous spirit and wisdom.

Finally, this work would never have happened without my loving wife and partner Connie Allison, who for reasons I'll never understand has tolerated me for many years. Connie's gentle demeanor, steadfast warmth, and sweet companionship have inspired and sustained me more than she'll ever know. Thank you, my dear Constance Rae.

INTRODUCTION

Unification at the Core of Heroism

SCOTT T. ALLISON

What lies at the core of heroism?

This book attempts to answer this daunting question. To understand the core of heroism – the forces underlying it – let's first examine what heroism is at its surface. On the outside, heroism is a behavior, or set of behaviors. These actions are directed toward helping others, and they go beyond expectation and are considered by most people to be extraordinary (Franco, Blau, & Zimbardo, 2011). In addition, heroism involves taking great risks and making exceptional sacrifices (Allison, Goethals, & Kramer, 2017). We observe these extreme helping behaviors and we admire them -- but where do these actions come from? What hidden, internal processes are at work and can explain why some people step up, take chances, and dare to do what most of us are unable to do? What lurks at the core of heroic action?

At its heart, out of sight but driving people's heroic behavior, lurks a heroic consciousness that "sees" the world through a broader, deeper, and enlightened lens. Heroic behavior is always a reflection of an expanded and mature consciousness. This highly developed consciousness lies at the core of heroism and makes extraordinarily positive, selfless, and inspirational behavior possible.

Let's be very clear: The idea that consciousness plays an important role in heroism is not new at all. For example, Joseph Campbell (1988) argued that the goal of the hero's journey in myth and literature is to bring about "a transformation of consciousness" in the hero (p. 155, italics added). Kinsella, Ritchie, and Igou (2017) argue that heroism heightens our conscious "awareness of ought selves and ideal selves" (p. 27). Heroism scientists have recently argued that the ultimate goal of heroic transformation is the attainment of a higher, or deeper, level of consciousness (Jones, 2019; Ross, 2019).

This type of "seeing" requires a fresh, heroic set of eyes, a new type of consciousness that involves viewing the world in a way that dares to deviate from our Western culture's emphasis on individualism, hyper-rationalism, and materialism. Ross (2019), for example, has conceptualized heroic transformation as the pathway to "higher or increased consciousness" (p. 5). A person with heroically transformed consciousness is "able to sense through division and experience the unity inherent in all, and will be able to unify perceptions and self" (p. 6).

FOUR SIGNS OF HEROIC CONSCIOUSNESS

From my review of the literature, I have identified four attributes of an individual who has experienced heroic consciousness. The four characteristics of the hero's consciousness include the tendency to show clarity and effectiveness in: (1) seeing the world from a nondualistic perspective; (2) processing transrational phenomena; (3) exhibiting a unitive consciousness; and (4) demonstrating the wisdom to know when to act heroically and when not to act when action would be harmful. Let's now examine each of these in turn.

1. Nondualistic Thinking

A central element of the hero's consciousness is the hero's use of the mental and spiritual approach to life known as nondualistic thinking (Jones, 2019; Loy, 1997; Rohr, 2009). Heroes are adept at both dualistic and nondualistic mental approaches. Heroes first master dualistic thinking, the ability to partition and label the world when necessary, and then they learn to go beyond this binary thinking by seeing a rich, nuanced reality that defies simple mental compartmentalizations. Cynthia Bourgeault (2013) describes this richer psychological mindset as third force thinking that transcends the rigid mindset of dualities. A third force solution to a problem is "an independent force, coequal with the other two, not a product of the first two as in the classic Hegelian thesis, antithesis, synthesis" (p. 26). Psychologists have known for a half-century that human cognition is characterized by a need to simplify and categorize stimuli (Fiske & Taylor, 2013). Because our lives include daily encounters with a range of phenomena that defy simple dualistic thinking, it is of crucial importance that we engage in third force approaches that access our deeper intuitions and artistic sensibilities. Third force solutions to problems are innovative and heroic solutions. In my view, it is crucial that we emphasize third force nondualistic thinking approaches in early education to help promote heroic mindsets in young children.

In contrast to dualistic thinking, nondualistic thinking resists a simple definition. It sees subtleties, exceptions, mystery, and a bigger picture. Nondualistic thinking refers to a broader, dynamic, imaginative, and more mature contemplation of perceived events (Rohr, 2009). A nondualistic approach to understanding reality is open and patient with mystery and ambiguity. Nondualistic thinkers see reality clearly because they do not allow their prior beliefs, expectations, and biases to affect their conscious perception of events and encounters with people. Abraham Heschel (1955) described it as the ability to let the world come at us rather than us come at the world with preconceived categories that can skew our perceptions. "Our goal should be to life live in radical amazement," wrote Heschel. "Wonder or radical amazement, the state of maladjustment to words and notions, is therefore a prerequisite for an authentic awareness of that which is" (p. 46-47, italics added).

Rohr (2009) describes nondualistic thinking as "calm, ego-less seeing" and "the ability to keep you heart and mind spaces open long enough to see other hidden material" (p. 33-34). According to Rohr, this type of insight occurs whenever "by some wondrous coincidence, our heart space and mind space, and our body awareness are all simultaneously open and nonresistant" (p. 28). Asian spiritual philosophies describe nondualistic seeing as the third eye, which is the enlightened ability to see the world with balance, wisdom, and clarity. Heroic protagonists in literature are often compelled to view the world at these deeper levels by traversing the hero's journey, which involves a descent into a desperately challenging and painful situation. During these darkest of times, heroes realize that their simple dualistic mindsets no longer work for them. The pre-heroic consciousness must be discarded, allowing heroes to achieve clarity and accumulate life-changing insights about themselves and the world (Allison & Goethals, 2014). We are all called to experience a transformative, expansive, nondualistic consciousness, and we usually get there through great love (Rohr, 2011) or great suffering (Allison & Setterberg, 2016). But not everyone gets there. Some remain sadly stuck at the level of dualistic consciousness. Dualistic thinkers have a split consciousness that contributes to perpetuating all the damaging "isms" of society – racism, sexism, classism, ageism, and nationalism, to name a few. Split people tend to split people.

I propose that dualistic thinking, the pre-heroic consciousness, is comprised of a two-step psychological process. First, people mentally divide the world into binary units, such as "us versus them", "true versus false", "big versus small", or "self versus other". This first step is a purely cognitive labeling process, quickly activated and largely reflecting a deep and well-practiced conditioned response. The second step in the process is less cognitive and more emotional. After making the initial dualistic assessment, the dualistic thinker then makes the evaluative determination that one component of the target of perception is good and the other component is bad. If the dualistic judgment is "self versus another", the tendency is to conclude that the self is better than the other, a phenomenon known as the self-serving bias (Alicke & Sedikides, 2009). If the dualistic judgment is "us versus them", the tendency is to conclude that one's own group is superior to another group, a phenomenon known as ingroup bias (Hewstone, Rubin, & Willis, 2002). This two-step process of dividing then ego-centrically evaluating resembles that of many psychological processes involving an initial quick heuristic judgment followed by a self-enhancing evaluation (e.g., Roch et al., 2000). It is a pre-heroic consciousness that allows our brains to go on autopilot, splitting the world mindlessly and then interpreting our mental division in a self-serving manner.

If nondualistic thinking reflects a more heroic consciousness than dualistic thinking, how does one adopt a nondualistic approach to the world? I believe there are at least two routes to attaining nondualistic thought. One route consists of Abraham Heschel's idea of approaching the world with an openness and receptivity to awe, wonder, and gratitude (Burhans, 2016). Heschel, you may recall, called this radical amazement. Our thoughts constrict what we can see, according to Heschel (1955, p. 47): "While any act of perception or cognition has as its object a selected segment of reality, radical amazement refers to all of reality." Research shows that training in mindful meditation can help quell the initial labeling and categorizing process and thus better enable people to see the world as it is rather than as we "think" it is (Jones, 2019). In his book Blink, Malcom Gladwell (2007) argues that spending less time thinking and relying upon one's immediate intuitions often engenders greater clarity about the world. This first route to nondualistic thinking requires us to adopt practices that encourage us to approach the world with more wonder, awe, openness, intuition, feeling, and artistic sensibility. Adopting these practices inhibits our predilection for forming quick mental partitions of the world that limit our ability to see the world more broadly, deeply, holistically, heroically, and with more radical amazement.

The second route to nondualistic thinking does not seek to reduce initial mental labeling but instead focuses on correcting for mental labels after they have already been generated. There is some evidence that the tendency to make quick, spontaneous categorizations of the world is wired into us and may therefore be very difficult to avoid (Pendry & Macrae, 1996). Awareness of this pattern is critical to remedying it. If we find ourselves dividing the world dualistically in our minds, we can become aware of this initial binary thinking and then pause to make the necessary corrections. Engaging in mental adjustments that help us see the world in broader, more unifying terms may indeed be the height of heroic consciousness. This two-step process of automatic judging and then correcting has been documented as a pervasive human decision-making process (e.g., Gilbert, 1998; Kraft-Todd & Rand, 2017; Tversky & Kahneman, 1974). We are all capable of heroic consciousness even if at first, as a result of deeply ingrained habit, we show a dualistic pre-heroic consciousness.

2. Processing of Transrational Phenomena

Encounters with experiences that defy rational, logical analysis are an inescapable part of life. A second major characteristic of the hero's consciousness is the ability to process and understand these experiences, as they often reflect the most important issues of human existence. These transrational phenomena are mysterious and challenging for most people to fathom, and thus they require a heroic consciousness to unlock their secrets. Rohr (2009) has identified five such phenomena, and I will add two more. Rohr's five are love, death, suffering, God, and eternity. The two that I am adding are paradox and metaphor (see also Allison & Goethals, 2014; Efthimiou, Bennett, & Allison, 2019). These seven transrational experiences are a ubiquitous part of human life, pervade good hero mythology and storytelling, and are endemic to the classic monomythic hero's journey as described by Joseph Campbell (1949).

To illustrate the importance of understanding the seven transrational experiences in storytelling, let's consider the role of each in the classic 1939 film The Wizard of Oz starring Judy Garland:

(1) Eternity: The hero of The Wizard of Oz is Dorothy Gale, who finds herself stuck in the land of Oz, possibly forever, unless she finds a way home.

(2) Suffering: Dorothy suffers from fear and doubt because she is seemingly trapped in a surreal and dangerous new world.

(3) God: Although never mentioned as divine per se, some magical force has sent Dorothy to Oz. There she encounters magical beings.

(4) Love: Dorothy has a deep love for her family of origin, and in Oz she establishes deep loving relationships with the scarecrow, tin man, and lion.

(5) Death: Dorothy accidentally kills both the Wicked Witch of the East and the Wicked Witch of the West.

(6) Metaphor: The metaphor of "home" is powerful; it represents more than merely a geographical location. Home is wherever you find the people you love. Home is also a metaphor for heroic consciousness.

(7) Paradox: Dorothy lacks the ability to return home, yet she always possesses the means to return home.

When we are young and not far along on our hero's journeys, all seven of these transrational experiences tend to overwhelm our ill-equipped pre-heroic consciousness. We need stories like The Wizard of Oz to help us awaken to a new, wiser, broader consciousness. Much like Dorothy, most human beings suffer until and unless they adopt a heroic consciousness that enables them to grasp the transrational world. The hero's consciousness is available to us once we realize that choosing to remain unconscious leaves us feeling alone, disconnected, frustrated, and miserable. The pre-hero's consciousness is insufficient for mastering life's biggest mysteries involving the seven transrational phenomena. These issues require a more dynamic and enlightened consciousness to understand, and until we understand them, we are doomed to struggle much like Dorothy Gale.

3. Unitive Consciousness

"A human being is a part of the whole, called by us 'Universe,' a part limited in time and space. He experiences himself, his thoughts and feelings as something separated from the rest — a kind of optical delusion of his consciousness. This delusion is a kind of prison for us."

- Albert Einstein (1950)

The hero's consciousness is a nondual, unitive consciousness, exactly like that described in the above quote by Einstein (1950). While recognizing and valuing individual separateness and multiplicity, the hero's consciousness sees and seeks unification. Joseph Campbell (1988) enjoyed telling the story about the two Hawaiian police officers who were called to save the life of a man about to jump to his death. As the man began to jump, one officer grabbed onto him and was himself being pulled over the ledge along with the man he was trying to save. The other officer grabbed his partner and was able to bring both men back to safety. Campbell explained the first officer's self-sacrificial behavior as reflecting "a metaphysical realization which is that you and that other are one, that you are two aspects of the one life" (p. 138). The hero's consciousness is the awareness of this truth. Campbell (1988) taught us that the classic, mythic initiation journey ends with the hero discovering that "our true reality is in our identity and unity with all life" (p. 138).

Einstein's metaphor of the mental prison is especially descriptive of the pre-heroic consciousness. The pre-hero is trapped in the "delusion" of tribal identity and of separateness from the world. Consistent with the mental prison metaphor, spiritual leaders have referred to our over-reliance on mental life as an "addiction" (Rohr, 2011) and a "parasitic" relationship (Tolle, 2005). Both the perseverance effect and confirmation bias in psychology refer to the troublesome tendency of people to hold onto their beliefs even when those beliefs have been discredited by objective evidence (Fiske & Taylor, 2013). The stories that we tell ourselves and cling to can hinder the development of our heroic consciousness (Harari, 2018). This is why hero training programs focus on strategies aimed at re-writing our mental scripts to bolster our heroic efficacy (Kohen et al., 2017). The trait of being open to new ways of thinking is considered by psychologists to be a central characteristic of healthy individuals (Hogan et al., 2012).

Heroes escape their mental prisons and experience a transformed consciousness when they engage in the process of self-expansiveness (Friedman, 2017), during which the boundaries between oneself and others are perceived as permeable. Many spiritual geniuses, including Thich Nhat Hanh, Eckhart Tolle, and Richard Rohr, deem unitive consciousness as core to their definition of spiritual maturity. Buddhist philosopher Hanh (1999) writes that human beings tend to believe that their fellow humans "exist outside us as separate entities, but these objects of our perception are us.... When we hate someone, we also hate ourselves" (p. 81). Rohr (2019) emphasizes that consciousness is the key to understanding the oneness of humanity: "The old joke about the mystic who walks up to the hotdog vendor and says, 'Make me one with everything,' misses the point. I am already one with everything. All that is absent is awareness" (p. 1).

In their list of features that distinguish heroes from villains, Allison and Smith (2015) argued that heroes seek to unite the world whereas villains seek to divide it. Unification in perception and in action tends to reduce human suffering, whereas division in perception and in action tends to produce suffering. The hero's consciousness thus operates in the service of ending human suffering, and the villain's consciousness (and also at times the pre-hero's consciousness) can operate in the service of producing human suffering. Harari (2018) suggests that the recognition of real human suffering may be the litmus test for distinguishing a high-level consciousness from a low-level one. According to Efthimiou et al., (2018), "the pre-heroic, unawakened state is characterized by comparing to others, criticizing others, and taking offense from others. There is a distinct lack of joy in the pre-heroic state, as untransformed individuals are destined to experience suffering and misery and will likely engender such suffering in others around them, too. Only by mentally and spiritually seeing the 'oneness' of humanity can personal wellbeing become possible" (p. 226).

Allison and Smith (2015) also point out another defining feature of heroes, namely, the tendency of heroes to transcend their pain and use their suffering to develop a heroic consciousness. Suffering promotes unitive consciousness (Allison & Setterberg, 2016). In contrast, villains are unable to use their suffering for transcendence. Villains tend to succumb to their pain and allow it to entrench them in the world of blaming, dualistic thinking, and a sense immature empowerment. Tolle (2005) has claimed that if evil has any reality, it is "complete identification with form – physical forms, thought forms, emotional forms. This results in a total unawareness of my connectedness with the whole, my intrinsic oneness with every 'other'" (p. 22). Villains, in fact, operate at such an unconscious level that they usually lack the awareness that they are doing any harm (Baumeister, 2012). Villains often deny they are villains, and heroes often deny they are heroes -- but these denials occur for completely different reasons. Villains are driven to bolster their egos, whereas heroes have no egos to bolster. The heroic consciousness is in ego-less union with everyone. Carl Jung (1938) also emphasized the importance of psychological wholeness, which can only be brought about by bringing unconscious material into conscious awareness. According to Rohr (2009) the pathway toward enlightened consciousness requires the healing of three things: our woundedness, our egocentricity, and our separateness. Only when we rid ourselves of these identifications and illusions can we see wholeness, unity, and reach heroic consciousness.

I argue here that heroism's primary aim is to unify people. The dictionary's definition of "unify" is to take actions that make people united and whole. Unification and wholes are the central mission of heroism. First, to unify is to unite people. Early in the COVID-19 crisis, ER nurse Allison Swendsen took a moving photo of an elderly man holding a sign at a window, thanking healthcare workers for saving his wife. These heroes allowed this woman to reunite with her husband. Heroism always involves bringing people together. Second, to unify is to promote wholeness, the mark of health and well-being. We witnessed that all heroic actions during the COVID-19 pandemic are aimed at reducing suffering and promoting the health and well-being of individuals and society. Heroes strive to promote the wholeness of all people, not just some of them. Heroism is always all-inclusive (Allison, 2020).

4. Wisdom of Tempered Empowerment

In the 1930s, a theologian and philosopher named Reinhold Niebuhr penned what is today commonly referred to as the serenity prayer (Shapiro, 2014). The prayer is as follows:

God grant me the serenity to accept the things I cannot change,

Courage to change the things I can,

And wisdom to know the difference.

The serenity prayer has enjoyed considerable worldwide recognition as a result of being adopted by nearly every 12-step recovery program. I believe the serenity prayer contains brilliant insight about heroic, behavioral self-regulation. George Goethals and I have written elsewhere about addiction recovery programs deriving their effectiveness from their use of the hero's journey as a blueprint for growth and healing (Allison & Goethals, 2014, 2016, 2017). Other scholars and healers have also noted the parallel between heroism and addiction recovery work (Efthimiou et al., 2018; Furey, 2017; Morgan, 2014). The serenity prayer is the centerpiece of recovery programs because addiction is largely a disease of control (Alanon Family Groups, 2008). The prayer works because it helps recovering addicts develop the wisdom to know when to exercise control over their lives and when to admit powerlessness.

Each of the three lines of the serenity prayer reflects the wisdom of heroic consciousness. First, the prayer asks for the serenity to accept people and circumstances that cannot be changed. This is a prayer for acceptance of non-action when action is pointless. It takes a deeper, broader, heroic consciousness to recognize the futility of action in a situation that seems to call for action. For example, if a chronic alcoholic is repeatedly arrested for disorderly conduct, and his partner repeatedly bails him out of jail, the partner may finally have had enough and decide not to bail out the alcoholic in the future. Not helping someone may at times lead to a better outcome than helping someone. After not being bailed out, the alcoholic sitting in jail may do some much-needed soul-searching that can lead to his recovery and healing. The partner who fails to help the jailed alcoholic may be more of a hero by doing nothing than by any action he can take. In terms of the serenity prayer, the partner accepts that he cannot change the alcoholic and that he cannot stop the cycle of repeated arrests for disorderly conduct. Passive acceptance and non-action are sometimes the wisest responses and reflect a nondualistic heroic consciousness.

Beggan (2019) would call this heroic non-action an example of meta-heroism. According to Beggan, "The meta-hero acts heroically by not acting heroically, at least in terms of a more narrow definition of heroic action. In this case, the right thing may actually create hardship and moral ambiguity" (p. 13). Beggan points out that there is a bias in heroism science toward taking action rather than inaction. His analysis puts the adage that "the opposite of a hero is a bystander" on its head. It seems there are times when heroes are indeed bystanders. But it takes an enlightened consciousness to discern these moments that call for heroic inaction.

The second element of the serenity prayer focuses on praying for the courage to change things that are changeable. After realizing that he is powerless over the alcoholic, the partner may recognize that he does have power over his own choices and attitudes. We can only change ourselves, not others. It takes heroic courage not to help a loved one when helping might be enabling the loved one's pattern of dysfunctional behavior. Moreover, it takes heroic courage to take charge of one's own life by confronting the alcoholic about the dysfunctional pattern, setting boundaries with the alcoholic, or perhaps even terminating the relationship with the alcoholic. In any difficult situation, there are always things one can change and options one can consider, although it may take great courage to try something completely different and outside one's proverbial comfort zone. It requires a heroic consciousness to consider all the things that can be changed with the goal of doing what is best for all concerned. In The Wizard of Oz, Dorothy could have given up her dream of going home and simply lived with her new friends in Oz for all eternity. Instead, she accepted her circumstances and musterd up the courage to do everything in her power to accomplish her mission of returning home.

The third and final component of the serenity prayer asks for "the wisdom to know the difference" between those things over which we are powerless and those things over which we do have power. This wisdom lies at the heart of heroic behavioral consciousness, healthy self-regulation, and sage empowerment. I call this the wisdom of tempered empowerment. Pre-heroes cannot easily distinguish between what they can control and what they cannot, nor are they adept at anticipating the efficacy of their efforts to control others or their environment. As a result, pre-heroes can easily become meddling or enabling individuals who do more harm than good (Beggan, 2019). People with heroic consciousness possess the wisdom of tempered empowerment by recognizing the difference between situations that call for action and situations that call for inaction. The heroically conscious individual has the courage to do great things as well as the courage to avoid the kind of helping behavior that may be harmful, futile, counterproductive, or unnecessary.

In summary, operating behind the scenes of heroism is heroic consciousness. Every hero has a consciousness – an ability to see, experience, and think about the world – in a way that is nondualistic, transrational, unitive, and empowered wisely. This is as true for one-time heroes who save people in burning buildings as it is for lifelong heroes who devote their entire existence to promoting large-scale social causes.

THE PALSGROVE SERIES OF STUDENT-AUTHORED BOOKS

A unique feature of this series of books, called the Palsgrove Series, is that each volume in the collection is authored by undergraduate students at the University of Richmond. This particular project is a two-volume set, with Volume 1 authored by first-year University of Richmond students and Volume 2 authored by senior Richmond students. All these student authors were instructed to compose a 5,000-word paper identifying and illuminating core concepts of heroism science. Each chapter in this book describes a core concept and then provides two or more case studies of heroes who illustrated the concept. As a collection we can see some extraordinary phenomena of heroism that lie at the heart of the phenomenon of exceptional selfless action. These core concepts emerge in the heroism in both fiction and non-fiction individuals; in the heroism found in both antiquity and in the present day; and in heroism across the globe, including Asia, Europe, North America, and the Middle-East. These core concepts of heroism are responsible for the prized and universal phenomenon heroism that is cherished and encouraged in all human societies (Allison & Goethals, 2017; Efthimiou & Franco, 2017; Efthimiou, Allison, & Franco, 2018a, 2018b).

It is my sincere hope that you, the reader, benefit from reading these outstanding essays crafted by students whom I got to know well. All these students are heroes-in-training and heroes-in-waiting, as I know they will go on to make positive and enduring contributions to the world. I hope you enjoy and benefit from their wise writings.

REFERENCES

Allison, S. T. (2015). The initiation of heroism science. Heroism Science, 1, 1-8.

Allison, S. T. (2020). The unification principle of heroism. Psychology Today. Retrieved from https://www.psychologytoday.com/us/blog/why-we-need-heroes/202005/the-unification-principle-heroism

Allison, S. T., & Goethals, G. R. (2011). Heroes: What they do and why we need them. New York: Oxford University Press.

Allison, S. T., & Goethals, G. R. (2013). Heroic leadership: An influence taxonomy of 100 exceptional individuals. New York: Routledge.

Allison, S. T., & Goethals, G. R. (2014). "Now he belongs to the ages": The heroic leadership dynamic and deep narratives of greatness. In Goethals, G. R., Allison, S. T., Kramer, R., & Messick, D. (Eds.), Conceptions of leadership: Enduring ideas and emerging insights. New York: Palgrave Macmillan. doi: 10.1057/9781137472038.0011

Allison, S. T., & Goethals, G. R. (2016). Hero worship: The elevation of the human spirit. Journal for the Theory of Social Behaviour, 46, 187-210.

Allison, S. T., & Goethals, G. R. (2017). The hero's transformation. In S. T. Allison, G. R. Goethals, & R. M. Kramer (Eds.), Handbook of heroism and heroic leadership. New York: Routledge.

Allison, S. T., Goethals, G. R., Marrinan, A. R., Parker, O. M., Spyrou, S. P., Stein, M. (2019). The metamorphosis of the hero: Principles, processes, and purpose. Frontiers in Psychology.

Allison, S. T., & Green, J. D. (2021). Nostalgia and heroism: Theoretical convergence of memory, motivation, and function. Frontiers in Psychology.

Allison, S. T., & Setterberg, G. C. (2016). Suffering and sacrifice: Individual and collective benefits, and implications for leadership. In S. T. Allison, C. T. Kocher, & G. R. Goethals (Eds), Frontiers in spiritual leadership: Discovering the better angels of our nature. New York: Palgrave Macmillan.

Allison, S. T. & Smith, G. (2015). Reel heroes & villains. Richmond: Agile Writer Press.

Brown, A. J. (2017). Whistleblowers as heroes. In S. T. Allison, G. R. Goethals, & R. M. Kramer (Eds.), Handbook of heroism and heroic leadership. New York: Routledge.

Campbell, J. (1949). The hero with a thousand faces. New York: New World Library.

Campbell, J. (1972). Myths to live by. New York: Viking Press.

Davis, J. L., Burnette, J. L., Allison, S. T., & Stone, H. (2011). Against the odds: Academic underdogs benefit from incremental theories. Social Psychology of Education, 14, 331-346.

Efthimiou, O. (2017). The hero organism: Advancing the embodiment of heroism thesis in the 21st century. In S. T., Allison, G. R., Goethals, & R. M. Kramer (Eds.), Handbook of heroism and heroic leadership. New York, NY: Routledge.

Efthimiou, O., & Allison, S. T. (2017). Heroism science: Frameworks for an emerging field. Journal of Humanistic Psychology. 10.1177/0022167817708063

Efthimiou, O., & Franco, Z. E. (2017). Heroic Intelligence: The Hero's Journey as an Evolutionary and Existential Blueprint. Journal of Genius and Eminence, 2(2), 32-43.

Efthimiou, O., Allison, S. T., & Franco, Z. E. (2018a). Heroism and wellbeing in the 21st century: Recognizing our personal heroic imperative. In O. Efthimiou, S. T. Allison, & Z. E. Franco (Eds.),

Heroism and wellbeing in the 21st Century: Applied and emerging perspectives. New York: Routledge.

Efthimiou, O., Allison, S. T., & Franco, Z. E. (2018b). Definition, synthesis, and applications of heroic wellbeing. In O. Efthimiou, S. T. Allison, & Z. E. Franco (Eds.), Heroism and wellbeing in the 21st Century: Applied and emerging perspectives. New York: Routledge.

Erikson, E. H. (1994). Identity and the life cycle. New York: W. W. Norton & Company.

Franco, Z. E., Efthimiou, O., & Zimbardo, P. G. (2016). Heroism and eudaimonia: Sublime actualization through the embodiment of virtue. In J. Vittersø (Ed.), Handbook of eudaimonic wellbeing. New York: Springer.

Freud, S. (1905/2011). Three essays on the theory sexuality. Eastford, CT: Martino Fine Books.

Friedman, H. L. (2017). Everyday heroism in practicing psychology. Journal of Humanistic Psychology. https://doi.org/10.1177/0022167817696843

Goethals, G. R., & Allison, S. T. (2014). Kings and charisma, Lincoln and leadership: An evolutionary perspective. In Goethals, G. R., Allison, S. T., Kramer, R., & Messick, D. (Eds.), Conceptions of leadership: Enduring ideas and emerging insights. New York: Palgrave Macmillan. doi: 10.1057/9781137472038

Haidt, J. (2003). Elevation and the positive psychology of morality. In C. L. M. Keyes & J. Haidt (Eds.), Flourishing: Positive psychology and the life well-lived (pp. 275-289). Washington DC: American Psychological Association.

Hanh, T. N. (1999). The heart of the Buddha's teaching. New York: Broadway Books.

Hayes, S. C., Strosahl, K. D., & Wilson, K. G. (2011). Acceptance and commitment therapy: The process and practice of mindful change. New York: The Guilford Press.

Hollander, E. P. (1995). Ethical challenges in the leader–follower relationship.
Business Ethics Quarterly, 5, 55–65.

Hoyt, C. L., Allison, S. T., Barnowski, A., & Sultan, A. (2020). Lay theories of heroism and leadership: The role of gender, communion, and agency. Social Psychology.

James, W. (1902). The varieties of religious experience. Boston, MA: Bedford.

Jones, P. (2017). Mindfulness-based heroism: Creating mindful heroes. Journal of Humanistic Psychology. https://doi.org/10.1177/0022167817711303

Jung, C. (1956). The archetypes and the collective unconscious. Princeton: Princeton University Press.

Kashdan, T., & Rottenberg, J. (2010). Psychological flexibility as a fundamental aspect of health Clinical Psychology Review, 30 (7), 865-878

Keck, B., Compton, L., Schoeneberg, C., & Compton, T. (2017). Trauma recover: A heroic journey. Heroism Science, 2, 1-17.

Kinsella, E.L., Ritchie, T.D., & Igou, E.R. (2015). Lay perspectives on the social and psychological functions of heroes. Frontiers in Psychology, 6, 130. doi: 10.3389/fpsyg.2015.00130

Kinsella, E.L., Ritchie, T.D., & Igou, E.R. (2017). Attributes and applications of heroes: A brief history of lay and academic perspectives. In S. T. Allison, G. R. Goethals, & R. M. Kramer (Eds.), Handbook of heroism and heroic leadership. New York: Routledge.

Latane, B., & Darley, J. (1969). Bystander "Apathy". American Scientist, 57, 244-268.

Le Grice, K. (2013). The rebirth of the hero: Mythology as a guide to spiritual transformation. London: Muswell Hill Press.

Lopez, S. J., & Snyder, C. R. (Eds.) (2011). The Oxford handbook of positive psychology. New York: Oxford University Press.

Maslow, A. (1943.) A theory of human motivation. Psychological Review, 50, 370–396.

Nisbett, R., & Wilson, T. D. (1977). Telling more than we can know. Psychological Review, 84, 231-259.

Phipps, R. (2011). My trip to Melbourne. Retrieved September 8, 2015 from http://quotationsbook.com/quote/35768/

Rendon, J. (2015). Upside: The new science of post-traumatic growth. New York: Touchstone.

Rohr, R. (2011). Falling upward. Hoboken, NJ: Jossey-Bass.

Rohr, R. (2014). Eager to love. Cincinnati, OH: Franciscan Media.

Sedikides, C. & Hepper, E. G. D. (2009). Self-improvement. Social and Personality Psychology Compass, 3, 899-917.

Seligman, M. E. P. (2011). Flourish. New York: Atria Books.

Simmons, A. (2012). The crab syndrome. San Antonio, TX: Antuan Simmons.

Swann, W. B., Jr. (2012). Self-verification theory. In P. Van Lang, A. Kruglanski, & E.T. Higgins (Eds.), pp 23-42. Handbook of Theories of Social Psychology. London: Sage.

Thomson, A. L., & Siegel, J. T. (2013). A moral act, elevation, and prosocial behavior: Moderators of morality. The Journal of Positive Psychology, 8, 50-64.

Turner, V. W. (1966). The ritual process: Structure and anti-structure. Ithaca, NY: Cornell University Press.

van Gennep, A. (1909). The rites of passage. Paris: Émile Nourry.

Wegner, D. (2002). The illusion of conscious will. Cambridge: MIT Press.

Worthington, E. L, & Allison, S. T. (2018). Heroic humility: What the science of humility can say to people raised on self-focus. Washington. DC: American Psychological Association.

Zimbardo, P. (2008). The Lucifer effect: Understanding how good people turn evil. New York: Random House.

Section 1: How To Make a Hero

HEROES AS MORAL MODELS: AN EFFECTIVE WAY TO MAKE CHANGE

JAMIE L. KATZ

"We feel that there are moral laws in the universe just as valid and as basic as man-made laws, and whenever a man-made law is in conflict with what we consider the law of God, or the moral law of the universe, then we feel that we have a moral obligation to protest."

– Martin Luther King, Jr. (1960)

These are the words that Dr. Reverend Martin Luther King, Jr., spoke while being interviewed on Meet the Press, a popular NBC broadcast. The question about where our morals come from still remains unanswered. Are government laws moral? Is there a higher power that decides what is right and what is wrong? What is more important when considering the morality of a decision: the consequences of the action or the intentions of the person? How can one moral code apply to every decision or situation that may arise? How does morality account for differences in culture and belief systems?

None of these questions can be answered, or at least they cannot be definitively answered. It is a common struggle among all humans to figure out what is intrinsically "good" and what is inherently "bad." Parents try to instill in their kids a sense of right and wrong from a young age, but when the child consistently probes asking why, the parent will eventually run out of answers. There are countless philosophers and theorists that have tried to justify the moral permissibility or prohibition of actions. Although there is no single theory or moral code that can account for all scenarios, there are some basic principles that seem to be universally true—for example, merciless killing is bad, you shouldn't steal, etc. Many of us continuously search for answers to these moral dilemmas in attempts to scratch at a sort of objective truth. Though we may never find an exact formula, many of us get our guidance from heroes and role models that have come before us who have set precedents. Heroes seem to have a strong sense of morality, and they influence society by modeling how such morality should be applied in real-world scenarios.

There has been considerable research conducted showing that heroes embody and impact the moral ideals of a society. Heroes are regarded as public figures that the population can identify with whose accomplishments can be celebrated by all (Allison et al., 2019; Hoyt et al., 2020; Pretzinger, 1976). Especially in today's day and age with technology and social media surrounding us at all times, heroes are more accessible than ever. Not only are their heroic deeds put on display via news and internet, but also their personal lives and updates on their thoughts are published through multiple different outlets. Although heroes seem to have lost their mysticism that they once had in the past, most public heroes are currently ubiquitous, accessible, and well-known throughout society (Pretzinger, 1976).

When heroes have such fame, influence naturally follows, especially if their fame is rooted in heroic and objectively good reason. Even an encounter with a hero whom people regard as moral can be enough to spark moral reflection and action in others. Heroes promote a sort of "moral elevation" in their followers that can be strong enough to inspire action. Moral elevation is described as a warm feeling similar to tranquility, and more importantly it drives people to become better versions of themselves (Allison & Goethals, 2016). Because they take such great risks to promote the wellbeing of others, heroes have the power to provoke feelings of awe and reverence that encourage others to act morally, too. This power is far reaching and has large implications for society as a whole. If heroes that model moral behaviors can influence the way that people can act in morally troubling situations, they can set the framework for the ideal moral code that should be followed.

When group situations of conflict or crisis arise, heroes fight the instinct to defer responsibilities to others, and they act to set a precedent for behavior and morality. There are many obstacles, both intentional and unintentional, that prevent heroes and heroic behavior from emerging. The bystander effect, one of the most well-known hurdles that leadership and heroism must overcome, occurs when some negative action unfolds in a large group, and because there are so many potential actors, each individual is less likely to take action (Parks, 2017). People have to overcome the tendency toward conformity in groups and take the risk that will set them apart from others.

 In addition, group settings can minimize the sense of urgency that one might feel in a dire situation. If no one else acts to prevent some negative conse-quence, the threat can be misinterpreted as a nonemergency and also hinder the likeliness of action from a general member of the population. It takes a special kind of person to act out against a wrongdoing when the vast majority of the population are sitting back doing nothing. These people are the heroes we need, and people turn to such heroes in times of conflict and crisis when they are unsure of which type of action to take. For example, in Asch's famous conformity study, participants were told to choose a line that matched the example. Though the answer was glaringly obvious in each case, the partici-pants more often than not went with the incorrect answer that their confeder-ate colleagues were giving so as not to go against the grain of the group.

However, in the condition where there was one confederate that gave the cor-rect answer, the participants were infinitely more likely to also give the correct answer (Asch, 1958). Often, people know the right course of action that needs to be taken, but they are afraid of being the person to take it. When there is someone that breaks the ice and decisively takes action against evil, people are more likely to act in response to that person. By rising above the daunting pull of the bystander effect, heroes encourage the population to do the right thing

in a negative circumstance. A hero is someone actively combats moral wrongdoings, and in the process, they can inspire others to act in the morally correct way
as well.

In addition to group pressure, people often face pressure from those in positions of authority, but heroes can inspire action against authority figures committing wrongdoings to citizens. Milgram tested men in a study to see how far
the researcher could push the subject through mere obedience to the authority
figure in the white lab coat (Milgram, 1963). About two-thirds of the participants
in the study were willing to deliver lethal doses of electric shock to the confederate behind the wall strictly because the experimenter told them to. However,
in a condition where there was another confederate in the teaching role and
he refused to deliver the shocks, almost no one would deliver them either. In
this case, the participants modeled their behavior in response to what the other
person in the room was doing. It can be daunting to stand up to someone in an
authority role, especially when there is a lot at stake, but scenarios like these are
what make a hero.

In fact, the definition of hero includes the willingness to take on extreme risk in
pursuit of the greater good. When there are people in society that are willing to
lead the charge against laws, policies, and treatment that is unfair and unjust,
they inspire others to action as well. Largescale changes in society would be
impossible without backing from huge quantities people. Heroes are the driving
force behind political movements and change because they speak out against the
authority figures that are committing wrongdoings. In times of moral, political,
or social unrest in a society, people will model their own behavior after heroes
that are brave enough to act and speak out against authority.

The people that push towards and inspire political change on a large scale are
often not appreciated or deemed heroes until after their deaths. Because they
are most likely speaking out against the majority or against an authority figure
or figures, they are putting themselves at risk for negative reactions as a result.
I will be talking about three examples a little later on in this paper, and two of
them were killed in pursuit of their causes. Premature death might be a contributing factor to why these people were hailed as heroes, and why their legacy is
so far reaching and long lasting. When people die, they lose the ability to fall

from grace. Simply put, they are not alive, so they cannot make any bad decisions (or any decisions at all for that matter). In addition, one of the criteria that makes a hero is that she willingly takes on the risks involved in her mission to better society (Zimbardo, 2011). Risking one's life is the ultimate cost, so the fact that someone died for his cause could make him even more heroic in the eyes of the public.

In addition, when someone important and influential dies, they likely draw more attention to themselves and their cause through their death. No one can consult them about their motivations or intentions anymore, and usually the best is assumed about a person posthumously. The heroes that I will be discussing in the following sections have strong moral codes that they adhere to, and they in turn inspire others to get on board their movements. These people have lost their lives, their privacy, and their autonomy among other things to pursue a cause greater than themselves. They created political and social unrest in a time of injustice, and they have called people to action to fight alongside each other for change. The heroes that I have chosen as exemplars of moral modeling have been exceptionally influential during and after their lives, and they have shaped and influenced the way people act in times of political and social unrest.

CHRISTINE BLASEY FORD: MAKING STRIDES IN "ME TOO" AMERICA

"My greatest fears have been realized – and the reality has been far worse than what I expected. My family and I have been the target of constant harassment and death threats. I have been called the most vile and hateful names imaginable" (Ford, 2018). This is an excerpt from Christine Blasey Ford's opening statement in her testimony against Brett Kavanaugh. When Christine Blasey Ford went public with the story of her attack, she knew she would be putting herself (and those closest to her) at risk for everything from harassment, insults, and even death threats, but she decided to move forward with her statement regardless because she felt that it was her civic duty to do so. She believed that the United States senate should have a full and uncensored account of Brett Kavanaugh's past behaviors before he got a lifelong appointment to the highest court in our country.

However, without steadfast evidence or supporting witnesses, Blasey Ford faced an uphill battle in a heated, partisan conflict. Dr. Ford started a movement that has inspired girls of all ages to come forward and tell their stories of harassment and abuse. Because of the bravery she has shown, there have been major pushes to improve the systems that silence girls and women who have been assaulted and moves towards a fairer process of justice appointment. By definition, Christine Blasey Ford is a hero, and she has made great strides towards equality and justice for women in the midst of fourth wave feminism in "Me Too" America.

There is much debate about the definition of a hero, and there is even debate about how to go about defining a hero. Many of the accepted definitions have a few things in common, though. A hero is someone who does large-scale actions to promote the greater good at some major cost or sacrifice to themselves (Allison et al., 2017). Christine Blasey Ford has decided to take her story of sexual assault to a very public setting: a live, nationally-televised testimony in a senate hearing. The scale to which she has exposed personal details of a traumatic event is so widespread that she has made every major news headline in the United States. In the process, she has made a major sacrifice. Her personal information including her telephone number, her address, and her place of work got disclosed to the press.

Although she wanted to stay anonymous throughout the process, she had been ambushed in her both her professional and personal life enough that she came forward and took ownership of her actions. People have attacked her from both sides of the aisle calling her a liar and a political opportunist, and her character and story have both been questioned. Her entire life has been thrown into chaos as she was forced to leave her family home and go into hiding for her and her family's safety and well-being. Her personal trauma is known to everyone now, and she has been exposed into the public sphere past the point of no return. She has assumed these risks for the benefit of the nation. Although it would have been much easier for her to stay quiet and keep her story to herself, she has fore-gone the role of a bystander and decided to publicly accuse Kavanaugh of sexual misconduct for a complete, ethical decision to be made about his Supreme Court appointment. In this scenario, she has much more at stake than she could ever personally gain, but the underdog professor still presses forward in her journey towards positive change and ethical conduct in our judicial system.

"You are opening up to open air hurt and pain that goes on across this country. And for that, the word I would use is it's nothing short of heroic," Senator Cory

Booker said to Blasey Ford towards the beginning of the hearing (Millstein, 2018). Blasey Ford has stood up to Brett Kavanaugh in the face of threats and harassment, and she shed light on a dark reality that exists in U.S. culture. Her bravery in testifying against Kavanaugh was a huge sacrifice, but she did it with a clear motive in mind—to make sure the senate knew exactly who they were appointing to the highest court in the U.S.A. She has also motivated other women across the country to come forward with their stories and demand justice and change for the future. Her testimony and deliverance in the court room will likely change the way the judicial system deals with cases of sexual assault (Maor, 2018).

With her case, she has brought undeniable attention to the inequality of men and women in positions of power in the United States government. The majority male senate committee that questioned her was heavily criticized and definitely noticed by the press, which would probably not have been the case ten years ago before the #MeToo movement.

Although Blasey Ford did not start the movement to call men out for the sexist and abusive behaviors they had so easily gotten away with in positions of power, she did a lot to press the movement forward at great personal cost. She has waited for years to bring her story to the public, which sent the message to women around the country that it is never ok to take advantage of someone, and that everyone's story is important no matter how long ago it happened. She is a woman coming forward to a male-dominated committee and hoping they will take her word against Kavanaugh's. Due to her underdog status, she has given disenfranchised women a platform to tell their stories, too. Her bravery, humility, honesty, and composure have sprung hope in others who have faced similar traumas.

Women are identifying with Christine Blasey Ford because so many of them have untold stories of sexual assault or harassment that they may not have been old enough to know were crimes. She has validated their experiences, and may have moved them past a point of doubting themselves to a point where they can share what happened to them and recognize how and why it is wrong. So many people have come forward with stories that they have been holding on to for years because they thought it was too long ago or too trivial to bring to the attention of friends, family, authorities, doctors, and/or mental health counselors. People are modeling their behavior after her sense of courage, bravery, justice, and truth, and they are helping themselves or others get the support they need for traumatic events. Dr. Ford is an underdog in the face of the justice system and her attacker, but she has stepped into the limelight and continues to heroically inspire a push for truth, justice, and equality for women in terms of power in America.

MARTIN LUTHER KING: DESEGREGATING AMERICA THROUGH CIVIL DISOBEDIENCE AND NONVIOLENCE

"I have a dream that one day my four little children will live in a nation where they will not be judged by the color of their skin but by the content of their character" (King, 1963). These words are some of the most famous in the United States of America. Reverend Dr. Martin Luther King, Jr., was an activist and a hero when it came to fighting for civil rights and desegregation in America for African Americans. He led the charge against the American government as first president of the Southern Christian Leadership Conference and the organizer of the Montgomery Bus Boycott that sparked a movement amongst marginalized citizens. In fact, he became the face for the civil rights movement because his speeches and messages were broadcast all over the world. He believed that everyone in America should be seen as equals despite the color of their skin, and that the separation clause in the fourteenth amendment was inevitably unjust.

Aside from ending government-backed segregation, he also pushed for the creation of the Civil Rights act and the Voting Act that helped end the systematic disenfranchisement of African-Americans ("Martin Luther King, Jr.," 2018). He was an underdog preacher who led a national movement against a racist, powerful, majority government. He was remarkably talented at communication, and he had an impressive slew of connections within the black community making him the perfect candidate for the leader of an African-American uprising movement. He risked his freedom, the safety of himself and his family, and his reputation to make a much-needed change in society. Although a villain took his life before he could see all the fruits of his labor, he is arguably one of the most well-known heroes in America, and he set the precedent for the way African-Americans and people of color are seen in the eyes of the law.

Martin Luther King, Jr., inspired others to action through his strong adherence to some higher moral code, and he popularized a belief system of tolerance, acceptance of diversity, community, and unity for American citizens. There had been a sense of injustice about racism in America before Dr. King took the stage, but no one had been able to make lasting, large-scale changes to the system. King wholeheartedly preached and practiced non-violence and civil disobedience even when faced with threats from black militants that thought his strategy was too slow-moving and whites who refused to give into the change he was promoting. His tactics were effective because they called for tangible actions performed by any citizen that was unhappy with the status quo. He encouraged students, children, families, workers, and people from all walks of life to join in his sit-ins, boycotts, marches, and protests.

Many criticized him for putting young lives in the face of harm, but he insisted that the only way to make large scale change was to call attention to the matter on a national level. The violence, arrests, and injustice that African-Americans faced in response to their peaceful protests caught the attention of middle and upper class white people that had previously been mere bystanders. By bringing the problem to light on a national stage, Martin Luther King, Jr., stirred up feelings of empathy and alarm in white people who formerly did not question the state of affairs. Once it became known that racism and discrimination were such wide-reaching, imminent problems, people's attitudes towards African- Americans began to change. Martin Luther King modeled and taught the morals that he believed in to his followers who demonstrated them to a vast American audience. His dedication to peaceful protest in the face of hate and violent backlash set the precedent for other protestors and ultimately broadened the civil rights movement to cover the outstanding scope that it reached.

MAHATMA GANDHI: FIGHTING FOR FREEDOM WITH FASTING

"Mahatma" literally translates to "great soul." Mahatma Gandhi was born into a very religious family of humble means, but he made a name for himself on an international level and is remembered throughout history as a hero and one of the most moral human beings to have ever lived. From a young age, Gandhi practiced values like minimalism, humility, nonviolence, discipline, and tolerance. He pushed for social change with strategies within his means, but he made waves on a level much larger than himself. His vision and leadership brought an end to unfair laws and treatment from British colonizers. His efforts eventually led to total independence of India from Britain so that its inhabitants could create their own laws that treated people in a more fair way.

To achieve such gargantuan results, Gandhi made many extreme personal sacrifices and was not afraid to put himself in harm's way in the name of justice. He would conduct multiple day fasts as a form of peaceful protest against laws or policies that he saw as unfair. In addition, he got arrested multiple times throughout his life from and was forced to watch his wife take her last breaths in his arms on a prison floor ("Mahatma Gandhi," 2018). He moved around between India, Britain, and South Africa, and in each place he stayed, he left a lasting impact. His tolerance and love for all people earned him some fierce backlash from other Hindu's who villainized him in his late life for loving and accepting Muslims in a time of conflict over communal land. He lost the trust of Hindus in India for siding with Muslims, and he was ultimately assassinated by a strong believer in Hindu supremacy.

He envisioned the world as a place where all peoples could live in peace and equality amongst each other, and no one would have more resources than necessary for personal survival and flourishing. He was extremely pacifistic and adhered to a strict vegetarian diet so as to reduce the suffering of other living beings. His work for social justice improved the quality of life for people all over the world suffering from the devastating aftereffects that colonialism, xenophobia, and discrimination that dominated the early twentieth century. Mahatma Gandhi sacrificed his own bodily needs, personal safety, and close relationships in pursuit of religious and ethnic freedom for marginalized people around the world, and he is the quintessential example of a hero.

Gandhi made a change by focusing his energy on peaceful initiatives, and his heroic actions and attitudes have influenced similar movements around the world that use him as a moral model. There have been many marginalized groups throughout world history, and to make a noticeable, lasting change, peaceful protest and civil disobedience has turned out to be one of the most effective and efficient means of making lasting change. Gandhi revolutionized the idea that non-violent fighting of the oppressing group or system is effective. His fight with the British colonizers provided inspiration for other famous civil rights movements around the world including those of Martin Luther King Jr. as explained above. Gandhi lived in a time full of hate and discrimination, but he chose to stand up to villains by leading by example. He called to action hundreds and thousands of people that didn't know how to take a stand, and they followed his examples of fasting and peaceful protesting to give the movement more momentum.

Without Gandhi's heroic sacrifice of his own wellbeing and life, the world could have turned into a much scarier place. He set the precedent for non-violent, peaceful protest to make necessary change and create more justice in society. He was and continues to be a moral model for people around the world looking to enact positive change through tangible, peaceful, and benevolent means. He was not willing to sit back and watch as his friends, family, and those around him were discriminated against and treated unfairly, but rather he took action and inspired action in his community. He practiced disciplined, pacifistic activism that pushed people enraged but stagnant to empowered and active.

CONCLUSION

There have been many noteworthy social justice heroes throughout history that have modeled morals and set precedents for the way we progress towards a more equitable and just world for all. Their heroic leadership provides a beacon of guidance for those who feel compelled to act but don't know the best course of action to take. Heroes provide a blueprint for behavior in times of social and political unrest, and they help to call bystanders and witnesses to action. Many times people are afraid to act according to their ideal moral code because there is pressure from the greater group or society that stifles individuality and action. Heroes break the mold and decide to act on behalf of everyone who believes an aspect of society needs to change. Because they are often the first ones to act and they do so decisively, they inspire others to action and allow for largescale protest and change to take place. Heroes serve an important function as moral models and leaders for enacting change, and the patterns of their emergence has the potential to give important insight into the status of society.

The heroic leaders that rise from the masses of society through their directed actions reveal meaningful information about the struggles that pervade daily life (Allison et al., 2017). The issues and exemplars that I have discussed throughout this paper target problems that had been around for a long time, but problems that weren't getting the attention needed to create massive change until these leaders of movements stepped on to the scene. These heroes would not have the magnitude of followership needed to reach their great levels of fame had the issues they stood for not been so far-reaching. By looking at the people that are starting to rise to popularity for supporting a certain issue, we can glean meaningful information about the problems that people are facing on an everyday basis.

The people who are moral models are typically of the first in the group to decisively take action against the villain or enemy so that others will follow their example and lead to widespread change. People tend to shape their behavior after what leaders or heroes exemplify, so a closer examination of emerging heroes for social change could potentially reveal predictive information about the direction in which the movement is headed. Oppositely, if there are obvious deficits in society in terms of equality, there might be some general predictive pattern that can be found about who will emerge as a hero. People who exemplify morals and values that strongly align with the shortcomings of the government or the people in power may be more likely to emerge as heroes. By taking a closer look at the heroes that come to fruition out of societal unrest, we can gain a deeper understanding of both the patterns of hero emergence and the problems that plague the population.

Although moral heroes adhere to strict ethical codes to encourage largescale mobilization for change, moral modeling can be effective on a micro level and create positive ripple effects, too. Many of the well-known moral heroes in history have lost their lives to their causes including both MLK and Gandhi. Although their legacies have continued past their physical lives on earth, the lethal risks involved in so strongly conveying a moral message are a huge deterrent from action for many people. While it would be ideal for everyone to follow in the footsteps of these notorious heroes, they still serve an important purpose for enacting positive change on smaller levels.

Heroes give people a standard to follow in terms of moral behavior in a world where morality and ethics are extremely subjective. In turn, people can apply the lessons that moral heroes teach us in their everyday lives to improve the circumstances within their own circles. While not everyone can rise to a position with elevated moral influence, people can feel moral elevation from watching or interacting with moral heroes and in turn make better day-to-day decisions. Whether its practicing courage, empathy, acceptance, discipline, nonviolence, integrity, or any other number of traits that moral heroes exemplify, following in the footsteps of moral heroes is beneficial to society.

REFERENCES

Allison, S. T. (2019). Heroic consciousness. Heroism Science, 4, 1-43.

Allison, S. T., Beggan, J. K., & Efthimiou, O. (2019). The art and science of heroism and heroic leadership. Lausanne: Frontiers Media.

Allison, S. T., Eylon, D., Beggan, J.K., & Bachelder, J. (2009). The demise of leadership: Positivity and negativity in evaluations of dead leaders. The Leadership Quarterly, 20, 115-129.

Allison, S. T., & Goethals, G. R. (2016). Hero worship: The elevation of the human spirit. Journal for the Theory of Social Behaviour, 46, 187-210.

Allison, S. T., Goethals, G. R., & Kramer, R. M. (2017). Setting the scene the rise and coalescence of heroism science. In S. T. Allison, G. R. Goethals, & R. M. Kramer (Eds.), Handbook of heroism and heroic leadership. New York: Routledge.

Asch, S.E. (1956). Studies of independence and conformity: I. A minority of one against a unanimous majority. Psychological Monographs: General and Applied, 70(9), 1-80

Davis, J. L., Burnette, J. L., Allison, S. T., & Stone, H. (2011). Against the odds: Academic underdogs benefit from incremental theories. Social Psychology of Education, 14, 331-346.

Ford, C. B.. (2018, September 26). READ: Christine Blasey Ford's Opening Statement For Senate Hearing. NPR.

Goethals, G. R., & Allison, S. T. (2019). The romance of heroism and heroic leadership: Ambiguity, attribution, and apotheosis. West Yorkshire: Emerald.

Gray, K., Anderson, S., Doyle, C. M., Hester, N., Schmitt, P., Vonasch, A., Allison, S. T., and Jackson, J. C. (2018). To be immortal, do good or evil. Personality and Social Psychology Bulletin, 44, 868-880.

Hoyt, C. L., Allison, S. T., Barnowski, A., & Sultan, A. (2020). Lay theories of heroism and leadership: The role of gender, communion, and agency. Social Psychology.

King, M. L. Jr. (1963). I Have a Dream. Washington D.C.

King, M. L. Jr. (1960). Interview on "Meet the Press."

Kinsella, E. L., Ritchie, T. D., & Igou, E. R. (2017). Attributes and applications of heroes a brief history of lay and academic perspectives. In S. T.   Allison, G. R. Goethals, & R. M. Kramer (Eds.), Handbook of heroism and heroic leadership. New York: Routledge.

Mahatma Gandhi: Anti-war Activist (1869-1948). (2018). (Biography). Retrieved from https://www.biography.com/people/mahatma-gandhi-9305898

Maor, D. (2018). Christine Blasey Ford's testimony is a heroic achievement for the #MeToo movement. Haaretz.

Martin Luther King Jr.: Minister, Civil Rights Activist (1929-1968). (2018). (Biography). Retrieved from https://www.biography.com/people/martin-luther-king-jr-9365086

Milgram, S. (1963). Behavioral study of obedience. Journal of Abnormal and Social Psychology, 67, 371-378

Millstein, S. (2018, September 27). Cory Booker's speech to Christine Blasey Ford praised her for being "Heroic." Bustle.

Parks, C. D. (2017). Accidental and purposeful impediments to heroism. In S. T. Allison, G. R. Goethals, & R. M. Kramer (Eds.), Handbook of heroism and heroic leadership. New York: Routledge. (pp. 438–458).

Pretzinger, K. (1976). The American hero: yesterday and today. Humboldt Journal of Social Relations, 4(1), 36-46. Retrieved from http://www.jstor.org/stable/44011695

Zimbardo, P. (2011). What makes a hero? Greater Good Magazine.

2

Motivational Heroism: A Phenomenon that Keeps the World Spinning

LAUREN A. LAMBERT

A shiny red tailcoat, white gloves, and a top hat can make any man appear to have the world at his fingertips. Add in a powerful song lyric and dazzling choreography, and suddenly you are presented with a charismatic character that has the capability to win over your heart and mind. P.T. Barnum, most recently depicted in the musical film *The Greatest Showman* by Hugh Jackman, used charm and inspiring lyrics to make the audience and his followers in the film view him as a strong and talented hero. He sings:

"You know you can't go back again to the world that you were living in, because you're dreaming with your eyes wide open... so come alive!"

In this lyric, Barnum displays his use of charisma and talent to inspire others to find the hero within themselves, establishing pride and power in their individuality. Receiving his heroic status was no easy task, however. Phineas Taylor Barnum was born into poverty; he was the son of a tailor and had nothing going for him other than a dream to create an unimaginably brilliant life for a wealthy young girl, Charity, that he was desperately in love with. With this dream as his driving motivation, he worked nail and tooth to make it reality, although arguably often at the expense of others. It is safe to say that P.T. is not a flawless character that embodies what society agrees to be heroic, but he perfectly emulates a sense of motivational transformation within himself and the society around him. His entire childhood was composed of negative event after negative event, and he refused to let that become the norm. As he sought after fame and fortune, P.T. found himself wanting to instill the attitude of not giving up on those around him. By gathering various types of societal misfits to perform in circus acts, he not only was achieving his dream of being financially successful but was also providing historically ostracized types of people with a job and a loving community. As seen above, Barnum encouraged his circus members to "come alive" and celebrate their oddities rather than putting them into shameful hiding (Gracey, 2017).

REALITY DOESN'T SPARKLE AND SING

While entertaining and inspirational, P.T. Barnum's story in The Greatest Showman is not meant to provide an authentic nor realistic account of motivational transformation. Negative events happen to everyone in various forms, but they aren't typically coupled by dramatic ballads and Broadway-level performances. Rather, events similar to P.T.'s impoverished childhood may be seen in everyone's own lives in the form of bad breakup, a miserable test failure, the loss of a loved one, or even an experience of violence or assault. Bad things happen to good people consistently and more often than we believe they should. Ruminating on the way in which this world presents such negative events can leave anyone feeling hopeless, empty, and purposeless. Regardless of the weight of the event described as negative, it has the potential to completely alter our lives for the worst. How is there still joy in this overwhelming, terrible world of ours? Is there a way for us all to make diamonds out of dust, to make a pleasant song and dance out of our despair as P.T. did?

Psychologists study a phenomenon defined as "learned helplessness" that illustrates the way in which individuals sink deeper into despair following negative life events. It was originally discovered as a detrimental behavior within neuropsychological experiments, in which rats already exposed to a negatively stimulating shock did not attempt to escape when given the opportunity a subsequent time. Since the initial discover of this behavior, the phenomenon has been studied in human behavior as well, especially in studies of psychological well-being and depressive symptoms. Following negative life events, especially if the event is one that has been repeated, individuals often give up on trying to better the trajectory of their life, accepting the notion that nothing they do will make their situation better (Nuvvula, 2016). At a personal level, learned helplessness and lack of perceived control within social and emotional situations fosters a harmful downward cycle comprised of diminished self awareness, negative psychosocial well-being, and failing relationships with others. Individuals suffering from learned helplessness do not see any way to reverse the downward spiral in their personal lives, so they give up (Maier & Seligman, 1976).

In creating the learned helplessness theory, Martin Seligman focused on the personal experience of individuals and the way in which the helplessness manifest itself on their experience of future negative events and emotional dysregulation. What is not as commonly addressed, however, is the potential for those internalized beliefs and behaviors to have a profound negative impact on the surrounding world. Imagine an individual that consistently succumbs to surrounding pressures-one that is unable to stand up, be bold, and make personal or relational changes. If the world was populated by individuals suffering from learned helplessness like the one you are picturing, there would be no way to see light at the end of the tunnel. Because it is often a symptom of depressive experiences, the state of learned helplessness is not something that can typically be overcome by pure will. It requires a form of combat from the outside-a form that fosters hope and a desire for change in a time of personal or societal downfall or stagnation.

As described previously, experiencing consistent negative life events can create a sense of hopelessness and despair, a spiraling negativity and loss of control that never stops moving downwards. This sentiment is widely understood and experienced by anyone that has ever encountered some sort of loss or tragedy. Those same events may also foster a dangerous sense of stagnation rather than downfall, however. Allison and Goethals (2017) explain stagnation as a different transforming outcome that is not necessarily a detrimental downfall but instead one that never reaches its fullness or potential. Remaining stagnant following a journey creates a "reluctant hero," one that is oblivious to his or her vital role in developing society, choosing to remain comfortable and set in the current ways of the world. Stagnation may be just as detrimental to society as downfall is; it disregards the potential for heroism in anyone and creates a deceivingly narrow focus of potential progress or growth. Ignorance is not bliss when it comes to developing heroes, and the motivational hero is a perfect example of how stagnation and hopelessness can be overcome.

MOTIVATIONAL TRANSFORMATION AS A FORM OF COMBAT

Motivation is explained as a desire and urgency to do something that works towards some ends. Intrinsically, individuals may be motivated to accomplish the ends because it is internally pleasurable. Extrinsically, however, they may feel an urge to work for something simply because of the positive consequences that arise from it. Regardless of the intention behind the desire, motivated individuals tend to have steadfast directionality and a defined purpose within their life trajectory (Ryan & Deci, 2000). Having motivation, however, is not in and of itself heroic. An individual's motivations may only satisfy their own self-serving bias or create some sort of temporary pleasure and feeling of accomplishment. The individual's altered motivations may serve as a precursor to heroism, but he or she only becomes a hero when the positive outcomes of the motivationally-driven actions are evident to the broader world and not just to the individual's personal development.

Motivational transformation describes the process of individuals developing into heroes by using their experienced negative events as a means to alter the trajectory of their lifetime motivation (Allison & Goethals 2017). Rather than allowing the event to negatively impact their well-being or even pretend that the event happened at all, individuals can become heroes by acknowledging that the event has forever altered their motivations. This change of motives into ones of heroic characteristics serves to counteract the negative event and the emotions that it caused. Overcoming the adversity can in and of itself be a heroic act, allowing those in similar situations to learn from the transformation of one who has overcome, instilling in others a desire to grow. More importantly, however, is the potential for motivational transformations to change society at large in some way. These heroes may work towards the prevention of events similar to theirs happening in the lives of others, which could be seen in the form of educational programming or increased awareness of the negative event or phenomenon.

Sharing their stories, serving as a spokesperson, and fighting for systemic changes in the fabric of society are just a few examples of how motivational transformations have the capacity to make profound differences beyond the individual experience. Whether or not his or her initial motivations preceding the negative life event were considered to be heroic, the individual fosters a newfound definition of heroism by allowing the negative event to create change for the better, combating the downward cycle of helplessness and despair that was previously described. Motivationally-driven heroes are resilient; they overcome adversity and serve as a vital example that their transformation can change the functioning of society for the greater good. Aly Raisman, a two-time Olympic gold medal gymnast, and Liz and Jay Scott, founders of Alex's Lemonade Stand Foundation, serve as realistic examples of the trials, triumphs, and profound impact that motivational transformations have on both a personal and societal level, leaving the world changed for the better.

The face of the USA Women's Gymnastics Team both in 2012 and 2016, Aly Raisman is recognized by all and highly regarded by most. She led the team to victory in the London 2012 Olympics, receiving a bronze medal for her performance on the beam and a gold medal for her floor routine. Aly was a leader among the group of five young girls who came to be known as the "Fierce Five" throughout the Olympic competition. The team won overall gold, defeating impressive and historically successful teams trained in Russia, Romania, and China. With three medals around her neck, Raisman became the most decorated American gymnast in London. Before participating in the Olympic trials, she had given up the opportunity to do gymnastics at University of Florida, and took a major risk in deciding to pursue professional gymnastics rather than higher education.

Her dedication and determination to succeed led her to impressively high achievements in London in 2012, and her success didn't stop there. Although she was injured in 2012 during a tour, Aly rose above and didn't let the injury stunt her future. She returned to Olympic training in 2014, and was named again to the USA Women's Gymnastics Team. The 2016 Rio Olympics brought even more success to Aly and her team, winning the team gold medal yet again. She was praised for her maturation both as a gymnast and a leader among her peers, and although she did not win the all-around gold medal in 2016, Aly continued to be highly regarded for her skills and courageous attitude in the sport, especially in times of intense competition (International Olympic Committee, 2017).

From an early age, Aly embodied many of the characteristics that researchers define as traits of a hero (Allison & Goethals, 2011). Raisman was heroic in her physical abilities ("strong"), her skills as a leader for her Olympic teammates ("selfless," "caring," and "reliable"), her strength in overcoming injuries ("resilient") and her ability to serve as a positive role model to countless young and aspiring gymnasts worldwide ("inspiring"). Especially evident is Raisman's physical heroism in achieving what others thought impossible in the tumbling pass of a floor routine. She took a major risk in performing a "round-off, one-and-a-half stepout, into a roundoff back handspring, arabian double front, punch layout" in her first tumbling pass of the 2012 London Olympics. Although it had never been accomplished by any other gymnast, Raisman humbly stated that "the first tumbling pass is crucial to the routine because it sets the tone" for success in the remaining movements of her routine (Wall Street Journal, 2016). She conquered new territory in the world of gymnastics without a boastful attitude and rather with a quiet confidence in her capabilities. Indeed, Raisman showed great heroic humility (Worthington & Allison, 2018).

Allison and Goethals (2014) describe the needs-based hero as one that arises from individuals finding heroic status in another figure due to their personal needs in that time of development. More than likely, Raisman served as this situational, needs-based hero to gymnasts who were lacking a drive to continue the intense training and rehearsal that gymnastics requires. With her trait of inspiration at the forefront, she displayed determination and commitment in her media appearances and performances, therefore potentially becoming a needs-based hero even without her knowing. Regardless of the various forms of heroism that Raisman may have fulfilled in her performance as a gymnast and service as an Olympic leader, the transformation that occurred two years after her last Olympics is what led to an unwavering distinction of Raisman being a hero to all. Nothing could have predicted the astounding impact that she would make some years later, uncovering that her moments in the spotlight were not as shiny as the gold medals hanging around her neck.

Inspired by the braveness of other gymnasts coming forward against a villain, Aly Raisman publicly came forward with a powerfully heroic statement on January 19, 2018 during a sentencing trial for US Olympic Doctor Larry Nassar. Nassar was discovered to have been sexually abusing the young women that he treated during their time competing with the US Gymnastics team, taking many of the gymnastics into private rooms for "treatments" to heal their injuries. Raisman stated, "Imagine how it feels to be an innocent teenager in a foreign country, hearing a knock on the door, and it's you. I don't want you to be there, but I don't have a choice. Treatments with you were mandatory. You took advantage of that. You even told on us if we didn't want to be treated by you, knowing full well the troubles that would cause for us" (Gajanan, 2018).

In watching the press coverage of the intense and emotional story that Raisman exposes in her sentencing statement, it was evident that she was resurfacing something difficult that had been creeping beneath the surface of her achievements for over 6 years. Although it took time and influence by other brave souls to confront the negativity in her Olympic experience, Raisman displayed insurmountable wisdom and a desire for change-for change that expanded far beyond having Larry Nassar punished for his actions. She addressed her personal drive towards healing from the anxiety that Nassar's abuse caused her. She looked Nassar in the eye, facing the enemy with full force.

This simple act of stepping out and wanting to overcome the tragic experience of sexual abuse allowed her to become a needs-based hero to those in similar situations, proving that it is possible to heal following abuse. Since the day of her sentencing trial statement, Raisman has been a prevalent and impactful figure in supporting victims of sexual violence, writing a book entitled Fierce: How Competing for Myself Changed Everything and partnering with Darkness to Light's #fliptheswitch campaign that encourages adults to properly educate children on how to recognize sexual abuse (Darkness to Light, 2018). Raisman could have stopped there, pleasantly settling with the fact that justice was served by getting Nassar locked up. Serving as a spokesperson for the awareness and prevention of sexual abuse highly regards her as a hero in and of itself, but the return to her familiar world signifies the profound impact of her motivational transformation.

In her statement, Raisman boldly addressed a systems-level change that was the overarching enemy across the negative events of sexual abuse for her and over 140 other girls- USA Gymnastics and the United States Olympic Committee. She explained the various ways in which Nassar's horrendous actions were covered up by officials, massively due to the fact that Nassar had aided in the creation of policies lasting over 30 years that were meant to protect the gymnasts from medical harm. Raisman powerfully stated, "I will not rest until every last trace of your influence on this sport has been destroyed like the cancer it is...to believe in the future of gymnastics is to believe in change. False assurances from organizations are dangerous, they make it easier to look away from problem and enable bad to happen" (Gajanan, 2018). With this statement, she exhibited urgency in her newfound motivation, abandoning any acceptance of stagnation within the system of creating policies that support athletes (Gajanan, 2018).

In Joseph Campbell's monomyth of a hero, the return to the hero's familiar world is of highest importance in the capability to make a difference to society at large (Allison, Goethals, & Kramer, 2017). In the conclusion of her statement, Raisman reminds Nassar that he has not taken gymnastics away from her, sharing that it "is stronger than the evil that resides in you, in the those that enabled you." (Gajanan, 2018). There's no denying that she found motivation and purpose in her time successfully competing as a gymnast. However, Raisman's transformations through the negative events of her experienced sexual abuse fostered within her a newfound motivation to not only hold the villain accountable for his action, but to return to her familiar world and make massive change. Since the day of the trial, three board members for US Gymnastics have resigned, the organization has been sued and it is being forced to make systems-level changes because of Raisman (Hobson, 2018). Her words, her desire to heal, and her urgency to remove Nassar's influences from gymnastics are already creating evident changes to society at large.

LIZ AND JAY SCOTT'S MOTIVATED HEROISM

Liz and Jay Scott were ordinary parents in Connecticut with four children, fighting to create the best life possible for their developing family. Following the first birthday of their daughter, Alex, they received tragic news that would alter the trajectory of their lives, but not in a typical nor desirable fashion. Alex was diagnosed with neuroblastoma, a type of cancer that develops within the early nerve cells of the sympathetic nervous system in children. Doctors informed the family that even if she was to survive the cancer, her condition would not allow her to walk for the rest of her life. However, Alex heavily surpassed their expectations, living until the age of eight years old. The Scotts were heroic to their daughter, consistently providing her support and resources to receive treatment and seek hope amidst the darkness of cancer. Their original motivations towards fighting to keep their daughter life were forced into an unexpected transformation after her passing in August of 2004.

Joseph Campbell's monomyth of a hero journey includes the help of a mentor that guides the individual towards finding their missing inner quality (Allison, Goethals, & Kramer, 2017). A young and tragically ill girl named Alex served as this mentor to her own parents, Liz and Jay Scott. She exhibited strength despite the consistent attack of cancer on her body, learning to walk at the age of two years old despite the doctors' prognosis. However, her physical strength could not always carry on, as the cancer spread and her life expectancy shortened yet again. Following a stem cell surgery at the age of four, Alex informed her mother that she wanted to have a lemonade stand when she got out of the hospital to help other children that were suffering from cancer like herself. Blown away by her altruism and dream to strive towards a better reality in cancer research, her parents agreed and they hosted the first of many "Alex's Lemonade Stand" events, raising over $2000. The lemonade stand became a tradition in the Scott household that eventually caught national attention. Even in her short eight years, Alex made a massive impact on the lives of many. She displayed many of the Great Eight traits of heroism, especially strength, resilience, and selflessness beyond her years (Allison & Goethals, 2011).

In a small way, Alex experienced a motivational transformation once the cancer began to take her away. Her work with running lemonade stands, while at first a charismatic and small effort to seek change as a child, surpassed expectations and became one of the largest national cancer fundraisers. However, Alex is not the hero experiencing motivation transformation in this narrative, but rather the mentor. She instilled within her parents, Liz and Jay, something vital to the trajectory of their lives, even if she didn't have the chance to witness that transformation while still on earth.

After the passing of their beloved young girl, Liz and Jay were faced with many options. Their hope and experience of happiness could have been profoundly shattered by the fact that they lost the love of their lives, causing a sinking downward spiral of depression. It could have fostered a development of learned helplessness due to their consistent efforts in trying to save their daughter that ultimately failed with her death. Such a reaction would not only have threatened their own well-beings but also those of their other three children and their surrounding community, as helplessness and perceived loss of control would be detrimental to all social relationships. The Scotts, too, may have chosen to avoid the word "cancer" for the rest of their lives, shutting out any negative memories that the disease brought to their family, remaining comfortably stagnant following Alex's death.

Stagnation may not have appeared to have any long-term consequences, as there could have been some form of discovered happiness from the removal of the negative stimulus "cancer." However, as Allison and Goethals (2017) explain, the experience of stagnation would remove the possibility of finding fulfilled purpose and a future life trajectory. While they may have been able to have positive life experiences that eliminated any sense of depression or perceived loss of control, the Scotts simultaneously would never have made a full transformation that welcomed the possibility of growing from the negative event in a way that changed the society around them. Luckily, Alex was a heroic mentor during her life and even after her death. Because of Alex's influence within her short but vibrant life, Liz and Jay were able to defeat both downfall and stagnation, instead carrying on Alex's legacy and continuing to raise money for childhood research in the form of nationwide lemonade stands.

Alex's Lemonade Stand Foundation is now one of the largest childhood cancer foundations that has raised more than $80 million since its establishment in 2006. The organization has not only supported over 450 research projects in hospitals, but also has a variety of programs aimed at bettering the lives of families struck by childhood cancer. Liz and Jay Scott serve as the co-executive directors of the foundation, and have more than 35 staff members supporting them. They are constantly striving to counteract the negative experience that they had in losing a child to cancer by raising money that goes towards preventing childhood cancer at the forefront. Rather than simply becoming needs-based heroes for other parents that might need an example of parents that grow from their grief, the Scotts are working to stop the initial cause.

Additionally, they do not shy away from reminders of Alex's life, and instead welcome any and all positive influences that her short but fulfilling life had on society as a whole. In this way, the Scott's have become examples of figures that create diamonds out of dust, demonstrating massive resilience, selflessness, and strength despite the barriers that loss and grief present. Alex's Lemonade Stand has recently been named one of Charity Navigator's "10 Best Medical Research Organizations" in the United States. Even more special is the way in which the foundation fosters the potential for heroism within everybody. Jay explains that anyone is capable of setting up a lemonade stand that supports Alex's desire to provide financial resources to the fight against childhood cancer. Fundraisers can be seen across the nation on college campuses, neighborhood streets, and everywhere in between (Alex's Lemonade Stand, 2018). When life gave the Scotts lemons, they not only made lemonade but allowed for society at large to do the same, fostering a vital sense of growth that spread beyond their initial desires to continue Alex's legacy.

CONCLUDING THOUGHTS

How can society find good in this tragic and complex world? While there has not yet been an answer revealing a way to prevent bad things from happening, it is evident that individuals overcoming their own negative experiences can display good by allowing their tragedy and grief to alter their lifetime motivations towards the greater good. Aly Raisman did so in the form of addressing not only the villain that is Larry Nassar, but by fighting for better policies within US Gymnastics as a whole. She was not required to come forward with her testimony, and even then did not have to address more than the internal experience she had with Nassar and his abusive actions (Beggan & Allison, 2018). However, the motivational transformation that occurred after years of abuse led her to attack the system with urgency and boldness (Davis et al., 2011).

Similarly, Liz and Jay were not required to continue Alex's lemonade stand following her death. No one would have blamed them for wanting to move on from the world of childhood cancer. Instead, however, the transformation they experienced altered their motivations in a way that served the greater good of the medical world, providing more financial resources towards research in preventing and treating childhood cancer. Motivational transformations provide a light in the darkness, allow others to find hope in hopeless situations, and create systems-level changes in society to prevent the dangerous state of stagnation. P.T. Barnum stated it perfectly in "The Greatest Showman," emphasizing the incapability of heroes to "go back again to the world that (they) were living in," but rather to use their altered motivations to create an improved world, one that brings their dreams to life.

REFERENCES

Allison, S. T., & Goethals, G. R. (2011). Heroes: What they do and why we need them. New York: Oxford University Press.

Allison, S. T., & Goethals, G. R. (2014). "Now he belongs to the ages": The heroic leadership dynamic and deep narratives of greatness. In Goethals, G. R., et al. (Eds.), Conceptions of leadership: Enduring ideas and emerging insights. New York: Palgrave Macmillan.

Allison, S. T., & Goethals, G. R. (2017). The hero's transformation. In S.T. Allison, G. R. Goethals, & R.M. Kramer (Eds.), Handbook of Heroism and Heroic Leadership. New York: Routledge.

Allison, S. T., Goethals, G. R., & Kramer, R. M. (2017). Setting the scene: The rise and coalescence of heroism science. In S.T. Allison, G. R. Goethals, & R.M. Kramer (Eds.), Handbook of Heroism and Heroic Leadership. New York: Routledge.

Darkness to Light. (2018, March 08). Aly Raisman partners with Darkness to Light to provide immediate training and support to gymnastics community. Retrieved from https://www.d2l.org/aly-raisman-partners-darkness-light-provide-immediate-training-support-gymnastics-community/

Davis, J. L., Burnette, J. L., Allison, S. T., & Stone, H. (2011). Against the odds: Academic underdogs benefit from incremental theories. Social Psychology of Education, 14, 331-346.

Gajanan, M. (2018, January 19). 'It's your turn to listen to me.' Read Aly Raisman's testimony at Larry Nassar's sentencing. Time Magazine.

Glista, K. (2014, September 26). When life gave their daughter cancer, she made lemonade. Hartford Courant. Retrieved from https://www.courant.com/courant-250/moments-in-history/hc-250-alex-lemonade-stand-20140926-story.html

Gracey, M. (Director). (2017). The Greatest Showman [Motion Picture]. United States: Twentieth Century Fox.

Hobson, W. (2018, January 24). Larry Nassar, former USA Gymnastics doctor, sentenced to 40-175 years for sex crimes. Retrieved from https://www.washingtonpost.com/.

Hoyt, C. L., Allison, S. T., Barnowski, A., & Sultan, A. (2020). Lay theories of heroism and leadership: The role of gender, communion, and agency. Social Psychology.

International Olympic Committee. (2017, April 27). Alexandra Raisman. Retrieved from https://www.olympic.org/alexandra-raisman

Maier, S. F., & Seligman, M. E. (1976). Learned helplessness: Theory and evidence. Journal of Experimental Psychology: General, 105(1), 3-46. doi:10.1037/0096-3445.105.1.3

Nuvvula, S. (2016). Learned helplessness. Contemporary Clinical Dentistry, 7(4), 426. doi:10.4103/0976-237x.194124

Ryan, R. M., & Deci, E. L. (2000). Intrinsic and extrinsic motivations: Classic definitions and new directions. Contemporary Educational Psychology, 25(1), 54-67. doi:10.1006/ceps.1999.1020

Wall Street Journal. (2016, July 08). Inside the floor routine once thought impossible. Retrieved from https://www.youtube.com/watch?v=2VX29jEkyhA

Worthington, E. L, & Allison, S. T. (2018). Heroic humility: What the science of humility can say to people raised on self-focus. Washington. DC: American Psychological Association.

3

ADHERENCE TO PRINCIPLES: THE HEROISM OF CHARLOTTE BRONTË AND EDITH WHARTON

SMARAGDA P. SPYROU

I was experiencing an ordeal: a hand of fiery iron grasped my vitals. Terrible moment: full of struggle, blackness, burning! Not a human being that ever lived could wish to be loved better than I was loved; and him who thus loved me I absolutely worshipped: and I must renounce love and idol.
- Charlotte Brontë (1998) p. 473

[...]let me ask myself a question – Which is better? – To have surrendered to temptation; listened to passion; made no painful effort – no struggle; - but [...] to have been now living in France, Mr. Rochester's mistress; delirious with his love half my time – for he would – oh, yes, he would have loved me well for a while. He did love me – no one will ever love me so again.[...]Whether it is better, I ask, to be a slave in a fool's paradise in Marseilles – fevered with delusive bliss one hour – suffocating with the bitterest tears of remorse and shame the next – or to be a village-schoolmistress, free and honest [...]? Yes; I feel now that I was right

54

when I adhered to principle and law, and scorned and crushed the insane prompt-ings of a frenzied moment.
- Charlotte Brontë (1998) p. 539

The very good people did not convince me; I felt they'd never been tempted. But you knew; you understood; you felt the world outside tugging at one with all its golden hands - and you hated the things it asked of one; you hated happiness bought by disloyalty and cruelty and indifference. That was what I'd never known before - and it's better than anything I've known.
- Edith Wharton (2006) p. 122

I couldn't have my happiness made out of a wrong—an unfairness—to somebody else.... What sort of life could we build on such foundations?
- Edith Wharton (2006) p. 105

These four quotations address the ultimate temptation: the possibility of happiness. The heroines of both of the above stories held happiness at the tips of their fingers and had to let it slip away because of the means necessary to fully grasp it. Sacrificing beliefs and principles was the price to pay for being with the men they loved, and as difficult as the decision was, neither of them could bear to pay that price. There are few cases in which it is perfectly justifiable to falter in this way, but love is definitely one of them. Neither woman had someone to hold her to any standards, both were given interpretations of the situation that made it seem okay to go against their beliefs in this case. Both of them had every reason to stay, but both of them chose to leave.

Reader, you may think this decision foolish, and that is your prerogative. After all, as they say, all is fair in love and war. Or is it? Millions have devoted their lives to love, making sacrifices they would not make for anything else, and most of the time, as humans, we allow such a stance to ourselves or others we see as our equals. But then why is it that humans are so inspired by such stories? Why do they keep being written? What heart string do they strum? And why do we idolize and glorify people who act as such? I argue that said heart string is none other than the awe of such strength of character in the face of temptation, and the desire to attain it, and we need these stories, and these people, to remind us and show us how. That is why we have higher expectations from our heroes and leaders.

Existing literature shows that we attribute moral integrity, conviction, and self-sacrifice to our heroes (Kinsella et al., 2015a), we think of them as strong and selfless individuals (Allison & Goethals, 2011, 2014, 2017) who model morality for us (Kinsella et al., 2015b), which means we expect them to uphold their values and moral beliefs in a time when most tempted not to – when love is at stake. The chapter you are about to read is intended to demonstrate that this adherence to principles is a necessary component of heroism. It does so through the stories of Jane Eyre, and Ellen Olenska.

DEFINING PRINCIPLES

The word principle comes from the Latin word princip, or princeps, which means first, or the source, beginning, or foundation. Similarly, in the Greek language, αρχή, the word for principle, is the same word used for beginning or source. What does that tell us about the meaning of principles? They are ideas or rules which constitute the basis for, or source of, our actions; the foundation of our behavior. Each individual forms and reforms his or her own principles throughout their lifetime, based on the principles they are taught at a young age to be more correct, their beliefs and understanding of the world, and their experiences thereafter. They are then used as a point of reference for deciding their behaviors.

The Role of Principles

Principles can be divided into several categories based on the context in which they belong; for instance, morality related principles like "it is not right to kill", priority based principles: "family comes before everything else", and so forth. They are meant to serve as a guide through tough times; usually pre-decided during a period of clear mind, to be referenced when in doubt or when judgement may be clouded. As Charlotte Brontë's character, Jane Eyre, eloquently reflects:

I will hold to the principles received by me when I was sane, and not mad—as I am now. Laws and principles are not for the times when there is no temptation: they are for such moments as this when body and soul rise in mutiny against their rigor; stringent are they; inviolate they shall be. If at my individual convenience I might break them, what would be their worth? They have a worth—so I have always believed; and if I cannot believe it now, it is because I am insane—quite insane: with my veins running fire, and my heart beating faster than I can count its throbs. [These principles] are all I have at this hour to stand by: there I plant my foot. (Brontë, 1998, p.475)

Very correctly put, principles are conclusions we reach after careful consideration and weighing of various options, behaviors, and feelings, during times when our mind is mostly clear, and sometimes even after having parsed and discussed them with others. They represent what we believe to be right and wrong. New experiences may sometimes be cause for reconsidering these values but, as a general rule, that would require another process of introspection and reflection. Their worth therefore stems from the thought and hard work that has been put into them during a state of soberness, and their representation of years of life experiences and reflection.

The Significance of Adhering to Principles

In the Christian religion, the Ten Commandments may constitute a basic set of principles which Christians should follow if they wish to find their way to heaven. These commandments are spelled out for the people, to make decisions easier in the face of temptation. When the individual has a very clear idea of the principle, in this case if the principle has been concisely and specifically stated, then there is no doubt, no room for interpretation based on circumstances. This is however rarely the case in people's lives. It is a common fallacy when faced with a difficult decision (temptation), and adhering to a principle results in consequences that the individual believes they cannot bear, to try and reason with oneself, and find an alternate interpretation of the principle, or an exception to it, such that would better fit the individual's preferred course of action.

If there is no room for interpretation however, like with the Ten Commandments, the individual only has two choices: re-evaluate the significance and correctness of the principle, or act according to it. Both choices require great internal strength: in one case the individual has to recognize and accept a mistake in a fundamental belief and, in the other, they have to show faith in said belief despite the potentially negative immediate consequences. In terms of humanity, I dare say the second decision is more difficult to make. Although admitting an error is one of the most challenging tasks for an individual, accepting negative consequences when there exists a seemingly more painless route is usually even more challenging. And when the painless route also includes a reward, this challenge significantly increases.

That is why adherence to principles and strength of character are so venerated in classic stories, with the hero always doing the right thing. "[W]e care about heroic stories because they serve as powerful reminders that people are capable of resisting evil, of not giving in to temptations, of rising above mediocrity, and of heeding the call to action and to service when others fail to act" (Phil Zimbardo as quoted in Franco et al., 2016).

Although it may seem unfair to hold them to such different standards than we hold ourselves, it is true and understandable. We look for qualities in heroes which we ourselves lack, because those individuals are what we strive to one day become, just like in the Christian religion, where God is the ideal, and believers spend their lives in an attempt to approach his perfection. We hold our heroes to the standards we want to hold ourselves but do not have the strength of character to.

THE EXEMPLAR OF JANE EYRE

Jane Eyre was raised as an orphan under the care of her uncle's wife, Mrs. Reed, and her three children, Eliza, Georgiana, and John. No one in that family treated her as a member of it, but John behaved especially cruelly to her, consistently mocking and terrorizing her. Jane disliked her situation, but never challenged it until one day, when John hit her in the head really hard, and her aunt punished her for fighting back by locking her in her late uncle's bedroom for several days. Following these events, Jane finally spoke up to Mrs. Reed and demanded to be sent away to school, an idea proposed by the family's apothecary. Soon after, Mr. Brocklehurst, the director of the Lowood School for orphan girls appeared at the Reeds' house to interview Jane for a place in his school.

Jane spent the next eight years of her life there, six as a student and two as a teacher. She went through many hardships including malnourishment, loss, and humiliation (Worthington & Allison, 2018), but she also gained a dear friend, and a lesson in perspective, patience, tolerance, and acceptance, as well as an education in all the feminine subjects of the time: knitting, music, and languages (mostly French). After her second year teaching there, armed with the tools and qualities she earned there, Jane decided to leave the world of Lowood, and left to work as a governess for a young girl at Thornfield Hall.

In Thornfield Hall, after conversations, arguments, and benevolent mind games, Jane slowly fell in love with the master of the estate, Mr. Rochester. The relationship developed between the two was made even more powerful by the fact that it remained purely platonic was platonic throughout, and was based solely on the mental connection they were able to establish as a result of their mutual psychological maturity and depth of thought. The connection they had was very rare; one which most people have never experienced and could not understand, mostly known today as "once in a lifetime". Soon the two expressed their feelings to each other, and Mr. Rochester proposed that Jane be his wife,

Jane accepted, and a month later their wedding took place. Unfortunately, during the ceremony, Jane Eyre's newly discovered uncle's lawyer, Mr. Briggs, professes that Mr. Rochester is in fact already married to another woman, Bertha Mason. Admitting the reality of this accusation, Mr. Rochester leads Jane to Thornfield's attic where Bertha resides. Jane witnessed a wild, disheveled woman with "a purple face" and "bloated features". Upon seeing her visitors, "the lunatic sprang and grapples [Mr. Rochester's] throat viciously, and laid her teeth to his cheek". They struggled for some time until Mr. Rochester managed to restrain her. Mr. Rochester's case for insisting to marry Jane although he was already married had been made – his wife had lost her mind many years ago, and was effectively not his companion anymore, not to mention he had been tricked into marrying her in the first place. Although Jane understood this, she also knew that it would still not be legal to marry Rochester. That meant that she would have to stay at his side as his mistress, a title very much against her beliefs.

Knowing that she couldn't see Rochester every day and act normally, she realized that to remain true to her principles, she would have to never see him again.

But she was too proud to ask her new-found uncle for his help, and didn't have anywhere else to go, or the means to sustain herself. She left despite that however, walked alone for almost a week with no food or shelter, or any reason to believe she had hope.

When Jane became aware of Mr. Rochester's mad wife, she was faced with two options. Either to make an effort to view things as Rochester did: that he was deceived into marrying his wife and has never loved her, that she is mad and has been so for years, and she never has and never will count as his companion in life, so in spirit Jane would not be his mistress, and be able to stay with the man she loved; or to listen to her instinct, that if she were to stay by his side she would never find comfort for the fact that she had consciously determined it wrong on principle to stay by Rochester's side while he was still married to someone yet still did so, but face the reality of a lifetime away from the love of her life. This dilemma is one of the most difficult ones any human being will ever have to face: a fight between the purest, most valuable, and most sought-after emotion we are capable of, and following a rule which we only have to answer to ourselves for.

Jane therefore identified the principle that was clashing with her desires and decided that, although a tough call, adhering to her principle was more important than giving in to her feelings for Rochester and her fear of what life would be without him. Right or wrong, good or bad, regardless of the outcome, the moment she made that decision she became a hero. In Jane's case, she was able to return and be with Rochester. However, that is not always the case. Most times we actually have to deal with the consequences of our decisions forever. This was the case with Ellen Olenska.

THE EXEMPLAR OF ELLEN OLENSKA

Ellen Olenska is one of the two main characters in Edith Wharton's The Age of Innocence, an ironically titled novel about the late 19th century New York elite. Ellen was born and raised in Europe, although her family was originally from New York. At the age of ten, upon her parents' death, Ellen moved to New York with her aunt, Medora Manson, who assumed responsibility of her upbringing thereafter. When Medora's husband passed away, she and Ellen returned to Europe. There, Ellen received an expensive but unconventional by New York standards education and eventually met and married the wealthy Polish Count Olenski. However, along with wealth came infidelity and presumably violence, which led Ellen to leave her husband and seek sanctuary back in New York.

Unfortunately, the title of divorcée, her European education, and her aunt's reputation did not work in Ellen's favor upon her reentrance to the New York society. Her name soon became associated with scandal, and it was frowned upon to allow young, unwed ladies alone in her company.

Upon her return to New York, Ellen reconnected with her grandmother, Mrs. Mingott, and people of her age with whom she was friends in her childhood. Among those, her cousin, May Welland, and the young Mr. Newland Archer, May's fiancé. Owing to the scandal surrounding her aunt, her education abroad, and her marriage, or rather, the termination thereof, Ellen was unwelcome in her family's circles, with the only exceptions being her grandmother, and Archer. Some kept up pretenses of being in her favor, either because it was proper for them to do so, or it benefited them in some way.

During her time there, Ellen interacted often with Archer, as no one else really sought out her company or conversation. Although a slave to the New York code of conduct, Archer was neither a believer nor a supporter of it. That constituted the main reason why he was the only one who could truly understand and connect with Ellen. For Archer, Ellen was genuine, brave, and wise. She was the polar opposite of his fiancé. She excited him and made him feel things no one else had before, and she showed him the problems in abiding by the social mandates. For Ellen, Archer was a breath of fresh air in the prison she walked into trying to escape from her husband. He was a friend, an arm to hold onto for support, and hope. Hope of a happy future away from her ex-husband, and away from New York.

However, being ostracized by everyone, or being forced to follow rules that were pretentious and aimed at changing her someone she was not, Ellen could not live in New York anymore. When Archer made his feelings for her clear, she initially asked him to come with her. In turn, he asked her to remain in New York under his protection. However, as it turned out, although they both developed strong feelings and cared deeply for one another, neither of them could accept the other one's offer. Archer, defiant though he was in theory, had been raised with the rules and regulations of the New York society, and was comfortable in them. He knew how to act, when to act, how to speak, when to speak, how to read the people around him. But above all, he had built a reality which would be shattered were he to leave the bubble that was New York. On the other hand, Ellen knew she would die inside if she were to stay in that place for the rest of her life. Despite all this however, Ellen's decision did not become absolutely clear until her cousin, Archer's wife-to-be, though yet unsure, confided with Ellen that she was expecting Arthur's son. After that, Ellen had no option but to leave not only New York, but most importantly Archer.

She hadn't always felt that way however. Ellen was a woman who generally obtained what she desired, and she had every intention of having Archer. However, meeting him, knowing him, loving him, she grew wiser and realized what was more important to her. To add to one of the opening quotes of this chapter:

I felt there was no one as kind as you; no one who gave me reasons that I understood for doing what at first seemed so hard and—unnecessary. The very good people didn't convince me; I felt they'd never been tempted. But you knew; you understood; you had felt the world outside tugging at one with all its golden hands—and yet you hated the things it asks of one; you hated happiness bought by disloyalty and cruelty and indifference. That was what I'd never known before—and it's better than anything I've known.... I can't go back now to that other way of thinking. I can't love you unless I give you up. (Wharton, 2006, p.122)

These were Ellen's words to Archer, explaining the change in her thought process, and her reasons for having to leave him. Ellen decided that once her eyes had been opened to the importance of adhering to her principles, doing things the right way, not sacrificing her morals for her desires, not achieving her goals by not taking any prisoners, she could not turn a blind eye to it. By telling Archer that she cannot love him unless she gives him up, she is telling him that the pure emotions required to feel true love, are the same as those which require her to love and forgive all people, and do what is right.

Similar to Jane Eyre, Ellen had to make a really difficult decision – to do what shed believed to be wrong to be with the man she loves, or to forsake that hope because the means to achieving it trespassed on her fundamental beliefs.

Unlike Jane however, Ellen's story did not have the happy ending a reader would yearn for. After leaving New York she did not return to her husband as she had told Archer she would, and had ended up living alone in Paris. Many years after their last encounter, Ellen and Archer were to meet again at her apartment in Paris, as arranged by Archer's son after May's death. However, once the two men arrived outside of the building, Archer sent his son up with the promise that he would join them soon, a promise he did not keep. Therefore, Ellen never saw Archer again after leaving him, and it is implied she never found another suitable companion either.

CONCLUDING THOUGHTS

If anything were to be taken as your understanding from this chapter, it would be that adherence to principles is a difficult task to undertake, especially in the face of temptation, and only those strong in character, like heroes, can achieve it (Allison & Cecilione, 2016). The research that has so far been conducted has mostly been concerned with understanding the lay people's understanding of heroes, and their perception of the qualities one must possess to be classified as such. People, therefore, have determined the results of that research. It is people who have decided that heroes must be held to higher moral standards than most, they must showcase strength, self-sacrifice, righteousness (Allison & Goethals, 2017). In this case, heroes have no choice but to sacrifice things most dear to them to ensure their actions are representative of the high moral standards to which they are held.

Fictional heroes will often 'earn' a happy ending as a result of adhering to their principles, a technique used to convey the message that with loyalty to principles comes reward. In the Christian religion, those who repent for their sins and believe in God will be rewarded by going to heaven, a reward they cannot experience until after they die, and which will likely be preceded by many occasions which may resemble punishments instead.

In real life however, this happy ending is not guaranteed. When a hero acts according to their values, in spite of other desires or temptations, they do so assuming that there may as well not be a happy ending, which is what makes their actions heroic in the first place. There is no guarantee of an ultimate reward for their actions, except perhaps the gratification they may feel from doing the right thing. In fact, more often than not, the immediate consequences of their righteous decisions may seem as punishment.

Jane had her happy ending, Ellen did not, but given the character given to them, if they were to go back in time, they would most likely make the same choice again; so would all true heroes. Which is why they are revered so and admired.

REFERENCES

Allison, S. T. (2019). Heroic consciousness. Heroism Science, 4, 1-43.

Allison, S. T., & Cecilione, J. L. (2016). Paradoxical truths in heroic leadership: Implications for leadership development and effectiveness. In R. Bolden, M. Witzel, & N. Linacre (Eds.), Leadership paradoxes. London: Routledge.

Allison, S. T., & Goethals, G. R. (2011). Heroes: What they do and why we need them. New York: Oxford University Press.

Allison, S. T., & Goethals, G. R. (2014). "Now he belongs to the ages": The heroic leadership dynamic and deep narratives of greatness. In Goethals, G. R., et al. (Eds.), Conceptions of leadership: Enduring ideas and emerging insights. New York: Palgrave Macmillan.

Allison, S. T., Goethals, G. R., & Kramer, R. M. (Eds.) (2017). Handbook of heroism and heroic leadership. New York: Routledge.

Brontë, C. (1998). Jane Eyre. Birmingham, AL: Sweetwater Press.

Franco, Z. E., Allison, S. T., Kinsella, E. L., Kohen, A., Langdon, M., & Zimbardo, P. G. (2017). Heroism research: A review of theories, methods, challenges, and trends. Journal of Humanistic Psychology, 58(4), 382-396.

Hoyt, C. L., Allison, S. T., Barnowski, A., & Sultan, A. (2020). Lay theories of heroism and leadership: The role of gender, communion, and agency. Social Psychology.

Kinsella, E. L., Ritchie, T. D., & Igou, E. R. (2015). Zeroing in on heroes: A prototype analysis of hero features. Journal of Personality and Social Psychology, 108(1), 114-127. doi:10.1037/a0038463

Kinsella, E. L., Ritchie, T. D., & Igou, E. R. (2015). Lay perspectives on the social and psychological functions of heroes. Frontiers in Psychology, 6. doi:10.3389/fpsyg.2015.00130

Principle. (n.d.). Retrieved from https://www.merriam-webster.com/dictionary/principle

Thompson, P. (2017, December). Timeline. Retrieved from
    http://jane-eyre.guidesite.co.uk/timeline
Wharton, E. (1996). The Age of Innocence (Penguin Classics). Penguin Books.
    Edited with an Introduction by Cynthia Griffin Wolfe
Wharton, E., & Orgel, S. (2006). The Age of Innocence (Oxford Worlds Classics). Oxford
    University Press.
Worthington, E. L, & Allison, S. T. (2018). Heroic humility: What the science of humility can say to
    people raised on self-focus. Washington. DC: American Psychological Association.

4

Wax On, Wax Off: The Transformative Effect of Mentors on Heroes

NATALIE R. SCHIANO

As the legendary Mr. Miyagi advised his apprentice, Daniel, there is "no such thing as bad student, only bad teacher. Teacher say, student do" (Avildsen, 1984). Human transformation is key to survival. You either adapt, or your legacy will go extinct. Humans, as social animals, have the capacity to teach and learn. Through mentors, human beings can grow and transform. We are moldable at birth. Mentors shape this clay into heroic or villainous versions of what it once was. Heroes and villains appear so similar because they are embarking on the same path. They are simply at different points within that path. We all have qualities of heroism and villainy within us and can fluctuate between the two social labels. Mentors offer guidance to ensure that our transformation is a positive one that leads us to heroism and morality.

Heroes originate through training and by embarking on a journey (Allison, 2019; Allison, Goethals, & Spyrou, 2019). Part of that journey is mentorship, or training by a wise individual. Rarely do people complete the journey alone. Receiving assistance from others plays a key role in developing that missing inner-quality and in maintaining a support system when persevering through difficult times. Heroes are usually marked by resiliency, which they develop through the experience of tragedy and desperation (Allison, Beggan, & Efthimiou, 2019). Humans are social animals. Despair is not easy to overcome alone. Mentors help heroes persevere through this despair and come out on the other end stronger and more resilient. Regardless of the story, the hero is always helped along the journey by the "actual, imagined, or implied presence of others" (Allison & Goethals, 2017). The Karate Kid depicts an implied mentor presence. Mulan portrays the dragon Mushu, whose actual presence accompanies Mulan throughout the entirety of her journey. After his father dies, Simba follows Mufasa's sage advice via his imagined presence in The Lion King. Mentors are vital not only in survival, but in transformation. They turn stories from survival stories to heroic transformation stories, as demonstrated in The Karate Kid, Mulan, and The Lion King.

Campbell (1949) identified the monomyth of the hero in which each hero must endure a departure, initiation, and return. Throughout their journey, they are summoned on an expedition, are missing an important quality, experience trials and tribulations, receive assistance from others, find their missing inner-quality, successfully complete their mission, and return to their familiar world to bestow a boon. However, no hero completes their journey alone. To gain their missing inner-quality, they need guidance. Life is rooted in transformation. Like the phoenix, we all must rise from the ashes, "renewed and reborn" (Brenner, 2015). Without mentors, the fire of their trials and tribulations remains destructive. With mentors, fire is transformative and burns the identity we need to shed to reveal who we truly are, as heroes. In this metamorphosis, heroes often gain the "Great Eight" characteristics. Under the careful guidance of their mentors, they become strong, smart, selfless, caring, charismatic, resilient, reliable, and inspiring (Allison & Smith, 2015).

From the moment of birth, humans undergo extreme transformation, from the "condition of a little water creature living in a realm of amniotic fluid into an air-breathing mammal" (Allison & Goethals, 2017). However, this transformation would not be possible without a mentor. Without a mother to catalyze the reaction, we could not begin a "lifetime of transformative journeys" (Allison & Goethals, 2017). We are dependent upon mentors and guides to incite our transformation from our very first moments on this earth. We move through various transformations as we age and shift our priorities. First comes the transformation of "setting, self, and society in that order" (Allison & Goethals, 2017). The fourth, and final, external source of transformation is the "social environment" of the hero. The hero's journey is ever populated by "numerous friends, companions, lovers, parent figures, and mentors who assist the hero on her quest" (Allison & Goethals, 2017).

When surveyed, people who were asked to name their heroes typically mentioned a "mentor or a coach who has a transformative effect on them" (Allison & Goethals, 2017). In this way, mentors themselves are a type of hero. Due to the cyclical nature of heroism, oftentimes mentors are heroes who bring their newfound wisdom back to society to continue transform those who are not yet at the later stages of their journeys. Allison (2019) summarized this effect by claiming that mentors transform heroes, who in turn "assume the role of mentor for others who are at earlier stages of their quests" (Allison & Goethals, 2017). To achieve self-actualization and fulfill the final stage of their quest, heroes must bestow a boon on the rest of society. This boon, in the case of mentors, is their newfound wisdom and guidance.

TYPES OF MENTORS

While mentors can take any form in a story, they usually fall under six general archetypes: traditional mentoring, role model, developmental mentoring, reciprocal mentoring, group mentoring, and coaching (Rolfe, 2017). Traditional mentoring occurs when a person with content-specific experience or achievements parallel to your own desires "shares their knowledge, introduces you to people or provides resources that will aid your progress." Similarly, a role model is someone whose "behaviors, attitude, and strategies you can emulate to achieve success." A guiding figure who "listens, questions, and enables" you to "set goals, create plans, make decisions, and solve problems" characterizes developmental mentoring. Reciprocal mentoring occurs when neither character dominates the role of "mentor." Each character serves as a resource, sounding board, and reality check for the other. Group mentoring is similar in structure and involves "tapping into collective wisdom and obtaining mutual support." The last category, coaching, is more specialized than the others. It hinges upon "personalized training to develop specific skills and improve performance" (Rolfe, 2017).

QUALITIES OF GOOD MENTORS

However, regardless of the archetype role, mentors represent the same common bond. Mentorship represents the symbolic value of the bond between "parent and child, teacher and student, doctor and patient, god and man" (Vogler, 2007). Mentors embody many of the same traits, similar to the way that many heroes possess the Great Eight traits. While prided on their communication skills of listening and questioning, mentors also excel in their skilled used of silence (Rolfe, 2017). The sign of a successful mentor is their hero's success long after the mentorship expires. Eventually, the hero must learn how to function independently from the mentor. Scheduled silence assists this process.

Furthermore, good mentors "give guidance without being directive." The goal of a mentor is not that of a drill sergeant. Transformation hinges upon learning, development, and growth. Heroes need to discern how to make tough decisions on their own. To cyclically become mentors themselves, they need to learn how to apply this knowledge to novel circumstances. Heroes learn this process through their own mentors "providing feedback, suggestion and options" (Rolfe, 2017). Successful mentorship requires a constant feedback loop that implements time commitment and willingness to contribute. Like in the case of reciprocal mentorship, each partner receives the benefits of and constructive criticism from the relationship. It is symbiotic in nature and leads to mutual metamorphosis. Through this relationship, they foster confidentiality and mutual respect for the other's personal privacy (Rolfe, 2017).

To begin with, Mr. Miyagi acts as the prototypical mentor, training Daniel until he can eventually function independently. Mr. Miyagi guides Daniel through a series of tasks designed to help him in his ultimate goals, without Daniel even realizing it at first. Mr. Miyagi is present for the training, but Daniel must eventually function successfully on his own. His training culminates in him demonstrating his newfound abilities. Mr. Miyagi in The Karate Kid demonstrates an implied mentor. He trains Daniel until the final battle. During the final stage of Daniel's journey, when he must prove his skill and determination,

Mr. Miyagi can only guide him psychologically. He cannot physically assist him or be present during this ultimate test. Instead, Daniel relies on his mentor's extensive previous training, supporting presence in the crowd, and implied presence via memory. The primary function of the mentor archetype is "to guide" (Voytilla & Vogler, 1999). However, guiding does not necessarily mean to explicitly direct or tell. As explained earlier, mentors use strategic silence to guide without being directive. In Mr. Miyagi's case, he utilizes strategic withholding of information through cryptic advice that only later becomes clear. Miyagi constantly guides Daniel through the gaps in his words. His vague morsels of advice, such as "Man who catch fly with chopstick, accomplish anything," still persist in conversation today (Avildsen, 1984).

The Karate Kid offers a prototypical example of a hero-mentor relationship. Mentors enter the plotline during the meeting stage of the Hero's Journey. The hero meets a mentor to "gain confidence, insight, advice, training, or magical gifts to overcome initial fears and face the threshold of the adventure" (Voytilla & Vogler, 1999). Daniel meets Mr. Miyagi, who instantly seems like a mystical being who could resolve all his issues with the Cobra Kai. Miyagi mystifies Daniel upon first glance. He remains focused on completing an incomprehensible task: catching a fly with a pair of chopsticks. Intrigued and captivated by his presence, Daniel instantly forms a mentorship bond with him.

The Karate Kid begins with a call to the Hero's Journey, when his mother informed Daniel that they will be moving cities (Vollbracht, 2018). In 1982, Daniel LaRusso moves from his established home in Newark, New Jersey, to the unfamiliar territory of Reseda, Los Angeles, California. After the death of his father, Daniel is left alone with his mother, Lucille. He has no father figure in his life to mentor him. However, his apartment building's handyman, Keisuke Miyagi, seems to instantly fill this role as his surrogate father. Daniel soon faces social issues when he becomes the target of Jonny Lawrence and his gang of karate practitioners from the Cobra Kai dojo. After being viciously bullied, Daniel meets Mr. Miyagi and remains "apprehensively in the doorway, shook by the presence of the man who will become his mentor, healer, and father figure" (Cooper, 2012). Needing some sort of superior guidance, Daniel begs Mr. Miyagi to be his teacher. Miyagi initiates their training with one final declaration: "We make sacred pact. I promise teach karate to you, you promise learn. I say, you do, no questions" (Avildsen, 1984).

Daniel's training seems to be an endless stream of menial household chores. Overcome by his desire to learn karate and complete his mission, Daniel quickly grows frustrated with the training process. Like most mentees, Daniel struggles with his "'this guy's full of crap' moments throughout the early stages" of his studies (Bancroft, 2012). Hours melt into days of tedious chores. Daniel is forced to "clean and wax all of the antique cars in Miyagi's lot, then sand his long and winding back porch, then finish both sides of his enormous fence, and finally, paint his house" (Cooper, 2012).

Again, Miyagi offers a clipped piece of wisdom to explain the process: "First learn stand, then learn fly" (Avildsen, 1984). Daniel is struck with the epiphany that "he wasn't just waxing cars and sanding a porch – he was learning muscle memory for defense. More than that, Miyagi was developing Daniel's personality; teaching humility and self-control" (Cooper, 2012). All of the tasks required specific motor movements and intense control of both physique and mentality. Miyagi cultivates Daniel to be not only skilled, but wise. Through "effortful training," Daniel becomes a hero who is "highly competent as well as highly moral; many [heroes] presumably have spent a good bit of time building up their self-regulation muscle" (Green, Van Tongeren, Cairo, & Hagiwara, 2017). Daniel becomes not only a hero, but a man.

Daniel highlights his newfound independence during the abyss and transformation stages of his journey. He must succumb to his fear of fighting and, potentially, losing in front of all his peers (Vollbracht, 2018). Each time he confronts the Cobra Kai, Daniel must "prepare himself for the greater ordeals yet to come" and "test his skills and powers, or perhaps seek further training from the mentor" (Voytilla & Vogler, 1999). Eventually, the final tournament arrives. Daniel can no longer rely upon his mentor to be with him physically. Although Miyagi could previously intervene if the trial seemed to overcome Daniel, there was no option for this aid in the final showdown. Both partners must rely on their faith that the training was comprehensive enough for Daniel to thrive on independently, with only the implied presence of his mentor to support him. Fulfilling the role of a typical mentor, Miyagi provided Daniel with tokens to support him on his journey. These talismans include Miyagi's supernatural healing power, the bonsai tree karate gi, and the now iconic tenugi (Cooper, 2012). Most essential is the transfer of knowledge of the Crane technique. While Miyagi never directly teaches it to Daniel, he "plants the seed in Daniel's mind" explaining "'if done right no can defense'" (Cooper, 2012). This kick allows Daniel to finally defeat his demons, and his opponents, in his last encounter with the Cobra Kai.

However, Miyagi himself depicts the cyclical nature of heroism. His own wisdom and experience developed after rising from the ashes of desperation and grief. Miyagi not only trains Daniel to be strong but reveals to him the power of being weak and embracing one's struggle. Miyagi allows Daniel to see him at his weakest, during the "heart-wrenching anniversary scene where Daniel learns about the death of Miyagi's wife and won in an internment camp" (Cooper, 2012). While serving in World War II overseas, Miyagi's pregnant wife was "shipped to a Japanese internment camp" where "she and her son died in childbirth, leaving Miyagi a widower. He never remarries" (Fenzel, 2008). The eternally wise Mr. Miyagi he drove home a "simple message to the Karate kid: build patience and willpower and guts will follow" (Malcom, 2013). Daniel instilled this advice not only in his dojo practices but in all areas of life. His mentorship was all-encompassing, even when Miyagi himself could not be there to support him.

MULAN: MUSHU AS AN ACTUAL MENTOR

Alternatively, Mushu serves as a mentor to Mulan at all times, not just during her hero training. Mushu offers his loyal guidance to Mulan. Often, the mentor is present during training and the hero reflects on their guidance and wisdom during trying times. Mushu is unique in that his size allows him to stay Mulan's companion throughout the entire film. He can literally whisper in her ear and offer guidance instantly. Mushu represents an actual mentor, acquired through an actual encounter. This encounter is one during which the hero befriends people or creates who "represent qualities that she lacks and must acquire to triumph on her quest" (Allison & Goethals, 2017).

Due to his size, Mushu can accompany Mulan through all stages of her Hero's Journey. They begin to act as a single unit, as opposed to a mentor-mentee relationship that only exists prior to the final trial. Transactive Goal Dynamics Theory proposes that "two or more individuals can exercise self-control jointly, as a single system" (Green, Van Tongeren, Cairo, & Hagiwara, 2017). Mushu and Mulan act symbiotically and help each other grow. They represent reciprocal mentoring. Through their relationship, they both grow and develop characters of successful mentors and heroes.

After the Huns breached the Great Wall, the Chinese government ordered a conscription requiring one man from each family to join the army. Mulan's father, the only man in her family, was left handicapped by a previous war. To protect her family, Mulan steals her father's armor and dresses up as a boy (Cook & Bancroft, 1988). Her family is left devastated by her departure. Mulan's grandmother prays to their ancestors for her safe return. Hearing her call, the ancestors gather and summon the forces of the "great stone dragon" to protect the protagonist. They task Mushu, a smaller, less respected guardian, to awaken the stone dragon. Mulan accidentally destroys the statue and decides to rescue Mulan and bring her back to safety himself.

Throughout her journey, Mulan relied upon the assistance of many mentors. Her commander, Shang, trained the army for battle. The other soldiers, Ling, Chien-Po, and Yao, support her in her endeavors and grow alongside her. However, Mushu steadfastly accompanies Mulan throughout her journey. He assists her in training and in the final battle. Initially, Mushu provides comfort and support through his guidance on how to behave like a man.

Although Mulan functions more efficiently as a man, she actually adopts a more "feminine approach to life's challenges" after adopting this persona (Hartman & Zimberoff, 2009). Mulan "immerses herself in the situation so as to become consciously aware of the ambiance of the environment, to gather experiential knowledge through relationships, and to submit to the wisdom and guidance from deep within" (Hartman & Zimberoff, 2009). Only by embracing the unknown can she unfold her "essence" and express it "within significant relationships" (Hartman & Zimberoff, 2009).

Even after Shang discovers her true identity and banishes her from the army, Mushu never deserts his hero. After a vicious battle during an avalanche, the army assumes they have defeated the Huns. However, Mulan quickly learns about the Hun's plan to attack the emperor. Mulan suddenly transforms from the hero to the mentor, once again demonstrating the cyclical nature of transformation. She switches roles with Mushu and instructs him to fire a rocket at the leader of the Huns. The ensuing explosion kills him and ensures safety for the entirety of the nation.

While Mushu did not direct Mulan's physical training, he did inspire her moral and character development. His constant and unwavering support motivated her to persevere even in the face of desperation. Mulan experienced many transformations during her Hero's Journey: from presenting as female to presenting as male, from valuing obedience to valuing independence, from being overlooked to being honored. Mulan's journey culminates in the Emperor honoring her efforts and confirming her expertise, knowledge, and foresight. Mushu's journey, on the other hand, concludes with his reinstatement as a family guardian due to his successful guidance and molding of Mulan.

The emperor, upon Mulan's completion of her journey, reminds her of all her failures along the way. However, he honors her for saving them all, demonstrating that all failure can be transformative and part of a larger developmental process. Without the guidance of her faithful mentor, Mulan's failure would have been just that – failures. We need guidance to transform our disasters into developments. Mulan's father confirms her hero metamorphosis by denying all her physical tokens of success and instead reiterating that the "greatest gift in honor is her" (Cook & Bancroft, 1988).

THE LION KING: MUFASA AS AN IMAGINED MENTOR

In contrast, Mufasa mentors his son not through his physical presence but through his spiritual guidance. Simba's father, Mufasa, dies early on in the film. However, he still serves as a spiritual mentor to Simba. Simba remembers his father's wisdom and guidance throughout a variety of pivotal scenes in the film. In difficult times, he relies on a spiritual and emotional connection with him. He often communicated with his father through reflections in the water or stars in the sky. He cannot literally call on him and gain a novel perspective, however. Any new insight Simba gains is by reinterpreting old information he previously received as a child.

According to Campbell, hero myths "inspire the possibility of the realization of your perfection, the fullness of your strength" and "carry the individual through the stages of life" (Allison & Goethals, 2017). Heroes do not need a mentor to be physically present at all times. Simply reflecting on the impact their mentor had is enough to inspire this greatness within them. Heroes must grapple with desperation. Oftentimes, the hero may "witness the death of an ally or mentor, or, even worse, directly cause that death" (Voytilla & Vogler, 1999). Simba did not cause his father's death, but he was led to believe he did by his villainous uncle, Scar.

Some heroes "may not have a physical mentor, but instead may be guided by an inner mentor, a code of honor, or justice that must be served" (Voytilla & Vogler, 1999). Mufasa represents this code for Simba. Simba constantly reflects upon his father's advice that "everything you see exists together in a delicate balance" and "as king, you need to understand that balance and respect all the creatures, from the crawling ant to the leaping antelope" (Allera & Minkoff, 1994). Mufasa guides his son during his childhood. In death, he serves as an "Inner Mentor, a strong code of honor or justice that guides him through the journey" (Voytilla & Vogler, 1999). Simba lives by his father's motto: "Remember who you are" (Allera & Minkoff, 1994).

Mentors are beings who can "mentor you, teach you, coach you, and awaken you" even "when they're not there physically" (Gilligan & Dilts, 2009). Mufasa, king of the Pride lands, trained Mufasa as his apprentice from birth. He prepared Simba to "be the hero by teaching him who he is meant to be," training him to hunt, and showing "him the importance of being a king" (Allera & Minkoff, 1994). As his father and mentor, Mufasa instilled in Simba a sense of meaning, purpose, and honor. Before his death, he advised Simba that kings of the past watch over their community from the sky. One day, he will watch over Simba as well. During the peak of Simba's self-doubt, Rafiki explains that Mufasa's spirits lives on in his son. Simba later sees his father's ghost reflected in the sky, telling him the path he must take. Simba understands he can no longer run from his past and instead needs to reclaim his rightful throne as king.

In life, Mufasa trained Simba on the policies of leadership and the practicalities of hunting. In death, Simba relies upon his father's guidance to dictate his moral code. Mufasa serves as an imagined mentor because he guides his son in spirit, not through physical presence. Simba calls upon the image and memory of his father in times of need but cannot directly ask him for mentorship. In Mufasa's death comes his skilled use of silence; he cannot physically communicate with his son and the pair must trust that Simba has all the knowledge he needs to succeed. In this silence also comes Simba's metamorphosis from son to king.

Mentors are pivotal in turning tales of destruction into tales of heroic transformation, as demonstrated in The Karate Kid, Mulan, and The Lion King. The mentors from each story depict an implied, actual, and imagined mentor respectively. As demonstrated previously, mentors are vital to the heroic transformation, regardless of what form they take (Eylon & Allison, 2005). A mentor is someone who "tells you what you don't want to hear, who has you see what you don't want to see, so you can be who you have always known you could be" (Allison & Goethals, 2017). Without exception, heroes begin to thrive only when they shed their doubt and instill full trust in their mentors. Heroes learn best when they succumb entirely to the knowledge of their mentors. The mentor "knows best" because they have "already been there. He or she knows more than you. That's why you are there" (Bancroft, 2012). According to Carl Jung, the most important task for a person is "to develop what he called a 'community of saints'" who "love and support us on our journey" (Gilligan & Dilts, 2009). Mentors make up this vital social network, although we might not understand their methods.

Like Daniel, we may question the necessity of waxing on and off. However, mentors are vital in propelling heroes forward into an external cycle of progress where they eventually become mentors themselves. All mentors are transformed heroes, now far enough along on their own journeys that they must bestow a boon on those who are just starting out. They represent the culmination of Erikson's seventh stage of development: generativity. Generativity includes a need to guide and mentor the next generation, to be needed, and to establish altruistic concern (Goethals & Allison, 2017). Without mentorship, we succumb to stagnation, feelings of insignificance, and the tragic fate of having "nothing to look backward to with pride, and nothing to look forward to with hope" (Goethals & Allison, 2017).

Inevitably, humans seek out a "benevolent presence that sees beyond the duality of hero and demon and of two separate worlds, who sees instead integration and wholeness" (Hartman & Zimberoff, 2009). There can be no heroes if there are no mentors. Characters would remain stagnant, without possibility for growth, redemption, or transformation. Mentors look beyond the dualities of heroism and villainy to recognize that all of us are capable of heroism – with the right guidance. Villains are simply heroes who have not yet been transformed by a proper mentor. We need these wise, experienced figures to see past our pasts and mold our futures. We are more than what we have done; we just need a guide to reveal our true inner selves to us.

REFERENCES

Allera, R., & Minkoff, R. (Directors). (1994). The Lion King [Motion Picture].

Allison, S. T. (2019). Heroic consciousness. Heroism Science, 4, 1-43.

Allison, S. T. (Ed.) (2019). Heroic transformation: How heroes change themselves and the world. Richmond: Palsgrove.

Allison, S. T., Beggan, J. K., & Efthimiou, O. (2019). The art and science of heroism and heroic leadership. Lausanne, Switzerland: Frontiers.

Allison, S. T. & Goethals, G. R. (2020). The heroic leadership imperative: How leaders inspire and mobilize change. West Yorkshire: Emerald.

Allison, S. T., & Goethals, G. R. (2017). The hero's transformation. In S. T. Allison, G. R. Goethals, & R. M. Kramer, The Handbook of Heroism and Heroic Leadership. New York: Routledge.

Allison, S. T., Goethals, G. R., & Spyrou, S. P. (2019). Donald Trump as the archetypal puer aeternus: The psychology of mature and immature leadership. In K. Bezio & G. R. Goethals (Eds.), Leadership and populism. Northampton, MA: Edward Elgar.

Avildsen, J. G. (Director). (1984). The Karate Kid [Motion Picture].

Bancroft, T. (2012). Character mentor: Learn by example to use expressions, poses, and staging to bring your characters to life. New York: Routledge.

Beggan, J. K., & Allison, S. T. (Eds.) (2018). Leadership and sexuality: Power, principles, and processes. Northampton, MA: Edward Elgar.

Brenner, G. (2015). Like a phoenix rising from the ashes. Retrieved from Dr. Gail Brenner: https://gailbrenner.com/2011/01/coping-with-challenging-life-circumstances/

Cook, B., & Bancroft, T. (Directors). (1988). Mulan [Motion Picture].

Cooper, P. (2012). Of bonsai and balance: The hero's journey in the Karate Kid. Retrieved from New Granada Recreation Center:https://newgranadarecreationcenter. com/2014/05/14/of-bonsai-and-balance-the-heros-journey-in-the-karate-kid/

Eylon, D., & Allison, S. T. (2005). The frozen in time effect in evaluations of the dead. Personality and Social Psychology Bulletin, 31, 1708-1717.

Fenzel, P. (2008). Reclaiming Miyagi: The most unjustly hated man in movies. Retrieved from Overthinking It: https://www.overthinkingit.com/2008/12/09/reclaiming-miyagi-the-most-unjustly-hated-man-in-movies/

Gilligan, S., & Dilts, R. (2009). The hero's journey: A voyage of self-discovery. Bethel: Crown House Publishing.

Goethals, G. R., & Allison, S. T. (2017). Transforming motives and mentors: The heroic leadership of James MacGregor Burns. In G. R. Goethals, & D. Bradburn, Politics, Ethics and Change. Northampton: Edward Elgar Publishing.

Goethals, G. R., & Allison, S. T. (2019). The romance of heroism and heroic leadership: Ambiguity, attribution, and apotheosis. West Yorkshire: Emerald.

Green, J. D., Van Tongeren, D. R., Cairo, A. H., & Hagiwara, N. (2017). Heroism and the pursuit of meaning in life. In S. T. Allison, G. R. Goethals, & R. M. Kramer, The handbook of heroism and heroic leadership. New York: Routledge.

Hartman, D., & Zimberoff, D. (2009). The hero's journey of self-transformaiton: Models of higher development from mythology. Journal of Heart-Centered Therapies, 12(2), 3-93.

Hoyt, C. L., Allison, S. T., Barnowski, A., & Sultan, A. (2020). Lay theories of heroism and leadership: The role of gender, communion, and agency. Social Psychology.

Malcom, S. (2013). From Mr. Miyagi to Dumbledore: The role of great mentors. Retrieved from The Redwood Project blog: http://redwood-project.com/Wordpress/2013/03/01/224/

Rolfe, A. (2017, March). What to look for in a mentor. Korean Journal of Medical Education, 29(1), 41-43.

Vogler, C. (2007). A practical guide. In C. Vogler, The Writer's Journey: Mythic Structure for Writers. Studio City, California: Michael Wiese Productions.

Vollbracht, J. (2018). Karate Kid. Retrieved from New World Culture: http://newworldculture.org/karate-kid/

Voytilla, S., & Vogler, C. (1999). Myth and the movies: Discovering the mythic structure of 50 unforgettable films. Studio City, California: Michale Wiese Productions.

Section 2: How To Break a Hero

5

Falling From Grace: From Celebration to Condemnation

JACOB W. ROBERSON

"Be careful who you choose as your hero or who you choose to deify... You put all you're hope and all your dreams and all your ideas about stuff into one human being. They're a human being they're going to let you down."
- Craig Ferguson

Starting at Le Puy du Fou and ending at Champs-Élyseés in Paris, the Tour de France in 1999 totaled a distance of 2,405 miles and was won in an impressive manner by a man of the name Lance Armstrong. Armstrong emerged victorious just three years after he had been diagnosed with stage-three testicular cancer, which actually had spread as far as his brain and lungs. He proceeded to win the next year, and the next year, and the next year, and so on until 2005 (USA Today editors, 2018). In 1997, prior to gaining international stardom from his athletic victories, he established Livestrong, a foundation built to help support cancer research and patients—his athletic successes coupled with his cancer initiative led to his emergence as a world-renowned hero. But then tragedy finally struck. Not a tragic death, nor traumatic injury, however. I use the adverb "finally" purposefully to insinuate that Armstrong's reign was ultimately going to come to an end, though I agree that all should be innocent until proven guilty.

Immediately after his first victory in 1999 of the Tour de France, Armstrong was questioned about his near-miraculous and dominant return to cycling (USA Today, 2018). In other words, had he used performance-enhancing drugs (PED's)?

Nonetheless, race after race, denial after denial, and win after win, Armstrong at this point had gained nearly as much "good" publicity as he had "bad", even though he had not been found guilty of doping... That is, until he was. In 2012, a year after retiring for the second time, Armstrong was officially accused of cheating by the U.S. Anti-Doping Agency (USA Today, 2018). A year later, he admitted on public television that he indeed used PED's for years, including during his streak of victories at the Tour de France. Consequently, all of his major sponsors dropped him including Nike and Oakley, and he was forced to pay millions of dollars in legal cases and settlements (USA Today, 2018). And a young boy like myself, who grew up during Armstrong's glory, wearing as many Livestrong bands as I could get my hands on, was left disappointed and confused on why this man, one of my heroes, had decided to cheat. I had had faith in him to always be great... But alas, no man is perfect... and, you know, perhaps it was naïve of eight year old me to have ever idolized a professional cyclist in the first place, but that's beside the point.

In his public confession and the subsequent millions of dollars worth of pay-ments, Armstrong apologized to his fans. However, since that first—and final—watershed moment, give or take some interviews and appearances here and there, Lance Armstrong, as a celebrity wave has subsided. What do we as "lay-people" make of scenarios like this when our heroes fall from grace? Do we our-selves breakdown in disappointment and mourn, or do we rise up, chin up and chest out, to show that our pride and wellbeing is not contingent upon a "strang-er's" (i.e. viewing the "hero" in a different light) immoral downfall. This idea of "hero worship" is fascinating, but it can be dangerous. In the most extreme cases, hero worship and idolatry can lead individuals to drastic ends, including death.

For example, the tragedy at Jonestown involved a cult leader whom individuals had become convinced was good and had all of their best interest in mind. Jones led all of them to drink the Kool-Aid -- and if you were wondering where the saying "don't drink the Kool-aid" or "they're drinking the Kool-Aid" in reference to folks blindly following or being brainwashed in a way -- well you're welcome. Hero worship can be good in that pride, joy, and fulfillment can be found in backing the heroes. However, when these heroes fail, fall, or flee, they leave their followers at bay, often times with no explanation or apology. And to be clear, these fallen heroes are those that stay down, as opposed to heroes who slip up, recognize their errors, apologize, and work to regain trust and prominence once more. No, no tragic heroes fall from grace with no return (Goethals & Allison, 2012). Though he may be living comfortably in solace at this point, Lance Armstrong exemplifies the taxonomy of a tragic hero because he never returned back to his once highly-regarded status of champion and cancer activist.

In explaining their social influence-based taxonomy of heroes, Goethals and Allison (2012) described "tragic heroes" as "a great individual whose character failings bring about his or her downfall" (p. 226). "Character failings" can range anywhere from a set of actions committed once, with grave consequences (e.g. assault or murder of another individual), to a recognized character flaw such as a sex addiction (Goethals & Allison, 2012). Almost similar to a romantic relationship, fans and supporters have a tendency to be so blinded by their heroes' successes and breakthroughs that it is easy for them, the fans, to ignore the warning signs, pitfalls, and missteps of their heroes.

THE DANGERS OF HERO WORSHIP

No man (or woman) is perfect but it seems as though it is human nature, regardless of culture, background, or upbringing, for us to idolize other humans. That is, we put seemingly random individuals, people we will never meet in our lifetime, on a pedestal as though they are more important than ourselves or the people closest to us. Whether it is a fascination with the life they have and we don't, or it's an appreciation for the art they produce or good service they administer, these "randoms"—otherwise known as "celebrities"—consume our attention and influence our social lives to the point where we are dependent on their actions for us to determine our own next actions. So what happens when this all breaks down? And by breaks down, I mean this celebrity no longer produces the same art they once did, or their ideological views finally drift too far past what we can morally accept, or at least let slide; or perhaps worst of all, they commit an act or crime so unfathomable, especially for someone of their status and notoriety, that it is quite literally unbelievable. You are heartbroken. This person you had let into your house and home, or at least your heart if you're not a homeowner yet, has left and taken all of their glory with them—the awards they won, the records they broke, the namesake they built—it is now all tarnished. You're left in a state of eminent nostalgia, and it's too hard to let go.

We're drawn to those we call our heroes because of what they provide for us. We seek (and seemingly find) things like wisdom and meaning—the epistemic function—and hope, inspiration, and growth—the energizing function—in our heroes that we otherwise are unable to obtain (Allison & Goethals, 2016). This Hero Leadership Dynamic (HLD), as Allison and Goethals refer to it, fulfills these cognitive and emotional necessities of the layperson: "The epistemic function refers to the knowledge and wisdom that hero stories impart to us. The energizing function refers to the ways that hero stories inspire us and promote personal growth" (Allison & Goethals, 2016). However, the issue remains that the individual is still vulnerable because he is finding his fulfillment outside of himself, and from another human being at that.

HEROES IN THE BLACK COMMUNITY

Leadership in the black community is ever valuable due to the systemic, historically low opportunities made available to black people in the United States. So when leaders come along, they often bear a psychological and emotional weight greater than their white counterparts, even if their position is of "lower caliber" so to speak in the grand scheme of things. The importance of their success matters not only for fulfilling the epistemic and energizing functions for their supporters and followers, but also for overcoming the odds and making it easier for the next leaders to breakthrough as well.

Now imagine living your whole life looking up to someone in such a way, and then, seemingly in an instant, you don't recognize the person you once looked up to anymore. Put plainly, these instances are particularly burdensome in the black community because, as has been stated, it is understood that black people in America do not get nearly as many "shots at the top" as white people. When a black man or woman fails and falls from the top, he is not only letting him or herself down, but also those closest to him, and the countless others who were closely rooting for him or her.

From Pride to Guilt

The story of OJ. Such was the case for fans of OJ Simpson. Orenthal James Simpson, born July 9th, 1947, grew up in the Bay Area of California. From a young age, he excelled in the sport of football eventually earning a scholarship to the University of Southern California Trojans. While at USC, he earned All-American honors two years in a row en route to a national championship victory in 1967 and a Heisman Trophy in 1968—he was the best player in college football (Biography.com editors, 2014). Not surprisingly he was drafted as the first overall draft pick in the 1969 draft to the Buffalo Bills and almost immediately had an impact on the brand of the Bills organization. Despite only ever playing in one playoff game during his time there, Simpson became the first player in NFL history to rush for over 2,000 yards—2,003 to be exact—in a single season (not surprisingly, this was the year he won the Most Valuable Player award) and he did so amidst five consecutive years of over 1,000 yards rushing (O.J. Simpson Highlights, n.d.). Although the Bills never won a Super Bowl, or had over 10 wins for that matter, during his time there, he had had a Hall of Fame career and was inducted in his first year of eligibility in 1985.

Many would agree that Simpson's story of coming from an underprivileged background and making his way to the top of the national football league is a story of heroic transformation (Goethals, & Allison, 2012). However, aside from his exemplifying all-star status on the football field, OJ did relatively little else for the black community as far as empowering and uplifting. This indifference, however, is what afforded him such greater favorability in the white community, who generally saw Simpson as the missing piece to bridging the racial gap. In other words, his willingness to deflect his blackness or choose to not speak up on racial issues granted him an "in" into white society that athletes such as Jim Brown or Muhammad Ali did not have due to their social justice activism (Demby, 2016; Wiley, n.d.). His provisions of leadership to the white community may have been separate but these dueling perspectives of his heroism status would soon become moot. Simpson's stardom and favor would hardly last 25 years because what transpired next was a rollercoaster of emotions for all of America.

Whether you see him as black or as OJ, before he was national news coverage via white Ford Bronco and a too-small leather glove, Simpson was a hall of famer who avoided confrontation—that is along racial lines at least. OJ was a hero to aspiring young boys, both black and white, everywhere from elementary school to college, and a fan favorite among many in some way, shape, or fashion. So when the news revealed him on a low-speed chase from cops (the car actually being driven by a former teammate, Al Cowlings), one could only have been at least somewhat surprised. But it didn't stop there because once it became known why Simpson was in the chase, the process of preparing to see your favorite football player possibly go down is not something you regularly prepare for.

OJ's estranged wife, Nicole Brown, along with her friend Ronald Goldman were found dead on June 12, 1994, in Brown's condo (Biography.com editors, 2014). When the bodies were found later in the day, Simpson was informed of his ex-wife's passing. Though he reportedly did not sound too terribly troubled, he returned back to California to assess the situation. Eventually the police began to question Simpson more thoroughly and it was at that point that he attempted to flee from police in the infamous white Ford Bronco (Biography.com editors, 2014). The chase itself was viewed by millions of viewers as a news helicopter captured the moment live. But the court hearings to follow became one of the most televised programs of all time.

OJ had been accused of murdering Nicole Brown and Ronald Goldman and there was a rather strong consensus from the white community that he had indeed done it. The black community, however, was more split (History.com editors, 2009). On one end, the evidence against him was so surmounting it would be almost ignorant and beyond naivety to try and construe the facts being presented as false. On the other end, here was a black man who had retired from a Hall of Fame career only 15 years ago, why with so much life left to live would he jeopardize it all in such a way as this (presuming he was not mentally unstable)?—"The System" was simply out to get another successful black male.

However, therein lies a rather counterintuitive question: was this "just another successful black male", or was it OJ Simpson, he who denied his blackness for the appeasement of whites (Demby, 2016)? Presumably, had this been any other black male in a low-speed chase, he would have been pulled over by force and likely removed from his car; from there, Lord knows what his fate could have been. But instead he was appeased, and thus ironically began OJ's fall from grace. At the end of a 252-day-long trial, with seemingly all evidence pointing against him except a glove that he was able to make appear not to fit, OJ Simpson was acquitted, freed of charges of the murder of his ex-wife and her peer (History.com editors, 2009).

One escape route for OJ perhaps could have been the suicide letter found that read, "To whom it may concern... Don't feel sorry for me. I've had a great life, great friends. Please think of the real O. J. and not this lost person. Thanks for making my life special. I hope I helped yours. Peace and love, O. J." (Linder, 2018). This message insinuates at the instability of an individual who is at or even past his or her breaking point. And whether it was a legitimate message or not, it very well saved Simpson's life. Alas, even with the amount of favor he seen in his life time, Simpson still managed to find his way into a jail cell. In 2008, Simpson was convicted of coordinating a gunpoint assault and robbery of two sports memorabilia dealers in Las Vegas in 2007. Simpson insisted that he was only looking to retrieve personal memorabilia that he felt was rightfully his, but the jury did not find favor with his claims. Simpson was sentenced 9 to 33-year for robbery, assault with a deadly weapon, and kidnapping (Biography.com editors, 2014).

Aside from "officially" becoming a criminal under the court of law, OJ had solidified his status as a tragic hero. From this day on, for an unforeseen amount of generations to come, Simpson will be remembered for his murder trial more so than his football greatness. Though his fall from grace may be particularly hard to take for those who grew up with OJ running down the sideline on their TV screens, what his productivity and heroic like play on the field did produce was a placeholder and precedent. Since OJ, the superstar backs we have seen in the NCAA and the NFL have increasingly gotten bigger, better, faster, and stronger, finally surpassing OJ who had set the mark for them to reach back in the 1970s. But even when his accomplishments are celebrated, the giant elephant in the room remains clear as day, overshadowing any positive impacts he made.

Little Bill, big problems. Bill Cosby brought one of the first representations of a full black family to television with his "The Cosby Show" (Kim, Littlefield, & Etehad, 2018). Lasting until the mid-90s, the shows successes propelled not only Cosby forward, but many of the actors and actresses who were once a part. The TV dad everyone claimed, whether you were white or whether you were black, you knew the name, you knew the distinct sound, and there were no ills against him. Cosby transcended generations even, partly in thanks to technology allowing younger fans to view his old material, shows, and movies, but also because there was a timelessness about his persona as well. A man so once highly regarded, praised by many—comedians and fans alike—as one of the original "Kings of Comedy", surely could never fall. With the ending of his spin off animated cartoon "Little Bill", a show I grew up with from 1999 to 2004, it seemed as though Cosby was set to ride off into the sunset, then at the retired age of 67. Little did we as his fans and admirers know, however, that he had some very big, rather disturbing secrets.

Fourteen years after the end of "Little Bill", at the peak of the #MeToo Movement, Cosby was accused of sexual assault (Chuck, 2018). 'me too', originally conceived in 2006 by Tarana Burke focusing on women of color, caught fire when, one by one, notable women in Hollywood, broadcasting, and show business began to come forward about their indecent experiences and encounters with men with whom they worked (Santiago & Criss, 2017). It started with one, and then caught fire as the hashtag, #MeToo, spread rapidly across Twitter and other news outlets in 2017 and 2018. Aside from the fact that he was not only the black community's favorite TV dad, but everyone's and a superstar comedic talent and trailblazer, what made Cosby's case—or should I say cases, plural—was the fact that it was just that, plural (Deggans, 2018). It was not only one victim, it was 60. Six. Zero (Mallenbaum, Ryan, Puente, 2018).

The villainy behind how one can bring himself to deliberately offend, harass, and/or assault 60 other human beings, I will not delve into within this chapter. However, I will point to the shock, awe, disgust, and utter disappointment that resonated throughout the nation at the coming of this news. Comedians who once looked up to Cosby as their heroes retracted their support; Millennials and Generation Zers more swiftly retracted their support than did say Generation Xers because they were more removed from a true era of Cosbyism through-out the comedic world. But Cosby's tragic fall from grace offers us as fans and laypeople many warnings and precautions for the future. First, do not put ill wills, wrongdoings, or negative and toxic characteristics past our heroes—or anyone. They are imperfect like the rest of us. Second, the saying goes that old age brings about wisdom, but it surely does not bring about innocence or ratio-nale. If anything, old age can bring about an abuse of power under the gauze of innocence; but Cosby did not commit many of his crimes at an old age, in fact, the earliest victim stories date back to 1965 (Kim et al., 2018).

Lastly, do not be surprised, and do not blame the victims of our heroes' vil-lainous acts. Perhaps you never thought you might have to rationalize such an instance, with them being your heroes and all. Sometimes you think you know someone, until you finally learn their whole truth. Being as removed from our heroes as we are places us in a vulnerable position. I am not here to discount the viability, importance, and joy of our heroes, but perhaps we could hold them accountable and to the same standards in earning our liking as we do say our romantic partners, or close friends.

This final exemplar once held arguably the highest prestige within the modern hip-hop and rap game. However, his mental and spiritual instability along with his new ideology has forcefully turned many of his fans against him. Now left with two versions of his art to appreciate or ignore—the old and the... con-fused—Kanye West fans and the greater black community debate how to move forward, and about just how many chances to allow him before deleting him from their playlists for good.

I miss the Old Kanye. If black heroes like Barack Obama, Oprah Winfrey, Martin Luther King Jr., or Jackie Robinson had ever did anything to fall from grace, there would have been or would still be great conflict and division in the black community in regards to continuing support of them, or retracting support. And it is here, in this back and forth limbo that we find attitudes toward Kanye West. Kanye Omari West, was born in 1977 just as Hip Hop was beginning to boom. A once in a lifetime talent, yet just as confused, hurt, and struggling as the rest of us, he would grow up to become one of Hip Hops greatest producers and artists of all-time. He caught his first big break after connecting with Hip Hop mogul Jay-Z in the mid-2000's. By 2010 he had five albums to his name, all of which had peaked number one in some fashion on the charts. His unique flows and masterpieces of production had cemented him as an all-time Hip Hop great. Ironically, it was a joint album with Jay-Z in 2011, "Watch the Throne", that marked his last time producing as "Old Kanye".

In 2007, tragedy struck West changing the trajectory of his music indefinitely—his mother, his rock, Donda West passed away unexpectedly. In the album he released the following year, "808s and Heartbreaks"—in many ways, an ode to West's late mother—a darker tone was present within the music as was the case in his 2010, "My Beautiful Dark Twisted Fantasy" (MBDTF) as well. Today, these two releases mark what many consider to be the transitionary period from "Old Kanye" to New—these, along with "Watch the Throne" were the pinnacle of overall music quality for West.

In 2013, Kanye released "Yeezus", a fusion of his own name and Jesus. In an interview just after the release of the album, Kanye is quoted as confidently saying, "I made that song ["I Am A God"] because I am a god... I don't think there's much more explanation... I am a god" (Cubarrubia, 2013). But the music within the album was far from Godly—both in spirit and quality. Though it still made its way to the number one spot on the charts, there is a distinct drop-off from the music of MBDTF to Yeezus. The disappointing release kept his fans at bay as they were forced to continue to listen to his previous releases (i.e. "Old Kanye"). In 2016, West, made plans to release a new album, "The Life of Pablo", and after changing the album artwork multiple times, and many false alarms and fake outs as to when the release date actually was, it was finally shared with the public. But again, reviews were questionable, as Kanye still had not found his "Old" sound yet.

It wasn't simply a decline in musical taste that would bring him among the likes of Bill Cosby and OJ Simpson, however. Kanye was once a shameless, bold, and charismatic figure, who did not care what others thought because he knew at the end of the day he was producing art by the people, for the people. As heroism research will tell us, however, resiliency and charisma are necessary characteristics of a villain just as much as they are of a hero (Allison et al., 2017). West had a few notable outburst, for example his version of advocating for black's equal rights—"George Bush doesn't care about black people"—he stated on a live, national Red Cross telethon during the aftermath of Hurricane Katrina (Braswell, 2009). He also stole the spotlight from Taylor Swift to defend Beyoncé and her album, which had been nominated for album of the year (Braswell, 2009). However, with just two outbursts amidst a thriving music career, these they were brushed under the table as a naïve and carefree young artist's stunts and only resurfaced as reminiscent jokes every so often. But, upon the arrival of Yeezus, Yeezy season—his grossly overpriced, hand-me-down-looking clothing line—and his somewhat controversial relationship with Kim Kardashian, West's decline started slow before crashing hard in a red sea of false freedom.

West was recorded saying that "slavery was a choice" and that he would never have allowed himself to be enslaved for 400 years because its all in the mind (Coscarelli & Ugwu, 2018). He furthered deepened his chasm from the black community by openly supporting Donald Trump and flaunting his MAGA hat, at one point defending that he appreciated the "fashion" of the hat (Henderson, 2018). But, to take it a step further, Kanye made his way to the white house to defend Trump and to thank him for being like the father figure that he never had growing up (Henderson, 2018). His affection and hugs for a man who has continuously disvalued lives of color in various capacities is not only disappointing, but in many ways unbelievable and disgusting.

Kanye's negative transposition—from glory to reject—offers us an abundance of insights into how we identify with our fallen heroes. First, it helps us consider "What made this person a hero in the first place?" If heroism is in the eye of the beholder as Allison and Goethals (2011) claims and supports, might there at least be a need for a more succinct and tangible categorization and qualification of our heroes? Or do requirements, minimums, and criteria foil any hope of subjectivity? Second, we ask, "What did they do to lose hero status?" Are each and every one of our subjective and personal heroes held to the same criteria both to enable and disable their heroism status? When objective heroes seemingly fall, but are still clung onto by some, where is the line drawn? And third, "Can this person ever return to hero status?" In the case of tragic heroes, the answer to this final thought would be "no". Might Kanye be a tragic hero? One can only hope he is instead only transposed, and that one day he will find his way back, but, until then, his current story remains a tragedy. As Allison and Goethals explained (2012), heroic transformation can in fact be villainous. In the case of Kanye, he went from a realm of sociocentricity, particular focusing on the advancement of ideas and music in the black and hip-hop communities, to that of egocentricity where only his thoughts, wants, and desires seem to be of importance (Allison & Smith, 2015). His social consciousness has continuously vanished since about 2010, the same time the quality and content of his musical production began to fade.

So why in the introduction even mention Lance Armstrong if the focus was tragic heroes in the black community? Well because Armstrong himself was a figurehead of a marginalized community—cancer survivors. And in the same way OJ brought joy to fans with his athletic prowess, or Cosby brought laughter with his talents, or Kanye brought entertainment with his art, Armstrong brought hope with his defeating of cancer followed by his athletic dominance and his rebranding of what it looked like to be a cancer survivor. Like most heroes, there is an argument to be made on whether or not Armstrong is simply a personal hero to many or a cultural hero that was once at least respected by all. An assumption can be made, however, that most cancer patients admired him; in the same way the three provided exemplars were once admired by the black community by in large. Such classifications of "black heroes" and "cancer heroes" are prime examples of cultural heroes; they were not just your hero or my hero, they were *our* heroes (Allison & Goethals, 2012).

CONCLUSION

Franco et al. (2011) operationally defined heroism as a social activity: (a) in service to others in need; (b) engaged in voluntarily; (c) with recognition of possible risks/costs; (d) in which the actor is willing to accept anticipated sacrifice, and

(e) without external gain anticipated at the time of the act. While arguing that heroism and altruism represent a "fundamentally different class of behaviors," (p. 6), paradoxically, their operational definition of heroism in fact, subsumes the construct of altruism, in its inclusion criteria that helping must be undertaken voluntarily, is motivated without expectation of reward and includes the potential for sacrifice. A proposed operational definition of heroism that includes voluntary, intentional, motivational, and potentially sacrificial aspects of behavior is predicated upon the construct of altruism, not distinguished from it. And yet, how often do our celebrity heroes act altruistically?

Once one reaches stardom, there is even more to gain at the top, and this exponential direction is usually the path most chosen. While we laypeople idolize or at least label these other former laypeople as our heroes we are playing with fire in that we provide them a cloak of near-invincibility. But does anyone really benefit from this? At some point in our lives, we will all be disappointed by someone: whether that someone is your best friend, your parent, your significant other, or yourself, it is going to happen. And so, I write this to remind you—as I have said numerous times throughout this chapter—that heroes are people, too. None of us were made perfect but there is still someone out there who sees us as "perfect", and perhaps we can find hope in this simple thought. We are all someone's hero. So why not act like it all the time?

REFERENCES

Allison, S. T. (2019). Heroic consciousness. Heroism Science, 4, 1-43.

Allison, S. T., & Goethals, G. R. (2016). Hero worship: The elevation of the human spirit. Journal for the Theory of Social Behaviour, 46(2), 187–210.

Allison, S. T., & Goethals, G. R. (2012). Personal versus cultural heroes. Retrieved from https://blog.richmond.edu/heroes/2012/09/12/personal-versus-cultural-heroes

Allison, S. T., & Goethals, G. R. (2011). Heroes: What they do & why we need them. New York: Oxford University Press.

Allison, S. T., Goethals, G. R., & Kramer, R. M. (2017). Setting the scene: The rise and coalescence of heroism science. In S. T. Allison, G. R. Goethals & R. M. Kramer (Eds.), Handbook of heroism and heroic leadership (pp. 1-16). New York, NY: Routledge.

Allison, S. T., Goethals, G. R., Marrinan, A. R., Parker, O. M., Spyrou, S. P., Stein, M. (2019). The metamorphosis of the hero: Principles, processes, and purpose. Frontiers in Psychology.

Allison, S.T., & Smith, G. (2015). Reel heroes & villains. Richmond: Agile Writer Press.

Andrews, T. (2018, April, 29). Kanye West's mom died in 2007. Judging by his tweets, it seems to still haunt him. Retrieved November 1, 2018, from https://www.washingtonpost.com/news/arts-and-entertainment/wp/2018/04/29/kanye-wests-mom-died-in-2007-judging-by-his-tweets-it-seems-to-still-haunt-him/?noredirect=on&utm_term=.7f24b2d76110

Biography.com editors. (n.d.). Bill Cosby biography. Retrieved November 1, 2018, from https://www.biography.com/people/bill-cosby-9258468

Biography.com editors. (2014, April 2). O.J. Simpson biography. Retrieved October 29, 2018, from https://www.biography.com/people/oj-simpson-9484729

Braswell, K. (2009, September 14). Kanye West's history of outbursts. Retrieved October 31, 2018, from https://abcnews.go.com/Entertainment/kanye-wests-outbursts/story?id=8568701

Chuck, E. (2018, April 26). Bill Cosby conviction is the first big win of the #MeToo movement. Retrieved October 31, 2018, from https://www.nbcnews.com/storyline/bill-cosby-scandal/bill-cosby-conviction-first-big-win-metoo-movement-n869381

Coscarelli, J., & Ugwu, R. (2018, May 1). What Kanye West said about slavery, Obama and mental health in his new interviews. Retrieved October 31, 2018, from https://www.nytimes.com/2018/05/01/arts/music/kanye-west-charlamagne-interview-tmz.html

Cubarrubia, RJ. (2013, June 24). Kanye West: 'I'm the number one living and breathing rock star' Retrieved November 1, 2018, from https://www.rollingstone.com/music/music-news/kanye-west-im-the-number-one-living-and-breathing-rock-star-246107/

Decter-Frain, A., Vanstone, R., & Frimer, J. A. (2016). Why and How Groups Create Moral Heroes. Handbook of Heroism and Heroic Leadership, p. 120-138.

Deggans, E. (2018, September 26). Bill Cosby and the #MeToo movement. Retrieved November 1, 2018, from https://www.npr.org/2018/09/26/651710715/bill-cosby-and-the-metoo-movement

Demby, G. (2016, June 29). On The Code Switch Podcast: 'I'm Not Black, I'm O.J.!'. Retrieved November 1, 2018, from https://www.npr.org/sections/codeswitch/2016/06/29/482796193/on-the-code-switch-podcast-im-not-black-im-o-j

Duntley, J. D., & Buss, D. M. (2004). The evolution evil. The Social Psychology of Good and Evil. Guilford, New York, 102-123.

The Editors of Encyclopaedia Britannica. (2018, October 20). Bill Cosby | Biography, TV Shows, & Facts. Retrieved October 31, 2018, from https://www.britannica.com/biography/Bill-Cosby

Francescani, C., & Fisher, L. (2018, September 26). Bill Cosby: Timeline of his fall from 'America's Dad' to 'sexually violent predator'. Retrieved November 1, 2018, from https://abcnews.go.com/Entertainment/bill-cosby-trial-complete-timeline-happened-2004/story?id=47799458

Franco, Z. E., Blau, K., & Zimbardo, P. G. (2011). Heroism: A conceptual analysis and differentiation between heroic action and altruism. Review of General Psychology, 15(2), 99–113. doi: 10.1037/a0022672

Goethals, G. R., & Allison, S. T. (2019). The romance of heroism and heroic leadership: Ambiguity, attribution, and apotheosis. West Yorkshire: Emerald.

Gordon, R. A., Bindrim, T. A., McNicholas, M. L., & Walden, T. L. (1988). Perceptions of blue-collar and white-collar crime: The effect of defendant race on simulated juror decisions. The Journal of Social Psychology, 128(2), 191-197.

Henderson, C. (2018, October 12). Here's every word of Kanye West's bizarre meeting with President Trump. Retrieved November 1, 2018, from https://www.usatoday.com/story/life/people/2018/10/12/heres-every-word-kanye-wests-bizarre-meeting-president-trump/1609230002/

Hoyt, C. L., Allison, S. T., Barnowski, A., & Sultan, A. (2020). Lay theories of heroism and leadership: The role of gender, communion, and agency. Social Psychology.

History.com editors. (2009, November 24). O.J. Simpson acquitted. Retrieved October 30, 2018, from https://www.history.com/this-day-in-history/o-j-simpson-acquitted

Kim, K., Littlefield, C., & Etehad, M. (2018, September 25). Bill Cosby: A 50-year chronicle of accusations and accomplishments. Retrieved November 1, 2018, from http://www.latimes.com/entertainment/la-et-bill-cosby-timeline-htmlstory.html

Kinsella, E. L., Ritchie, T. D., & Igou, E. R. (2016). A Brief History of Lay and Academic Perspectives. Handbook of heroism and heroic leadership, 19-35.

Kohen, A., Langdon, M., & Riches, B. R. (2017). The making of a hero: Cultivating empathy, altruism, and heroic imagination. Journal of Humanistic Psychology, 1-17.

Levenson, E., & Cooper, A. (2018, September 26). Bill Cosby sentenced to 3 to 10 years in prison for sexual assault. Retrieved October 30, 2018, from https://www.cnn.com/2018/09/25/us/bill-cosby-sentence-assault/index.html

Linder, D. (2018). The trial of Orenthal James Simpson: An account. Retrieved October 31, 2018, from http://famous-trials.com/simpson/1862-home

Mallenbaum, C., Ryan, P., Puente, M. (2018, September 26). A complete list of the 60 Bill Cosby accusers and their reactions to his prison sentence. Retrieved October 31, 2018, from https://www.usatoday.com/story/life/people/2018/04/27/bill-cosby-full-list-accusers/555144002/

O.J. Simpson Highlights | Pro Football Hall of Fame Official Site. (n.d.). Retrieved October 30, 2018, from https://www.profootballhof.com/players/oj-simpson/highlights/

Santiago, C., & Criss, D. (2017, October 17). An activist, a little girl and the heartbreaking origin of 'Me too'. Retrieved October 31, 2018, from https://www.cnn.com/2017/10/17/us/me-too-tarana-burke-origin-trnd/index.html

USA Today editors. (2018, April 19). A timeline of Lance Armstrong's cycling. Retrieved November 1, 2018, from https://www.usatoday.com/story/sports/cycling/2018/04/19/a-timeline-of-lance-armstrongs-cycling-career/33994779/

Wikipedia contributors. (2018, August 11). 1999 Tour de France. Retrieved November 1, 2018, from https://en.wikipedia.org/wiki/1999_Tour_de_France

Wiley, R. (n.d.). White lies: HBO gets it half right. Retrieved October 29, 2018, from http://www.espn.com/page2/s/wiley/021113.html

6

Tales of the Flawed: An Examination of Anti-Heroism Across Media

TAI L. HO

Brave. Honorable. Moral. In practice, the ideal hero is righteously good through and through. Although weathered by the challenges they face, such lionhearted heroes remain true to what is right. They are our humble leaders, our knights in shining armour, and our pure-hearted princes who have come to rescue us in our darkest hour. These heroes are exemplary role models and serve as a beacon of virtue for all.

However, in many ways, ideals heroes are just that: ideal. They are paragons of their class and set unrealistically unattainable standards for heroism because they serve to be "an idealised version of the self" (Kinsella, Ritchie, & Igou, 2017). In many cases, these quintessential heroes exist only in the realm of childhood fantasy and those who are real tend to be portrayed in a perfect light by the media (Franco, Blau, & Zimbardo, 2011). While there is a faint sense of relatability in their character, their lack of grounding flaws renders the ideal hero beyond the reaches of the common man.

Amoral. Unprincipled. Imperfect. However, usually acting on the side of good. Anti-heroes are deeply flawed luminaries that the everyman can identify with. Often times, even highly esteemed heroes may possess qualities that may tarnish their title (Allison et al., 2019; Franco et al., 2011). Although their title suggests that they are the antithesis of a hero, they are not villains in that they do not come from a place of cruelty, evil, and corruption. Rather, while they are distinguished by their heroic deeds, these heroes lack many of the traditional qualities of the idealistic hero; they are "the rebel-victim who is alienated from his culture and society [...] at times he may be a clown; at other times a grotesque combination of criminal and saint; but his essential marks are his alienation and estrangement" (Barksdale, 1966) and historically, anti-heroism has been "born out of a rebellious desire to subvert what the author considers the standard conventions of fiction" (Simmons, 2008). They may be self-interested, unethical, or evenly merely apathetic – their heroic actions may be selfishly driven or may not carry great personal sacrifice (Goethals & Allison, 2019; Kinsella et al., 2017).

In other cases, these antiheroes may even lack the conventional ability to enhance, morally model, and protect the lives of others (Kinsella et al., 2016) as a result of their fatal flaws tarnishing their name. Such individuals' heroism is measured simply by the veneer of their actions in spite of the deeply acute character flaws. Though conventional heroes possess a certain moral and physical high ground, anti-heroes often fail to be blessed with both. Subdivisions of this class of hero include, but are not limited to, the cynical hero, the nominal hero, and the sociopathic hero.

The tale of the anti-hero has long been told time and time again across many cultures. Its rise in popularity has been attributed to people no longer believing in traditional heroism "as a declining society was inadequate for it and as man had a sense of powerlessness in the face of a blind technology" (Neimneh, 2013). Films, video games, and novels have provided platforms from which profound anti-heroes have emerged. Produced from the iconic mind of Ingmar Bergman, the character of Jöns from Det sjunde inseglet, a classic of world cinema, epitomises the archetype of the cynical hero. Meanwhile, in what is considered one of the most critically acclaimed video games, one assumes the role of Geralt of

Rivia, the quintessential nominal hero, in CD Projekt Red's critically acclaimed The Witcher series. Lastly, in the realm of great absurdist literature, Albert Camus' L'Étranger features Meursault, who embodies the spirit of the sociopathic hero. Such works have not only generated influential exemplars of anti-heroism but each telling of the anti-hero's narrative is a unique reflection of the ever-shifting needs and desires of society.

CYNICAL HEROES

In a day and age where idealistic thinking is a scarce commodity and true optimism is often considered foolish and naïve, cynical heroes emerge from the depths of a bleak, comfortless world. Some cynical heroes are born idealists whose bitterness is forged by world callousness while others are simply natural-born defeatists. These individuals are marked by their jaded world-weariness and plagued by pessimism, disenchantment, and negativity. Despite their mistrust in the world, the cynical hero continues to act on the side of good. However, this will to fight is not driven by the hope that their actions will provide some transformative good to the world and positively impact those around them. Rather, the detached and deeply neutral commitment to upholding justice is enough.

These heroes, while profoundly cynical in nature, recognise the harshness of the world but do not seek to exacerbate such problems. With the exception of their signature disillusionment, cynical heroes subscribe to many of the same just virtues typically associated with other conventional heroes. Such overlap lies in the shared devotion to moral and ethical codes of conduct. Often, rules are broken only when necessary and the drive to do what is right is deeply ingrained within.

Fierce cynicism provides a stark contrast to idealistic behaviour. Hence, when heroes whose cherished hopes and dreams have been crushed by a grim reality behave in ways that are indicative of moral integrity and a genuine concern for the wellbeing of others, it is considered more noteworthy and significant. This type of behaviour is the hallmark of Jöns, the nihilistic squire of Ingmar Bergman's iconic film Det sjunde inseglet. As the nobleman following in the footsteps of Antonius Block, a knight whose duty is to the law, Jöns proves time and time again his propensity for goodwill despite his inherent cynicism towards the world. Because it is typically characteristic of individuals who lack a certain compassion for life to also lack a drive to act benevolently and for the greater good of others, the juxtaposition between the mindset of a world-weary pessimist and the actions of a caring altruist is what is particularly moving about Jöns' portrayal as the archetypical cynical hero.

CYNICISM AS EXPRESSED THROUGH DEATH AND RELIGION

The Danse Macabre is an artistic allegorical representation originating from the late Middle Ages in which the personification of death is emphasised as a universal equaliser as he is leading living people from all walks of life, in order of social precedence, in a dance to their graves. These artistic, literary, and musical pieces were constructed as a means of symbolising memento mori, or the remembrance that one must die, and typically reminded people of the fragility and futility of human life. The Latin phrase memento mori promotes not only a pragmatic and grounding mindset about mortality but a grim and cynical one as well. It is this fresco that Jöns walks into an artist painting, to which he remarks that his work is a piece of nonsense that won't cheer anyone up.

Rather, the painting will frighten people and "if you scare them...they'll think... and the more they think...the more scared they get...and run into the arms of the priests" (Bergman, 1956). Jöns then expresses strife regarding an unprincipled theologian who convinced his master of going on a crusade, protesting how "[they] spent ten years in the Holy Land letting snakes bite [them], insects sting [them], wild beasts maul [them], heathens attack [them], bad wine poison [them], women infect [them], lice eat [them], and fever consume [them] [....] all for the glory of God" (Bergman, 1956). Jöns' cynicism appears most apparent when he claims, "[their] crusade was so stupid that only a true idealist would have thought it up" (Bergman, 1956).

In his conversation with the artist, Jöns claims that both meaningless crusades in the name of God and fear, especially in light of realising the fragility of life, drives people into blind religious devotion. While for many, religion is a beacon of hope for those who are suffering from a lack of direction or purpose in life, he is unaffected by such motivations, as manifested in his blatant bitterness and dismissal of God. Though Jöns' character is sullied by his spite and his cynical nature is apparent in his lack of respect for the idealist and in all his further interactions, he is redeemed in his inclination towards heroism. In fact, while he is considered a deuteragonist, he consistently behaves in ways that are more practically heroic than that of his master, who is primarily focused on introspection rather than those around him.

TWO SIDES OF A CYNICAL COIN

Benevolence and mortal empathy. Though, unlike other heroes, he expresses little fear for death, resentment for religion, and pity for humanity, Jöns is not black-hearted. He has been shown to save a mute girl from being raped by a pilferer and subsequently taking her away from a troubled life, where it is speculated her family had recently died from the plague, by having her join him and his master. Furthermore, he has shown altruistic compassion when he intervened a public shaming aimed at humiliating Jof, an actor who had been falsely accused of stealing another man's wife and consequently was forced by the attendants of the bar to dance like a boar. In both situations, Jöns solidifies his role as a hero when, without hesitation or reward, he assumed the role of the upstander when no one else did. However, his actions may seem even more heroic given it juxtaposes the typical behaviour of an individual who lacks faith in humanity.

Selfish drives and retributive justice. However, Jöns, like any other anti-hero, is not without his flaws. While he has demonstrated the ability to be kind, Jöns lacks the capacity to be truly idealistic and altruistic all the time; rather, he displays a sense of pragmatic yet harsh realism. After he saves the mute girl from trouble, he brashly jokes about raping her and begins telling her of her new duties, such as cooking and cleaning, without any consideration from her condition or if she truly consents to go with him. In addition, Jöns, when faced with the same theologian who was found looting corpses, attempting to rape the mute girl, and convincing his master to join the crusade, dying of the plague and begging for water, watched silently as he succumbed to his affliction. These instances of callousness reveal another, darker, side of the cynical hero archetype.

Even in the face of cynicism, many conventional heroes err on the side of the morally righteous and are generally driven by a noble cause. Rather than sharing a traditional lawful leaning disposition, nominal heroes are, at their very core, neutral. This class of anti-hero is neutral in their motivation to act heroically and in their concern for those who they are helping as well as those they are hurting; they are a hero only in name. There exist a number of possible motivators for a nominal hero's benevolent actions, including external rewards or promise of solitude, but none are purely altruistic in nature.

Such anti-heroes are highly inward thinking as evidenced by their selfish motivations and the absence of unadulterated self-sacrifice conflicts with the standard nature of ideal heroes. In spite of this egocentricity, nominal heroes are not evil for they lack the brutality and callousness that define villains. While nominal heroes have the opportunity to temporarily align oneself with villainy in times of unrest given their impartiality, it commonly results in added complications that impede their desire to return to a state of neutrality. It is often the case that these heroes default to aiding the side of good simply because it is typically the side of evil that threatens to uproot them from their place of peace and consequently, it is necessary to act morally to eliminate such dangers.

HEROISM AND NEUTRALITY

Neutrality is the abstaining of actively supporting one side or another. In the case of examining heroism, this endorsement refers to either helping the side of the morally just or the side of the morally corrupt. The very notion of neutrality tends to imply impartiality and, in some cases, inactivity. Failure to take a strong moral standpoint and engaging in passivity heavily contradicts the traditional notion of heroism in that heroes as typically portrayed as individuals who actively fight for the moral values they have personally internalised. However, it is debatable whether or not one is considered a hero, as defined by their valiant actions, or not a hero, as defined by their moral neutrality regardless of their actions.

In Slavic mythology, vĕdmáks – or "warlocks" – embody the spirit of neutrality in that, if absolutely necessary, they are both just as capable of protecting humanity and acting with a high moral sense as they are at cursing it and working on behalf of the Devil but are otherwise inherently impartial. Influenced by the Polish fantasy novel series Wiedźmin (The Witcher), the term vĕdmák, or "wiedźmak" in Polish, can also be loosely translated as "witcher". This series has since given rise to one of the most accomplished and widely acclaimed games of all time: The Witcher 3: Wild Hunt; however, its prequels The Witcher and The Witcher 2: Assassins of Kings are also relevant in the context of anti-heroism. The branching system of moral choices presented within the game's storyline stresses a lack of black and white morality. Although players may choose to make any decision they wish, regardless of the ethical and moral perspective, the protagonist, Geralt of Rivia, is canonically neutral. Though his individual actions may suggest heroism or villainy, his ultimate motivations and goals are at best impartial. In the truest sense and the spirit of how he was intended to be portrayed, Geralt is a model nominal hero and typifies many of the behaviours that are representative of such kind of heroism.

The notion of 'witcher neutrality' is a prominent characteristic of the dying class of monster slayers who possess supernatural powers known as witchers. These highly trained individuals are subjected from a young age to a variety of extreme alchemical processes, mutagenic compounds, and physical and magical training to hone their strength, speed, reflexes, and endurance such that they are prepared to professionally hunt and kill any inhuman prey that may plague the land. This elite caste of warrior-monks first emerged as protectors of humanity and served to safeguard them from the dangerous monsters that roamed the wild. Though the need for them has largely died out as a result of the declining rate of monsters. Many humans began to fear their mutated form and contact with such witchers are limited only to business.

As a result of their taxing training and their ostracisation by humans, many witchers are frequently cited to be emotionless and lonesome in nature. During times of violence, witchers are faithfully removed from taking a side unless their loved ones are threatened or if they are swayed financially. As with all nominal heroes, witchers are characteristically neutral and only engage in altruistic and heroic behaviour as a consequence of selfish drives.

Amongst the most legendary of witchers is Geralt of Rivia. Across the course of The Witcher series, he is faced with a number of socially demanding situations where he is forced to determine whether an individual lives or dies at his hand. Furthermore, he is allowed to side with either given racial faction during times of political instability or remain truly neutral because ultimately, for a witcher, the act of fighting on one side or another makes little difference in their lives because it is seen less as a moral commitment and more of a job. Though his isolated decisions cannot be neutral in that it is difficult to classify any action as neutral when forced in heavily polarised environments where every undertaking can be seen as heroic or villainous, he is morally detached from the situation and cares only to finish his job and return to a life of normalcy.

PERCEPTUAL CONSEQUENCES OF NEUTRALITY

While witchers, and Geralt in particular, are not usually concerned with the public's perception of their kind, given their history of undesirability to humans in lore, their actions, and consequently, their character, are not immune to judgement. How one chooses to approach each branching decision shapes the type of hero they wish to be in that it is possible to be a neutral hero who has a disposition toward virtuousness or a neutral hero who is prone to wickedness or indifference.

Certain decisions, such as the choice of defending a town witch against a mob of angry townspeople or siding with the villagers and killing her, may alter whether or not Geralt is played as a hero who actively entwines himself in others' lives to help them or as one who is passively altruistic and prefers not to mettle in the business of others. Situations such as this are primary experiences that contribute to the shaping the of one's standards of behaviours and beliefs.

Other decisions, such as ones to directly or indirectly kill or not kill a prominent political or social figure, only results in whether or not said individual makes a reappearance in a later portion of the game and is essentially insignificant in the end. These consequences demonstrate that while heroes are faced with a number of moral obstacles, not every decision or perception of them will be meaningful.

As described in the lore, witchers are, by trade, beast hunters. The killing of monsters as a means of keeping humanity from harm is done almost exclusively through "witcher contracts" wherein townspeople request the help of a witcher to slay beasts for a monetary reward. These pleas can be ignored or accepted for a fee which serves to remind the player that witchers are nominal anti-heroes who fundamentally lack a drive for pure altruism and though they may frequently act on the side of justice, it matters little who they work for. Hence, although one may choose not to get involved or intervene in civilian suffering, it is not unreasonable for any witcher to act in ways that may seem heroic to the people they are protecting but at heart, it is the selfish financial reward that drives such heroism forward.

Though conventional heroism implies acting altruistically and in ways that inherently selfless, even if those who reap the benefit of heroes insist on a reward, it can be argued that using putting oneself in danger to protect the livelihood of others, regardless of recompense, is heroic to a certain degree (Bennett, Efthimiou, & Allison, 2020).

SELF-SERVING HEROISM

Many, if not most, of the moral and ethical choices Geralt is forced to make are of little consequence to his own life and carry little bearing on the lives of those he truly cares about, such as his potential lovers, Triss and Yennefer, or those tied to him through destiny, such as Ciri. In fact, in the latest instalment of the series, there exist 36 possible endings one may experience given the choices they have made throughout the Geralt's heroic journey. However, in a game filled with numerous situations that demand numerous instances of moral judgment, very few decisions truly affect Geralt and those he cares most for. Otherwise, whether or not one received a "good" ending or a "bad" ending is dependent on having done more positive interactions than negative and does not give too much weight on the moral context of each individual decision.

For many players, it is those few, selfishly driven choices, that matter the most because they contain the consequences most relevant to themselves. This self-absorbed thinking can be seen as a reflection of the many parallels in society in that they may aspire to be heroes, but when they are placed in the shoes of one, they may prioritise acting in ways that are self-indulgent over supporting one side or another.

SOCIOPATHIC HEROES

Some anti-heroes merely lack a sense of faith or interest in the world while other anti-heroes lack compassion for it altogether. Lacking in complete empathy for the world, those who inhabit it, and the moral and ethical rules that structure it, sociopathic heroes are a class of heroes who are heroes only in name. These heroes may act on the side of justice but are characterised by their sociopathic inability express concern for the feelings and needs of others and their lack of moral responsibility and social conscience. Even in their commitment to justice, sociopathic heroes may be prone to employing unscrupulous tactics and manipulation to achieve their end goal.

For such heroes, torture, murder, and other wicked practices that are typically characteristic of the villains they are rivalled against are valid methods of doing good. In fact, despite the moral, ethical, and social consequences, such evil actions do not appear to rest heavy on their conscious as a result of their dearth sense of right and wrong. The absence of empathy manifests as a total disregard for both the villains they face as well as the people they save and their acts of heroism are driven by selfish motivators or for other reasons that are unrelated to the well-being of others and upholding the need to do what is right. Often times, such actions are motivated by boredom, bloodlust, or prior engagements that necessitate the doing of good, such as devotion to one's personal honour code or to another person.

Given their bleak nature, existentialist works undoubtedly breed sociopathic heroes. Because the concept and function of anti-heroes have evolved to serve as an instrument of social criticism, it is not unusual that a literary genre influenced by a philosophy that rejects societal emphasis on life's meaning has produced a number of such heroes. Amongst one of the most notable names in existentialist and absurdist literature is Meursault, the principal protagonist of French philosopher and author Albert Camus' L'Étranger. He is a phlegmatic and self-interested French Algerian who is inherently psychologically and socially detached from the world around him. Though it may appear ironic and contradictory to his motivations, Meursault, plagued with indifference and neither positively nor negatively morally motivated, is an atypical hero for a narrow scope of individuals who seek guidance in the form of acceptance of the futility of life.

THE ROLE OF APATHY IN HEROISM

"Maman died today. Or yesterday maybe, I don't know. I got a telegram from the home: 'Mother deceased. Funeral tomorrow. Faithfully yours.' That doesn't mean anything. Maybe it was yesterday" (Camus, 1993). These are the opening thoughts of a man who is numb to sorrow during conventional times of sadness and when asked if he had loved her, he, without shedding a single tear, stoically believed he loved her "the same as anyone" (Camus, 1993). Immediately, L'Étranger lays the groundwork for Meursault sociopathic indifference with his apathy regarding the death of his mother. However, this detachment extends beyond that which is adverse; neither positive nor negative experiences affect his demeanour and he is not encumbered with emotions.

From the day directly following Madame Meursault's funeral, Meursault indulged in an untroubled day of swimming, watching comedic films, and having sexual relations with his former employee, Marie, seemingly unfazed by what many would consider an emotionally devastating loss. Yet, even during times of joyfulness, he is unable to generate a sense of compassion for others; when asked by Marie if he loved her, Meursault states that "it didn't mean anything but that [he] didn't think so" (Camus, 1993). He is not only callous and lacking in remorse, but he also displays a sociopathic incapacity for love and absence of empathy.

As the archetypal sociopathic anti-hero providing a beacon of comfort for those affected with existential apathy and a pronounced disinterest in the universe, Meursault reflects that our decisions, though we are forced to make many in our lifetime, are meaningless in consequence. When confronted by an Arab bearing a knife, Meursault pulls out a gun and shoots once, killing him. He then fires four more bullets into the Arab's motionless body. During this split-second decision, "it was then that [he] realised that you could either shoot or not shoot" (Camus, 1993), emphasising the meaningless of life and implying that regardless of the choice, there exists no difference between either reality. Furthermore, he recognises that the universe, much like himself, is indifferent to what happens. Consequently, there is a certain solace that comes with acknowledging the senselessness, futility, and triviality of the world and that by attempting to aimlessly search for meaning in the people one meets or the events one experiences, one is only creating unnecessary societal and personal pressures and furthering potential anguish.

Apathy is often considered the antithesis of heroism because internalising a sense of indifference typically results in the lack of heroic action, as seen in many cases of the bystander effect. Though the events of L'Étranger appear inherently self-absorbed, the apathy Meursault displays in the face of adversity allow him to be his own hero as it shields him from the psychological and sociological burden of misfortune. In doing so, he sets an example for all those who feel lost in life and can be seen as a hero whose ability to ignore the existential crisis of mortality is to be admired.

HEROISM IN REJECTING THE SEARCH FOR MEANING

Meursault's final act of rejecting moral and social norms comes during his imprisonment and later execution for his crime of murdering the Arab. While many turn to religion as a source of direction, hope, and comfort during trying times and as a means of rationalising the world (Kinsella, Igou, & Ritchie, 2017), Meursault wholly spurns the whole concept of faith and applying any sort of logical sense to one's existence. When met with an examining magistrate who urged him to believe in God, Meursault believed that "he was wrong to dwell on it, because it really didn't matter" (Camus, 1993). Meursault's apathetic defiance serves as a threat to the magistrate and all those who shared such passionate convictions about the universe because "that was his belief, and if he were ever to doubt it, his life would become meaningless" (Camus, 1993). The denial of God's existence and the belief that nothing has meaning incited frustration and indignation from not only the magistrate but also the God-fearing chaplain who tells him that even the worst criminals have seen a divine face during their darkest hour and that because he is unwilling to do so, "his heart is blind" (Camus, 1993). This insistence of a greater purpose inspires rage within Meursault who simply disagrees on a moral principle for the chaplain's certainties were pointless when "he wasn't even sure he was alive, because he was living like a dead man" (Camus, 1993). Rather, it was Meursault, with his absurd certainty in the nothingness of death, that has allowed him to leave the world with a greater understanding of life.

As he nears his execution, Meursault admits that he finds the callous insouciance of the universe to be much like a brother and consequently opens himself to "the gentle indifference of the world" (Camus, 1993). In these last moments, he hopes for a large, hateful crowd to be present at his beheading so that he feels less alone. While ideal heroes typically "prompt reflection on important questions about one's own purpose and contribution in life" (Kinsella et al., 2017) and inspire others to act in ways that are meaningful, Meursault's perspective that there does not need for a greater purpose to exist for life to be fulfilling gives those who do not subscribe to conventional beliefs a hero to venerate – this opposition acts the fatal anti-heroic flaw that drives Meursault to behave indifferently to the euphoria of love and the deep-seated fear of death.

It is in this callous, uncaring, and deeply sociopathic flaw that gives readers a sense of relatability during times of adversity and a reason to find comfort in death when they are forced to yield under the pressures of society. What Meursault lacks in traditional heroic qualities, he makes up for in the ability to ground demoralised or otherwise unorthodox individuals who may be lost in trying to find the meaning that society argues will solve their existentialist problems. Apathy is quintessentially the antithesis of heroism as it suggests inaction and impassivity during times that necessitate it, but Meursault demonstrates that sociopathic indifference can be an alternative source of comfort in the face of death and suffering.

CULTURAL MANIFESTATIONS OF ANTI-HEROES

Anti-heroes carry with them the negative connotation of being amoral and the glaring social blemishes they possess often detract from their heroism. Despite their tremendously unfavourable portrayal, these heroes have gained great popularity in both modern and historic media. In fact, the concept of anti-heroic characters has existed since the early days of Ancient Greece, though the term was not conceived until the 18th century. The wide-scale adoration of anti-heroes, and consequently, unprincipled role models as a whole, has begun to rival that of traditional, ideal heroes – the question is: why do we enjoy these morally tarnished narratives? One explanation is that that art imitates life (Jonason, Webster, Schmitt, Li, & Crysel, 2012); the world is filled with heroic individuals who, in spite of their valiant actions, lack "largeness, grace, power, and social success" (Neimneh, 2013). While traditional heroes may possess these qualities, the upsurge in anti-heroic representation is in part due to their ability to captivate our attention through their atypicality, their relatability, and their uniqueness.

The rise of anti-heroism tales may also stem from the idea of moral disengagement (Raney, Schmid, Neimann, & Ellesohn, 2009). People have been observed resolving the cognitive dissonance of liking a traditionally unlikeable character by granting "moral amnesty" (Raney et al., 2009) under certain circumstances to those who are demonstrating otherwise unacceptable behaviour because they like them and want them to succeed. Hence, their interest and investment in a character may quite often override traditional moral beliefs.

CONCLUSION

The tale of the anti-hero is a "response to the uncertainties of people about traditional values; it is a response to the insignificance of human beings in modernity and their drab existence" (Neimneh, 2013) and it is through the narratives of these individuals that others are able to interpret the world with greater clarity and live more purposefully. However, heroism is a fluid abstraction whose meaning can shift, change, and evolve over the course of history in order to meet the needs of the people at that particular moment in time. As a result, it is not unusual that the ideal hero is now in competition with a different class of exemplar given the ever-metamorphosising troubles of the masses.

Heroism is not a static concept and what it means to be heroic has adapted in such a way that it buffers individuals from the psychological threats and burdens of everyday life (Allison, Goethals, & Spyrou, 2019). While there exist certain enduring universal themes regarding heroism, the particular nuances that classify one as a hero are often subject to change. What it means to be a hero today is different from what it meant to be a hero long ago and it will be different from what it will mean to be a hero in the future.

REFERENCES

Allison, S. T. (2019). Heroic consciousness. Heroism Science, 4, 1-43.

Allison, S. T., Eylon, D., Beggan, J.K., & Bachelder, J. (2009). The demise of leadership: Positivity and negativity in evaluations of dead leaders. The Leadership Quarterly, 20, 115-129.

Allison, S. T. & Goethals, G. R. (2020). The heroic leadership imperative: How leaders inspire and mobilize change. West Yorkshire: Emerald.

Allison, S. T., Goethals, G. R., & Spyrou, S. P. (2019). Donald Trump as the archetypal puer aeternus: The psychology of mature and immature leadership. In K. Bezio & G. R. Goethals (Eds.), Leadership and populism. Northampton, MA: Edward Elgar.

Allison, S. T., Goethals, G. R., Marrinan, A. R., Parker, O. M., Spyrou, S. P., Stein, M. (2019). The metamorphosis of the hero: Principles, processes, and purpose. Frontiers in Psychology.

Allison, S. T., & Green, J. D. (2021). Nostalgia and heroism: Theoretical convergence of memory, motivation, and function. Frontiers in Psychology.

Barksdale, R. K. (1966). Alienation and the anti-hero in recent American fiction. CLA Journal, 10(1), 1-10.

Bennett, D., Efthimiou, O., & Allison, S. T. (2020). The role of heroic creativity and leadership in creative work. In A. de Dios & L. Kong (Eds.), Handbook on the geographies of creativity. Cheltenham, UK: Edward Elgar.

Bergman, I. (Director). (1956). Det sjunde inseglet [Video file]. Sweden: Svensk Filmindustri.

Camus, A. (1993). The Stranger (M. Ward, Trans.). New York: Knopf.

Franco, Z. E., Blau, K., & Zimbardo, P. G. (2011). Heroism: A conceptual analysis and differentiation between heroic action and altruism. Review of general psychology, 15(2), 99.

Goethals, G. R., & Allison, S. T. (2019). The romance of heroism and heroic leadership: Ambiguity, attribution, and apotheosis. West Yorkshire: Emerald.

Jonason, P. K., Webster, G. D., Schmitt, D. P., Li, N. P., & Crysel, L. (2012). The antihero in popular culture: Life history theory and the dark triad personality traits. Review of general psychology, 16(2), 192.

Kinsella, E. L., Ritchie, T. D., & Igou, E. R. (2017). Attributes and applications of heroes: A brief history of lay and academic perspectives. In S.T. Allison, G.R. Goethals, & R.M. Kramer (Eds.), Handbook of heroism and heroic leadership. New York: Routledge.

Kinsella, E. L., Igou, E. R., & Ritchie, T. D. (2017). Heroism and the Pursuit of a Meaningful Life. Journal of Humanistic Psychology, 0022167817701002.

Neimneh, S. (2013). The Anti-Hero in Modernist Fiction: From Irony to Cultural Renewal. Mosaic: a journal for the interdisciplinary study of literature, 75-90.

Raney, A. A., Schmid, H., Niemann, J., & Ellensohn, M. (2009). Testing affective disposition theory: A comparison of the enjoyment of hero and antihero narratives. In annual meeting of the International Communication Association, Chicago, IL.

Simmons, D. (2008). The anti-hero in the American novel: From Joseph Heller to Kurt Vonnegut. Springer.

7

Transposed Heroes: Supporting Evidence for Subjective Heroism

CHLOE L. ZALOOM

Have you ever found yourself in a debate with friends or family, disagreeing over the moral character of a hero turned villain/villain turned hero, in a classic movie or story? You two just can't agree on whether that person is truly a hero or villain. While there has been a recent push for research into the science of heroism, there remains a similar divide amongst scholars. There are those who believe that heroism can be defined by certain objective criteria. There are others who vehemently oppose this notion and claim that heroism is extremely subjective. These scholars will argue that there is no standard method of measuring heroism; that heroism and villainy are actually in the eye of the beholder. Those who are proponents of the objective approach to heroism have agreed upon certain heroic standards that need to be met. These include the notion that heroism involves taking extremely risky and exceptional actions, for the greater good of society, and in spite of great personal sacrifice (Allison & Goethals, 2016). While there have been slight modifications or tweaks to these criteria, these standards are generally agreed upon amongst those who prefer the objective approach to heroism science.

Those who lean towards a more subjective perspective to heroism tend to challenge these strict specifications. They point out that most of the criteria are open to vast interpretation and are very much subjective. Subjective heroism scholars will debate how "exceptional" an action has to be, what determines "great risk", as well as question who sets these thresholds. Moreover, there are often instances where the line between what is considered good versus evil and who is considered heroic versus villainous is quite blurry. Joseph Campbell, a scholar known for contributing ideas that developed critical theories of heroism science, points out the rigidity of the objective approach saying, "You could be a local god, but for the people whom that local god conquered, you could be the enemy. Whether you call someone a hero or a monster is all relative..." (Campbell, 1991).

Campbell brilliantly points out a major flaw to the objective approach: when an individual can considered be both a hero and a villain. This belief is fascinating to scholars who adopt the subjective approach, prompting them to focus on how the people and society perceive and judge heroes and villains, compared to objective scholars who focus mainly on defining heroism. Through this research, subjective scholars have identified three main taxonomies of heroism; situational demand-based, social influence-based, and a social-structure based taxonomy (Allison, Goethals, & Kramer, 2017).

In Goethals and Allison's examination into dimensions of influence, they devised the social-influence based taxonomy of heroism. This taxonomy divides heroes into the following subtypes; trending, transitory, transitional, tragic, transposed, transparent, traditional, transfigured, transforming and transcendent (Allison & Goethals, 2013). In support of the subjective approach, these subtypes attempt to account for the various degrees and forms of heroism that defy objective standards. Specifically, Allison and Goethals' proposal of the transposed hero is a phenomenal example of how the criteria of heroism can be relative.

Transposed heroes generally "undergo rapid change from either villain to hero or from hero to villain" (Allison et al., 2017). These are individuals who experience a reversal in their status, and either transition from hero to villain or vice versa. These occurrences emphasize the fine line between heroism and villainy. Heroes and villains embody many of the same qualities, yet it is truly a sense of moral obligation that differentiates the two. Transposed villains to heroes exemplify how even those who seem irredeemable can feel this sense of moral obligation, then transition towards becoming a hero and making the right decisions.

In contrast, transposed heroes to villains are also an interesting point of study being that they are epitomes of moral righteousness that have lost their way and turned towards dark and evil actions. Additionally, transposed heroes are a prime example of how heroism is in the eye of the beholder specifically because of this reversal in status. An individual who is regarded as a villain to group A yet a hero to group B, but is then transposed, could very well be considered a new foe to group B and a sudden hero to group A. These two aspects of transposed heroism speak to both the fact that the objective evaluative methods used to define heroism are not so consistent, as well as pokes holes in the idea that everyone in society perceives an individual to be of same heroic or villainous nature.

Transposed heroism often refers to these two types of individuals: the hero turned evil or the villain who found the path to redemption. These two paths are not always the case, however, and there are also instances when a single individual can cycle through states of good to bad and bad to good (Goethals & Allison, 2013). The same individual can be considered either a villain or hero at various stages of their life. This type of transposed hero is especially powerful evidence in favor of adopting a subjective approach to studying heroism. With an in depth look into four case studies; those of Severus Snape, Jerry Givens, the Grinch and Oskar Schindler, this chapter aims to reinforce the subjective approach to studying heroism using transposed heroes as supporting evidence.

As Goethals and Allison (2012) point out that, "transposed heroism is quite common in fictional accounts of heroes, particularly in the superhero and horror genres" (p. 131). Furthermore, they argue that "writers of fiction know that people are transfixed by stories involving sudden displays of magic and supernatural power. When these powers are unleashed, heroes are either born or undergo instant transformations" (Goethals & Allison, 2012). Goethals and Allison make a strong point when they state that readers are captivated by stories involving heroes and magic, as evident by the popularity of author, J.K Rowling's, Harry Potter series. Based on Goethals and Allison's point regarding how people obsess over magical heroes, it is unsurprising that readers have fallen in love with many of Rowling's fictional characters, including Harry's sinister professor, Severus Snape.

Severus Snape is a professor of Defense Against the Dark Arts and the Potions Master at Hogwarts, a prestigious magical school of wizardry. Time and time again, Snape is referenced as mysterious, and is a known threat that undermines the progress of heroes Harry, Ron and Hermione. A little background into Snape's life history reveals his evil tendencies; it is implied that Snape is friendless and uncared for by his parents, he became interested in the dark arts at a young age, and he ended up involved with pure-blood supremacists. Snape's passion for the Dark Arts increased his desire for revenge against his childhood nemesis, James Potter, for stealing the love of his life, Lily Evans (Potter). In a misguided attempt to win back Lily's affections, Snape joins the Death Eaters; a name given to followers of the ultimate villain in Rowling's novels, Voldemort. A lack of love and support system largely shaped his bitter disposition and unusually cruel behavior later in life. In his mission for vengeance, Snape takes some truly evil measures that brand him as a traditional villain.

When Snape had first joined the Death Eaters, he was the spy responsible for notifying Voldemort about the prophecy foretelling the dark lord's destruction. Voldemort realized this prophesized hero was the child of Lily and James Potter, Harry, and decided to exterminate the threat. Through great sacrifice, Lily and James managed to protect their son, but at the expense of their lives. Snape had joined the Death Eaters and spend countless years loving Lily

Evans (Potter), only to end up the party responsible for her death. Snape is capable of murder himself when he brings about the demise of his longtime ally Dumbledore, towards the end of the series. In fact, Snape actually revels in creating potions and spells that can be used to torture and kill people. He is credited with creating a charm to make someone mute, enchantments that hoist victims in the air by their ankle and even a spell that causes horrible gashes and uncontrollable bleeding in victims. Unsurprisingly, throughout his time at Hogwarts, Snape was regarded as a harsh disciplinarian.

In his Defense Against the Dark Arts course, Snape was known for terrorizing his students with potions, magic and vicious jabs, all in the name of "education". The reality of the situation was actually that Snape got some satisfaction out of bullying his students, who are the children of people who had harassed him. Snape's torment of Harry and his friends continues throughout the entire series until the last book, when Rowling reveals the reality of Snape's situation to the readers.

Eventually it is disclosed that while Snape may have been the spy that gave information leading to the Potter's death, he also aimed to thwart Voldemort's attempts to kill his beloved. Snape actually confessed his betrayal to Dumbledore and begged for his assistance. While Dumbledore was unable to protect Lily and James, he recruited Snape to watch over Harry throughout his life, a vow that Snape kept until his very last day. Snape was able to work as a double agent, deceiving the Dark Lord and gaining inside knowledge into his plans. It is even revealed that there was a prior arrangement in which Dumbledore agreed to Snape taking his life to protect Harry. Every action that Snape has taken, despite appearing mis-intentioned, was actually for the greater good and out of his love for Lily Potter. Snape pays the ultimate price and sacrifices his life in order to deceive Voldemort and give Harry a fighting chance at saving the world.

Furthermore, Snape acted extraordinarily with no expectation of recognition or respect. Harry, his friends, and many respected wizards despised Snape and believed the worst about him. Snape let his reputation suffer and continued to spy for Dumbledore and protect Harry's life, despite knowing all too well that many people hated him. Snape expected no admiration in return and acted solely out of the goodness of his heart. It is for these reasons that Severus Snape can be considered a transposed hero.

While Snape is a transposed hero, he is a rather unique example. In the classic sense Snape was a villain; he was a pure-blood supremacist, a Death Eater, and committed crimes with the intent to harm others, namely those who had wronged him. As stated early, transposed heroes are those that have undergone a transformation from villain to hero. This "transformation" for Snape began upon the realization that the woman he loved was dead and it was his doing. From that moment on, Snape adopted new motives and principles in an attempt to right his wrongs. He took great risk in playing double agent and protecting Harry, all based on his sense of moral responsibility to atone for his past. Snape knew the consequence of his decision would be his death but proceeded anyway. Following this line of thought, Snape is the classic transposed hero.

Snape is a transposed hero not only due to his moral epiphany and shift in character, but also based on the perception of his heroism. While there is some debate amongst Harry Potter fans as to whether or not Snape is genuinely a hero or villain based on his past intentions and inner qualities, the debate stems from the fact that it is unclear as to whether or not he was pretending to be evil all along. Assuming this is the case, Snape is still considered a transposed hero to the readers. Even if Snape was never ill-intentioned or evil, he certainly appeared that way to the readers. Appearances are reality and to fans of the series, Snape was in fact a villain. After Rowling reveals his backstory and clues readers in that Snape has given up his evil ways in the name of good, readers perceive Snape as a hero. He has been transposed in the eyes of the reader. Severus Snape, exemplifying the transposed hero, is a convincing example of how heroism and villainy are truly in the eye of the beholder.

CASE STUDY II: JERRY GIVENS

While Goethals and Allison (2012) are accurate in saying that transposed heroism is common in fiction and literature, there are also real instances where individuals have been transformed from villain or "monster" to "hero". A great example is that of Jerry Givens, a renowned executioner who worked for the

Virginia Department of Corrections for 25 years. From 1982-1999 he served as the chief executioner for the Commonwealth and was responsible for 62 death row executions (Jouvenal, 2013). During these 17 years, Virginia actually fulfilled more capital punishment sentences than any state besides Texas (Jouvenal, 2013). Givens often used lethal injection and the electric chair to end prisoner's lives. The whole procedure involved praying with the death row inmate, preparing their last meal, shaving their head and then administering the execution (Nour, 2016). Throughout this entire process, Givens conviction never wavered.

When Givens took the job in 1982 he was somewhat ignorant to the prison and judicial systems of the United States. In a recent memoir of his career, Givens recalls that he could not understand why people would consciously commit crimes knowing the risk of getting caught was death. He is quoted as saying "a person [has] to be foolish to commit that kind of crime knowing they could be put to death. It's like volunteer suicide" (Givens, 2013). What really drew Givens to the job was an incident that occurred in his childhood that continued to influence him. When he was just 14 years old Givens was at a house party, standing in the corner and admiring a girl. He was gathering up the courage to ask her to dance when a man with a gun burst into the room and open fired; killing the girl. From that moment on, he firmly believed that those who commit crimes like this shooter had, deserved to die (Jouvenal, 2013). He carried this conviction with him throughout his career as an executioner.

Givens' life was shattered in 1999 when he was subpoenaed to appear before a grand jury. Givens and an old friend were charged with money laundering and perjury for purchasing cars with what prosecutors claim Givens knew was drug money. During his trial, Givens alleges that the U.S attorney told the jury, "he is by no means the worst criminal any of us will ever meet, but he did cross the line" (Givens, 2013). The jury voted to convict Givens, who spent at least four years behind bars while maintaining his innocence the entire time. After being forced to resign from the Department of Corrections, the prison guard and executioner who spent countless years enforcing the law suddenly had the law enforced on him. With time to reflect as an inmate, he looked to strengthen his Baptist faith in hopes of making sense of what had happened to him.

Givens has said that he spent much time in jail reading the Bible, specifically the story of Jesus's crucifixion, which holds a special meaning to the man whose job was putting people to death. He reflected back to all the people he had taken the lives of and wondered how many of the 37 individuals executed via chair and 25 by lethal injection, were actually innocent (Givens, 2013). Over the course of those years Givens realized that the judicial system, upon which he had placed so much faith, was flawed.

After serving his sentence, the former executioner emerged from prison in 2004 as an adamant opposer of the death penalty (Jouvenal, 2013). Not long after his release, a lawyer and former executive director of Virginians for Alternatives to the Death Penalty (VADP) named Jonathan Sheldon, had heard about Givens' story and decided to reach out. It was a remarkable discussion between an activist and a former chief executioner; one that paved the way for Givens future path as a vocal opponent and protestor of the death penalty. Givens became involved in VADP, attending regular meetings and actually joining the board around 2009 (Jouvenal, 2013). He began to travel the United States, giving talks about his experiences as a chief executioner and the epiphany where he realized his actions were truly wrong. In 2010, Givens gave a critical and powerful testimony at a state legislative hearing, challenging a bill designed to expand the use of capital punishment to accomplices in murders (Jouvenal, 2013). He told senators that "the people who pass these bills. They don't have to do it. The people who do the executions, they're the ones who suffer through it" (Jouvenal, 2013). Senators have said his raw and emotional testimony moved representatives, who ultimately voted to reject the proposed bill.

Givens' journey is an inspiring one and shows how even people who have been on a dark path can find the light towards redemption. What makes Givens' story so powerful is that it is a factual one rather than fiction or fantasy. Givens started out as a villain of the State, not just witnessing the horrors of capital punishment, but actually being the man responsible for "swinging the sword". His resolve never wavered and his faith in the U.S legal system remained solid. Yet having experienced this horrible injustice, he emerged from prison not as a bitter or angry man set on revenge, but as an enlightened man determined to bring about peace. This is the journey of a true transposed hero. Givens was transformed from someone capable of taking another human life, to someone devoted to educating others in the value of life. When asked what the biggest mistake he ever made while on the job was, Givens replied "biggest mistake I ever made was taking the job as an executioner. Life is short. Life only consists of 24 hours a day. Death is going to come to us. We don't have to kill one another" (Givens, 2013).

Yet Givens heroic status as someone who has been transposed from villain to savor is up to interpretation. Those who are proponents of the death penalty might argue that Givens was never a villain to begin with. These people would debate that capital punishment is just, and that Givens was dutifully upholding the law. These same people might also say that as a reformed executioner now a determined activist in opposition of the death penalty, Givens is a villainous traitor to his country. Givens as a transposed hero emphasizes the blurry distinction between hero and villain. While Givens may have been a hero to some and a villain to others, he is now a hero to others and a villain to some, highlighting the subjectivity of heroic status.

CASE STUDY III: THE GRINCH

While real life transpositions make for meaningful exemplars, the influence that fictional heroes have on our understanding of heroism should not be underestimated. These fictitious stories are the ones that children hear while growing up. These tales have the lessons that we want young children to internalize. One such classic narrative is the transformation of the Grinch, which is often told around the holiday season. In his tale, there is a villainous green monster, known as the Grinch, who has a severe hatred for Christmas and all things joyful or festive. The Grinch lives on top of a mountain above a city called Whoville. The Whos are fun-loving people who take extreme delight in celebrating the holidays with feasts, gifts, decorations and cheerful Christmas singing. At the start of the story, the Grinch is watching the Whos prepare for Christmas while plotting a way to damper the holiday cheer. The narrator informs the readers that the Grinch's heart is two sizes too small, indicating that he is evil and incapable of love.

Brooding on his mountain top, the Grinch is horrified of the festivities going on below and decides he must put an end to them. The Grinch formulates a plan to dress up as Saint Nick, sneak down into Whoville and prevent Christmas from being celebrated by confiscating all the holiday decorations. The Grinch, stuck in his evil ways, needed every Who in Whoville to be as unspirited and bitter around the holidays as he was. He makes his way down to Whoville and ransacks houses of all their holiday spirit, a move that is very much illegal. He stole all the presents, stockings, food for feasts, and even Christmas trees.

Taking his loot up to his lair, the Grinch was determined to get rid of the Christmas spirit once and for all by throwing all the decorations and goodies off the side of the mountaintop. Just as the Grinch is about to get rid of the Christmas supplies, he is suddenly hit with the notion that he has not heard the Whos crying for their lost presents and trinkets. He lifts an ear to hear for the sobs but is surprised when he hears a slight Christmas tune. Led by a young Who, named Cindy Lou, this tune grew louder and was bursting with cheer until all of Whoville was joining in the Christmas carol. The Grinch was taken aback with disbelief. He could not fathom how the holiday spirit could live on when he had stolen all of their Christmas belongings. Then the Grinch has an epiphany as he realized Christmas was not about the presents or the gifts, but about the spirit and joy one gets from being around family and friends. Realizing the error of his ways and inspired by the jubilee, the Grinch rushes to return all the stolen goods to the Whos down in Whoville. It is said that the Grinch's heart grew three times that day and he transitioned from evil villain determined to ruin the holidays to a hero that saves Christmas day. He discovers that what he was missing in his lonely life, was a sense of community and friendship during the holidays.

While the story of the Grinch may be fictional and a little far-fetched, it serves as a great example of transposed heroism for both children and adults. As Goethals and Allison put it, "the transpositions that occur in fictional literature do not occur in the real world, yet somehow they fascinate us. We are emotionally drawn to instantaneous shifts in morality and how these shifts play a role in creating or destroying heroes" (Allison & Goethals, 2016). The Grinch, a villain transposed to hero, is a prime example how not everyone is truly good or evil. The heroic deeds that the Grinch took cannot be objectively measured as heroic based on traditional standards, indicating that a subjective approach is more useful in deciphering the heroism in this Christmas tale.

The final case study to be analyzed in this chapter is the true story of an Austro-Hungary business man who saved hundreds of lives during the twentieth century tragedy of the Holocaust. In 1908, Oskar Schindler was born in a German province of the Austro-Hungarian Empire, now a part of the Czech Republic (Byers, 2005). Schindler grew up in a deeply Catholic household, to well respected and extremely wealthy parents, Hans and Louisa Schindler, who owned a successful machinery business. Schindler was an attractive man who was used to getting what he wanted, which resulted in impulsive philandering and an excessive drinking problem. Schindler was also known as an opportunist and strategic business man. In the 1930's, he sensed that the political landscape was changing with the rise of Adolf Hitler and the Nazi Party (Byers, 2005).

Schindler used this opportunity to join a pro-Nazi activist group and started collecting information as a spy for the German military. He continued to spy until just before 1940, at which time Schindler traveled to the newly invaded Krakow, Poland in search of "get rich quick" scheme (Oskar Schindler Biography, 2015). A sleazy business man with a lack of moral compass, Schindler hoped to profit from the impending war at the expense of the Jewish people. He purchased a former Jewish enamelware factory with the intent on producing goods for the German military. Schindler viewed the Jewish people not as people at all, but rather as a source of cheap labor. He dehumanized them and reduced them to nothing but a means to make more money.

Through many of his Jewish workers, Schindler discovered that many of the local Krakow Jewish people were being sent to Plazow labor camp. He was told of the brutalities and atrocities that occurred there, and he believed the plans for mass extermination of millions of people were terrifying. Using his connections with the German government to convince officials to set up a portion of the Plazow labor camp in his factory. Schindler employed those who were unqualified and unfit to work, in turn sparing roughly 900 Jewish lives with this one action (Oskar Schindler Biography, 2015). Similarly, he negotiated with officials and was allowed to transfer over 700 Jews from the

Grossrosen concentration camp and roughly 300 women from Auschwitz, over to his factory (Oskar Schindler Biography, 2015). Under his care they received the food, clothing, shelter and medical attention; all at the expense of Schindler. Once they had been relocated from the camps to Schindler's factory, they were not forced to work. Schindler purposefully weakened the manufacturing process to make sure his products failed quality-control tests (Byers, 2005). He did this to hide the fact that his workers were not actually producing goods, but actually being rescued. Not only did he spend large amounts of money on the upkeep of his "workers", but he spent obscene amounts of money bribing the German military and government.

Schindler is another great example of a transposed hero in real life. He started out as a selfish individual who was only concerned with making money. He dehumanized the Jewish people and reduced them to nothing more than a means to make money quickly. After being faced with the injustices and hearing tales of brutalities against the Jewish people, Schindler came to recognize his workers as humans who had been exposed to ruthless slaughter. This came to be his only motivation Schindler had for risking his life, fortune, and the safety of his family. He was arrested twice and had to bribe officials to avoid punishment (Byers, 2005). Schindler takes great personal risk and sacrifices much, with the aim of alleviating the suffering of as many Jewish people as possible. He has been transposed from a greedy businessman to a humanitarian and hero in this inspiring story of redemption.

DIRECTIONS FOR FUTURE RESEARCH

This chapter does not aim to discredit the objective approach to heroism or undermine its value. There are benefits to analyzing heroism using an objective approach, which include clear standards and guidelines for determining an individual's status as hero, villain, or bystander. Furthermore, it is beneficial that some aim to objectively define heroism, since a clear definition could expand the knowledge and growth of heroism science. Instead, this chapter seeks to explore the idea that there are instances of heroism or villainy that cannot be accounted for by the current objective definition of heroism. Transposed heroes are exemplars for why it is valuable to consider a subjective technique when evaluating acts of heroism (Bennett, Efthimiou, & Allison, 2020).

The case studies in this chapter serve to identify various types of transposed heroism. There are instances when someone has committed genuinely evil actions with the intent to harm or exploit others. These people have had some kind of epiphany or revelation and realize the error of their ways. They then shift their behavior to act heroically. People will debate whether an individual who is making up or preventing an evil action of their own doing, can really be considered a heroic savior (Allison, 2015). Some will argue that this redemption makes the individual a hero, while others will disagree. This conflict is a great example of the type of transposed hero that emphasizes the fine line behind villainy and heroism. Likewise, there are instances where an individual is considered both a hero and a villain to different groups of people. When this individual undergoes transposition, they then hold the opposite heroic or villainous status in the eyes of those groups, further stressing that heroism is more subjective rather than objective. There are also cases where an individual may appear to be the villain, but they are actually the hero all along. They have been despised by people until it is revealed that their actions have heroic intentions. This highlights how easy it is for someone who is viewed as a villain to suddenly be regarded as a hero. This idea also hints that while transposed heroes can either be morally, spiritually and physically transformed, they can also be transposed in their perception as a hero.

This chapter briefly mentioned Goethals and Allison's idea that transposed heroism is often seen in fictional circumstances or in literature (Goethals & Allison, 2013). This is an interesting point that hints at the idea that transposed heroism might occur more frequently in fictional narratives compared to real life. An interesting point of future research could be to validate or reject this notion, and perhaps aim to decipher why. Are literary transposed heroes a reflection of the authors desire to transpose themselves? Is there some major obstacle in the real world that does not exist in fiction that prevents or dissuades transposition? These are valid questions that could guide potential research directions.

Furthermore, in both reality and fiction alike, there seems to be more cases of a villain transposed to become a hero than vice versa. Time and time again there are stories of a villain or terrible human who has committed some heinous actions, then ends up finding redemption and atoning for their past mistakes. This theme of redemption is very prominent for transposed villains to heroes.

However, there seem to be far less cases where a hero or saint gives into their dark temptations and turns evil. This could indicate that there is some quality that heroes possess, that villains do not, that makes them less susceptible to corruption and evil temptations. Future research into the rate of hero to villain, versus villain to hero transpositions could prove invaluable. Further studies could also aim to identify if heroes possess such an incorruptible quality, and what that attribute is. While these subsequent directions for heroism research are compelling, the objective of this chapter is not to overanalyze traits of transposed heroes. Rather this chapter is designed to use case studies of various types of transposed heroes to stress how these heroic courses cannot simply be explained by the objective definition of heroism. Instead, adopting a subjective approach to studying heroes proves to be effective in interpreting varied heroic journeys.

REFERENCES

Allison, S. T. (2015). The initiation of heroism science. Heroism Science, 1, 1-8.

Allison, S. T., & Goethals, G. R. (2013). Heroic Leadership: An Influence Taxonomy of 100 Exceptional Individuals. New York: Routledge.

Allison, S. T., & Goethals, G. R. (2016). Hero worship: The elevation of the human spirit. Journal for the Theory of Social Behaviour, 46, 187-210.

Allison, S. T., Goethals, G. R., & Kramer, R. M. (Eds.) (2017). Handbook of heroism and heroic leadership. New York: Routledge

Allison, S. T., & Green, J. D. (2021). Nostalgia and heroism: Theoretical convergence of memory, motivation, and function. Frontiers in Psychology.

Campbell, J. (1991). The Power of Myth. Anchor Books.

Bennett, D., Efthimiou, O., & Allison, S. T. (2020). The role of heroic creativity and leadership in creative work. In A. de Dios & L. Kong (Eds.), Handbook on the geographies of creativity. Cheltenham, UK: Edward Elgar.

Byers, A. (2005). Oskar Schindler: saving Jews from the Holocaust. Berkeley Heights, NJ.: Enslow.

Givens, J. (2013, November 21). I was Virginia's executioner from 1982 to 1999. Any questions for me? The Guardian. Retrieved from https://www.theguardian.com/commentisfree/2013/nov/21/death-penalty-former-executioner-jerry-givens

Goethals, G.R. & Allison, S. T. (2012). Making heroes: The construction of courage, competence and virtue. Advances in Experimental Social Psychology, 46, 183-235

Jouvenal, J. (2013, February 10). Ex-Virginia executioner becomes opponent of death penalty. Washington Post. Retrieved from https://www.washingtonpost.com/local/ex-virginia-executioner-becomes-opponent-of-death-penalty/2013/02/10/9e741124-5e89-11e2-9940-6fc488f3fecd_story.html

Nour, S. (2016, January 24). 10 Incredible Real-Life Stories of Redemption. Retrieved November 2, 2018, from https://listverse.com/2016/01/24/10-incredible-real-life-stories-of-redemption/

Oskar Schindler. (n.d.). Retrieved November 2, 2018, from https://www.ushmm.org/collections/bibliography/oskar-schindler

Oskar Schindler Biography. (2015, May 15). Retrieved November 2, 2018, from https://www.biography.com/people/oskar-schindler

Shulleeta, B. (2015, September 25). Former Virginia executioner Jerry Givens expresses regret. Richmond Times-Dispatch. Retrieved from https://www.richmond.com/news/local/crime/former-virginia-executioner-jerry-givens-expresses-regret/article_25f6e244-a8c3-58bc-9836-56999230b4ec.html

Zanna, M., P., & Olson, J., M. (2012). Advances in Experimental Social Psychology (Vol. 46). Academic Press.

8

Citizens or Heroes: The Fall – and Rise – of Heroic Martyrdom

MEGAN R. WIRTZ

"She died like a heroine."

The words, uttered by a German chaplain, sum up the life of Edith Cavell in many ways ("Account by Reverend H. Stirling Gahan," n.d.). Cavell's heroism began when she was tending to two wounded soldiers. A British nurse herself, she was stationed in Brussels (occupied by Germany) during World War One. These two wounded, British soldiers begat a massive "ring" that Cavell smuggled out of German territories; they started her heroism. Less than a year later, her efforts were squashed as she was arrested; she was executed two months later ("Who Was Edith Cavell?," 2018).

Here's the thing about Cavell, though: she was not partisan in regards to her job. Despite her heroism with smuggling the Allied men, she treated all of the wounded soldiers just as if they were themselves: men ("Who was Edith Cavell?," n.d.). Although her "heroic deed" was sided on the side of the Allies, she actively attempted to make sure all of the soldiers felt cared for and safe with her. Yet, the German government found her guilty of treason, turning her from being a hero for both sides into a villain on one – and a hero and martyr on the other (Rigby, 2015). Thus, she wasn't a hero in the eyes of the Germans until they renounced Nazism.

Cavell is not alone in this sort of reverse-heroism, where one begins as a villain and ends up a hero. That is, due to revolutions and changes in society, those who promoted something previously "villainous" return as heroes after their death, once society has changed. They serve as martyrs, giving up their lives to successfully cultivate change in their society. Thus, their death begets and creates their heroism; the challenges they are faced with on the journey to becoming heroes become too much, and they pass away before their heroism is fully realized.

In other words, those who "fail" before their heroism is fully discovered hit a block at the initiation phase of the hero's journey. Joseph Campbell, the founder of the study of heroism, was the one who initially discovered the hero's journey, the pattern behind every heroic life in classic mythology. Every hero, Campbell posited, undergoes a process – the hero's journey – in which they are transformed through three phases. The first phase is separation (departure), when the hero becomes separated from their familiar world. The second is initiation, when heroes go through painful experiences that will help them to grow. The third stage is the return, in which the hero makes his or her triumphant return to society as a changed person (Campbell, 1949).

However, there is a small, but very interesting, subset of heroes who initially seem to fail the initiation phase. That is, the initiation phase becomes too much for them, and they pass away during their initiation. Often, they are the outliers and outcasts of society who don't fit in to some given societal norm, and as the pressure of being the antithesis of society mounts on them, they are forced to leave their lives too young. Years later, however, these heroes make a triumphant return as martyrs of the cause they often died from – the societal pressure that had weighed them down during their lives is now lifted. For instance, Cavell was executed by the Germans for helping smuggle Allied soldiers across the German border. Germany, since, has disavowed Nazism; thus, they have implicitly disavowed Cavell's execution.

This essay will delve into the lives of two more exemplars of this phenomenon. Both were deemed hero's under one of society's greatest examples of cultural change: the LGBTQ movement. Previously, nearly everywhere across the globe repudiated the concept of homosexuality; no matter what the culture or religion, homosexuality was a sin and went against all norms. Both men wound up dead or destitute because they were accused of gross acts of indecency – that is, homosexuality – which was illegal when they were alive. However, both of them returned in the 21st century as role models and martyrs for a flourishing LGBTQ community that is no longer illegal. This essay will take a detailed look at two of the world's most popular LGBTQ martyrs, Alan Turing and Oscar Wilde. This essay will look at how society can, at the time of the hero, consider the hero a villain – only to have that same villain return to society a half century later as a martyr for the cause for which they were originally killed or silenced.

ALAN TURING: HERO OR VILLAIN?

We'll start with Alan Turing. Turing's journey as one of the world's foremost mathematicians began when he enrolled as an undergraduate student at the University of Cambridge. After much success there, he completed a fellowship at the prestigious King's College, where he would meet a mentor and future collaborator, Alonzo Church, whom he would follow to Princeton University. One of Turing's greatest inventions, the Turing Machine, was adapted from his time as a fellow at King's College. In 1939, he joined the British government in fighting World War Two, working behind the scenes as a code breaker (Copeland, 2018).

Here is where Turing rose to fame. The governments of Poland, France, and England had been working to try to crack the Enigma – the principle encoder of the German army. Turing's arrival helped spur the Brits to the invention of the Bombe, a massive code-breaking device that would eventually decipher nearly 2 messages per minute every day. For his efforts, he was recognized with honors and awards (Copeland, 2018).

Unfortunately, Turing's story then turned somewhat bleak. In 1952, Turing was convicted of acts of gross indecency – that is, homosexual acts – which were illegal in Britain at the time. He was sentenced to a year of hormone therapy (chemical castration) – an act that labeled him a criminal, and immediately ended his governmental career. This conviction led to his presumed suicide, and it was not until 2009 that the British Prime Minister apologized for Turing's treatment, and it took four more years for him to be granted an official pardon (Copeland, 2018). However, one important thing to note is that Turing was never necessarily upset about his punishment – he was, however, worried that his reputation would mar his discoveries and inventions for the future. In a letter to a friend, he is quoted as describing the discovery of his sexuality in this way:

"Turing believes machines think
Turing lies with men
Therefore machines do not think." (Couch, 2014)

It is horrific, especially in the decade of the 2020s, to think that one's sexual orientation may "prove" them to be a liar, or a fraud. However, because of society's borders, Turing had to worry himself about the idea that people might consider his discoveries unusable due to his sexual orientation. He was not worried about his reputation, nor about what would happen to him as a homosexual individual, but was instead worried about what his reputation would do to the advancement of society.

Here, then, is where we round back to the hero's journey, in which society plays a major role. The first interesting aspect of Turing's life is that he had not one, but two, heroic journeys that he was taken on. His first occurred during his life, when he joined the war and fought as a code breaker. He was thus removed from society, as much of society was not actively trying to contain and halt the war. He was then faced with the initiation of breaking the Enigma, which would have been a massive hurdle and obstacle on his way to becoming a hero. He then returned to society, with honors and awards being bestowed upon him.

Then, though, Turing is forced to undergo another hero's journey. Just at the peak of his career, he is called a criminal on the basis of acts of indecency. He is separated from society via his criminality, and is faced with the initiation and obstacle of being forced to undergo chemical castration – an action that will ultimately kill him. Herein, then, is the most fascinating part of his second hero's journey: his return to society. As activism surrounding the legalization of LGBTQ marriages and relationships begins, Turing becomes a martyr for this culture, someone who died for the cause that others are fighting so hard for. Thus, his return to society occurs when his name is cleared in the early 21st century, transforming him from someone who used to be the antithesis of societal morals to one who displays the best of them.

Thus, Turing has become a hero anew; he has, even post-mortem, completed the final lap of the hero's journey. But how was that leg completed? It's interesting to think about the fact that Turing's journey might not have been completed without some help from others along the way – namely, the shifting of societal norms. That is, had society not shifted, Turing might have not become a hero, and would have remained a villain in the eyes of many.

Thus, we have an example of what has occurred with so many who "push the boundaries" of society. Although they may be seen as a villain, as someone un-idealistic, they become a hidden leader of a societal shift and change; they become sparks for a communal change in morals and ideals. We've seen this shift time and time again, in different scenarios: feminism, civil rights, voting rights. One person, or one group of people, pushing the pendulum so far in the other direct that society has to take a hard look at where its values currently lay. These people can be as normal as Cavell, going about her daily work as a nurse while secretly smuggling soldiers across the border to safety; they can be as prominent as Turing, who hid his secret life away from the public while rising to becoming one of the most important theorists and inventors of our time; or they could be as flamboyant as Oscar Wilde, who changed the course of history by showing that even exceedingly accomplished artists did not always adhere to the morals that their societies set forth.

OSCAR WILDE: REPUTATION IS THE DEMISE

"Most people are other people. Their thoughts are someone else's opinions, their lives a mimicry, their passions a quotation" ("Oscar Wilde," n.d.). There is no better way to introduce our next exemplar, Oscar Wilde. Unlike Turing, Wilde was born into a family with two parents who were already somewhat well-known: his father was a well-respected doctor, his mother a poet and author. He studied, on scholarships, at Trinity College (Dublin) and Oxford (Beckson, 2018).

It didn't take long for Wilde to create a reputation for himself. When he was in his late 20s, he found himself the subject of a periodical, who cited Wilde for his "unmasculine" affinity for the arts. He peaked with the publication of his only movie ("The Picture of Dorian Gray") in 1891. Many of his publications dealt with the concealment of some major immorality or secret, which eventually led to his characters' demise. In fact, in an 1889 poem, Wilde insinuated that he himself was one of these characters (Beckson, 2018).

And here is where Wilde's initiation occurred. The Marquess of Queensberry, whose son was close with Wilde, accused Wilde of sodomy. Wilde then sued the Marquess for libel – an act that led to his ultimate demise. When the case turned unfavorably on Wilde, he was arrested, with two years of hard labor in prison. When he was released, he was completely bankrupt, and fled to France. He died a few years later (Beckson, 2018), but was pardoned in 2017 (McCann, 2017).

So, again, one could say that Wilde had a double journey – except Wilde's journeys were parts of other journeys. He was separated from society when he received a well-rounded education; his initiation occurred when he began to be ostracized for his affinity for the arts; and his return occurred with his literary success. However, he underwent a second hero's journey, as well. He was separated from society when he began to be ostracized for his affinity for the arts. He was initiated when the case against the Marquess flipped on him. And his return – post-death – occurred when he was pardoned, becoming a hero for a burgeoning LGBTQ community. Thus, once again, also, his heroism came about through changes in society – when society changed, so did his status as a hero (or a villain).

SOCIETY AS A FORCE OF CHANGE

Now, it feels necessary to clarify why these two exemplars have become "reborn" heroes. The fact that these two exemplars are both heroes for the LGBTQ community is not mere coincidence; neither, though, were these two chosen simply because they recognize that branch of the population. Those two were chosen because they only became heroes because society changed course. When they died, they were seen as villains in the eyes of society because their actions were illegal;

when they reemerged as heroes, it was because society had, by then, accepted and legalized acts of homosexuality (Allison et al., 2019; Goethals & Allison, 2019). In that same vein, we can look at famous feminists (think Susan B. Anthony) or those that fought for civil rights and integration (e.g., Martin Luther King, Jr.). There is a remarkable distinction we must make between how these exemplars became heroes. It is not, necessarily, that society changed them; it is that they changed society. Though neither Anthony nor King were necessarily "villains" in the eyes of society prior to their deaths, both of these sects of protestors fought the status quo. They both became heroes because they defied society, and thus they changed it.

While Turing and Wilde did not necessarily change society while they were alive, society changed while they were dead – and thus they transitioned posthumously from a villain into a hero. They gave their lives so that other might understand the depths of their despair and inequality, that they might incite a form of change. It is clear, then, that there is a bit of a chicken-before-the-egg puzzle here: did these heroes change because of their community changing, or did their community change because of them (thus making them heroes)?

This paradox is absolutely fascinating, and one that will be focused on for quite a bit more of this paper. The interesting thing about Turing and Wilde is that they did not transform society; society transformed them. They did not actively seek out their heroic status – how could they, when they passed away too soon to realize that they were even remotely heroic? And they were not the ultimate, catalyzing force that drove society to change. So, how did they become heroes?

TRANSFORMING SOCIETY – OR TRANSFORMED BY SOCIETY?

Here, then, is where we run into another intriguing paradox: can heroes be heroes if they themselves do not transform society? Here is where the concept of heroic martyrdom comes into play. By giving their lives to incite change, they served as martyrs for their community. A lot of the current research overlooks is the concept of heroic martyrs, because they tend to be the antithesis of the "prototypical" hero. They don't necessarily transform society. They don't necessarily win glory immediately. They typically aren't idolized or admired when they are alive.

However, there needs to be a shift in how we perceive these heroic martyrs, and we need to view them in the same light as other, more "obvious" heroes.

One of the reasons for this oversight of heroic martyrdom is that these are heroes who have initially failed. They weren't immediately successful, and when compared with people who developed cures for diseases or pulled someone from the wreckage of a car crash, they don't immediately strike one as heroes. Allison and Goethals (2017) argue that one of the benefits of the heroic transformation – which many would undergo during the initiation phase – is that this transformation allows for the ability to transform society. They also argue that the two types of transformation applicable are the self and society (Allison & Goethals, 2017). Thus, we land ourselves in a perfect in-between: how can we argue that these two were heroes, if their hero's journey was halted in the initiation phase, and therefore they weren't able to experience a transformation of their society?

Parks (2017) has an idea: what if their tendency toward heroic action was inhibited due to, say, societal pressures, or cultural norms? Both Turing and Wilde were forced to reckon with the fact that their way of being and their life ran against the cultural norm. In fact, Britain, at the time of Turing, was undergoing a something akin to a "witch hunt", wherein men who called in crimes were often found at the guilty end of gross indecency. Police were quick to arrest any man who displayed any amount of homosexual tendencies. No matter what the crime was that the police had been called in for, they would disregard it if there were the chance to make an arrest for the crime of "gross indecency" (Bedell, 2007).

There was a similar feeling toward homosexuals in Ireland in the 1800s. In fact, the Offences Against The Person Act of 1861 deals with the idea of homosexuality explicitly under its "Unnatural Offences" section: "Whosoever shall be convicted of the abominable crime of buggery, committed either with mankind or with any animal, shall be liable...to be kept in penal servitude for life...". In fact, the Act goes even further: "Whosoever shall attempt to commit the said abominable crime, or shall be guilty of any assault with intent to commit the same, or of any indecent assault upon any male person, shall be guilty of a misdemeanor..." (Offences Against The Person Act, 1861). Thus, not only did committing homosexual acts come with a life sentence, but simply being regarded as having attempted to commit an act of homosexuality would be seen as a crime. And, if it were not already obvious, there is a clear opening here for arrests to be made on the mere assumption that one is a homosexual.

Thus, what Turing and Wilde were doing was inherently illegal. They were pushing the boundaries of society while hiding behind the shadows – they did not want to necessarily change society so that it would adapt to them, but they did want to enjoy their lives the way they pleased. Thus, the cultural norms of Britain stopped the men from advocating for LGBTQ rights while they were alive, as they would have been arrested for their acts of gross indecency and had their reputations marred, and their advocacy would have been disregarded.

ARE MARTYRS HEROES?

This concept, then, is the first example of how heroic martyrs should be considered "heroes" just as much as any other hero. Even if a transformation of society is necessary to be considered a "hero", one cannot disregard those who were forced to evade society for their own personal well-being. In fact, it's fascinating that the one thing that the men ended up as martyrs for was the thing that stopped them from being heroes at the time they were alive.

Unfortunately, we cannot simply determine "heroism" by proving that the cultural norms of society impeded their attempted heroism; we must first acknowledge that their heroism was involuntary. Franco, Blau, and Zimbardo (2011) stated in their initial definition of heroism that heroism: 1) is directed toward others in need; 2) is voluntary; 3) acknowledges possible risks and costs; 4) is pursued while willing to accept the anticipated sacrifice; and 5) is pursued with the hero accomplishing their action without the inherent necessity of external gain. While both Turing and Wilde served others in need and recognized the potential risks of the intimate relationships, we cannot validly argue that any of these other criterion of "heroism" are true of them. Their heroic actions were not voluntary (unless we can count Turing's suicide as a heroic action that turned him into a martyr), nor were they prepared to accept or acknowledge any potential sacrifice or external gain because they were unaware that they were heroes. The way that society viewed them was as villains, as the antithesis of "normal"; they were not trying to fight against this notion.

So here we are, caught in a place of wondering whether heroic martyrdom makes one a hero. We can argue that their heroic actions were potentially impeded by cultural norms, but we cannot argue that their heroism was voluntary. There is a fundamental gap in the literature in regards to heroes who have become heroes post-death; do their actions count as voluntary? Do we acknowledge that any obvious heroism may have been precluded by cultural norms?

Thus, there must be a new definition of heroes created, one that includes those who have only recently come heroes due to the ever-changing society. To do so, we need to look at some of the current principles of heroism as they do or do not relate to both Turing and Wilde, and begin to dissect and unravel the notion that heroic martyrdom is somehow below other forms of heroism.

WHAT THE RESEARCH SAYS

Both of these characters were social heroes, which are described by Kinsella et al. (2017) as persons who risked personal sacrifice in the face of their society. This idea is different from the aforementioned theory that stated that a necessary facet of heroism was the recognition that heroic actions require personal sacrifice, because in this case, this theory is simply stating that social heroism involves some kind of personal sacrifice, not that the person necessarily needs to acknowledge that their actions are potentially sacrificial. In fact, the article gives the explicit example that martyrs are considered social heroes (Kinsella, Ritchie, & Igou, 2017). Thus, we can retain the idea that they are social heroes.

Both Turing and Wilde also meet the criterion for the functions of heroes. Kinsella et al. (2017) describe that a hero must have an enhancing, moral modeling, and protecting function. In the enhancing function, heroes will motivate, inspire, and provide roles models to society; I don't think we can argue that both Wilde and Turing have those functions. The moral modeling function of heroes argues that heroes help people understand society's norms, virtues, and models, and decide for themselves whether they want to adhere to these established norms. This argument is very important to note – it does not say that heroes encourage people to act toward the established norms; rather, it simply says that heroes provide a moral guideline from which people can determine their own actions. Thus, because Turing and Wilde went against the morals of society, they can be seen as heroes – they provided society with that mirror on which to reflect themselves. The protecting function involves "doing what no one else will, helping, saving, guiding, and acting against evil or danger". It is important, especially in the case of heroic martyrs like Turing and Wilde, to look at how they acted against evil or danger. Both of them were jailed or treated with chemical castration due to their lifestyle – a lifestyle that they were told was illegal. Thus, they were, in a way, acting against what they deemed to be evil or dangerous, or at least dangerous to what they believed in.

Both men also meet the criteria for heroic transformations, as defined by Allison and Goethals (2017). The heroic journey implies that this transformation occurs directly after the initiation phase; but how can these exemplars be heroes if they did not complete the initiation phase, and therefore did not have a self-transformation? In the heroic journey, I think there is a general over-conceptualization that heroes must transform themselves so that they may be considered heroes. Nothing could be further from the truth. Allison and Goethals (2017) argue that there are specific subtypes of heroic transformation, the first being the transformation of the self or of society. It is not necessary that the hero experience this transformation unto his or her self; perhaps the hero, as the authors say, "serves as the catalyst for the transformation in others". This concept, then, would go along with the fact that society transformed them; when heroes serve as the catalyst for societal change, that societal change will loop back around and make them a hero.

In an interesting way, we can also apply some of Kohen et al.'s (2017) steps to heroic development. Expansive empathy – the idea that one acts heroically because they feel empathetic toward someone – is often associated with heroes, the ones who complete the heroic actions. In the case of heroic martyrs, however, the expansive empathy is retroactive, and something that is actually placed in the hands of the non-heroes – those who are making the martyrs a hero. By feeling empathetically toward the hero, they make the hero a hero – they recognize the sacrifice that the hero made for them, and feel empathetic to their plight, thus making them a hero.

Both Turing and Wilde fit the criteria for heroism throughout much of this research. The only facet that they really do not fit into is the idea of their heroism being voluntary – something that is quite literally impossible for them, given their circumstances. But isn't it fascinating that we are establishing that heroism is based on the concept that one is in the right place at the right time, and not on how much a person contributes to society?

There are a few directions in which I think this question could be resolved. Future research should delve further into the hero's journey, especially the possibility of expanding the initiation phase. It is possible for one to, essentially, fail their initiation phase, and become reborn as a new hero. The hero's journey tends to establish that one must make it through the departure stage and through the initiation phase before returning to society. However, the hero's journey needs to be readjusted to account for those who fail in their initiation phase – there needs to be room for them as a hero, as well.

Which leads us into the next categorization of heroism we need to account for: martyrdom. There is very little research on those of those who failed their initiation phase but returned as a hero through societal changes. Without taking these persons into account, we are probably missing several people who fought the status quo in their day, but whose names go unknown because they were held silent in their time.

What everything boils down to is the fact that there needs to be a change in the perception in our society of what makes a hero a hero. Heroes aren't always the ones who have biopics made of them, or the ones who make the front cover of newspapers because they foiled a terrorist-bombing plan. We need to recognize that there are heroes who are giving their lives on a regular basis to help us understand that certain societal changes must be enacted to progress our society further. We could argue that those children dying of cancer are martyrs for the cause of cancer research, because they are giving up their lives so that cancer research can progress further. We don't yet call them heroes, because our society has not yet developed a cure for the cancers that have caused them to pass away. However, I guarantee that when that cure is found, those children who have passed will be considered heroes to the families of future children who have been diagnosed with the same type of cancer and are now saved.

Just because one passes away should not be an exclusionary criterion for how whether or not they are seen as heroes. We must expand our vision to be inclusive of those who have passed away, and those who are not "obvious" heroes. Those who have become martyrs for society through changes in the status quo deserve just as much importance and infamy as the others.

REFERENCES

Account by Reverend H. Stirling Gahan on the execution of Edith Cavell. (n.d.). Retrieved from https://edithcavell.org.uk/edith-cavells-life/account-by-reverend-h-stirling-gahan-on-the-execution-of-edith-cavell/

Allison, S. T. (2015). The initiation of heroism science. Heroism Science, 1, 1-8.

Allison, S. T. (2019). Heroic consciousness. Heroism Science, 4, 1-43.

Allison, S. T., & Burnette, J. (2009). Fairness and preference for underdogs and top dogs. In R. Kramer, A. Tenbrunsel, & M. Bazerman, (Eds), Social Decision Making: Social Dilemmas, Social Values, and Ethical Judgments. New York: Psychology Press.

Allison, S. T., Eylon, D., Beggan, J.K., & Bachelder, J. (2009). The demise of leadership: Positivity and negativity in evaluations of dead leaders. The Leadership Quarterly, 20, 115-129.

Allison, S. T. & Goethals, G. R. (2020). The heroic leadership imperative: How leaders inspire and mobilize change. West Yorkshire: Emerald.

Allison, S. T., & Goethals, G. R. (2017). The hero's transformation. In S. T. Allison, G. R. Goethals, & R. M. Kramer (Eds.), Handbook of heroism and heroic leadership (1st ed., pp. 379–400). New York: Routledge.

Allison, S. T., Goethals, G. R., & Spyrou, S. P. (2019). Donald Trump as the archetypal puer aeternus: The psychology of mature and immature leadership. In K. Bezio & G. R. Goethals (Eds.), Leadership and populism. Northampton, MA: Edward Elgar.

Allison, S. T., Goethals, G. R., Marrinan, A. R., Parker, O. M., Spyrou, S. P., Stein, M. (2019). The metamorphosis of the hero: Principles, processes, and purpose. Frontiers in Psychology.

Beckson, K. (2018). Oscar Wilde. In Encyclopedia Britannica. Retrieved from https://www.britannica.com/biography/Oscar-Wilde

Bedell, G. (2007, June 24). Coming out of the dark ages. The Guardian. Retrieved from https://www.theguardian.com/society/2007/jun/24/communities.gayrights

Campbell, J. (1949). The hero with a thousand faces. New York: Pantheon.

Copeland, B. J. (2018). Alan Turing. In Encyclopedia Britannica. Retrieved from https://www.britannica.com/biography/Alan-Turing#ref214877

Couch, A. (2014, November 29). Alan Turing's 5 most powerful quotes. The Hollywood Reporter. Retrieved from https://www.hollywoodreporter.com/news/alan-turings-5-powerful-quotes-752669

Efthimiou, O., & Allison, S. T. (2017). Heroism science: Frameworks for an emerging field. Journal of Humanistic Psychology, 58, 556-570.

Franco, Z. E., Blau, K., & Zimbardo, P. G. (2011). Heroism: A conceptual analysis and differentiation between heroic action and altruism. Review of General Psychology. https://doi.org/10.1037/a0022672

Goethals, G. R., & Allison, S. T. (2019). The romance of heroism and heroic leadership: Ambiguity, attribution, and apotheosis. West Yorkshire: Emerald.

Hoyt, C. L., Allison, S. T., Barnowski, A., & Sultan, A. (2020). Lay theories of heroism and leadership: The role of gender, communion, and agency. Social Psychology.

Kinsella, E. L., Ritchie, T. D., & Igou, E. R. (2017). Attributes and applications of heroes. In S. T. Allison, G. R. Goethals, & R. M. Kramer (Eds.), Handbook of heroism and heroic leadership (1st ed., pp. 19–35). New York: Routledge.

Kohen, A., Langdon, M., & Riches, B. R. (2017). The making of a hero: Cultivating empathy, altruism, and heroic imagination. Journal of Humanistic Psychology. https://doi.org/10.1177/0022167817708064

McCann, K. (2017, January 31). Turing's Law: Oscar Wilde among 50,000 convicted gay men granted posthumous pardons. Retrieved from https://www.telegraph.co.uk/news/2017/01/31/turings-law-thousands-convicted-gay-bisexual-men-receive-posthumous/

Offences Against The Person Act (1861).

Oscar Wilde. (n.d.). Retrieved from http://www.bbc.co.uk/worldservice/learningenglish/movingwords/quotefeature/oscarwilde.shtml

Parks, C. D. (2017). Accidental and purposeful impediments to heroism. In S. T. Allison, G. R. Goethals, & R. M. Kramer (Eds.), Handbook of heroism and heroic leadership (pp. 438–458). New York: Routledge.

Rigby, N. (2015, October 12). Nurse Edith Cavell and the British World War One propaganda campaign. BBC News. Retrieved from https://www.bbc.com/news/uk-england-norfolk-34401643

Who was Edith Cavell? (2018, February 5). Retrieved from https://www.iwm.org.uk/history/who-was-edith-cavell

Who was Edith Cavell? (n.d.). Retrieved from https://www.cavellnursestrust.org/edith-cavell

9

Sexism, Gender Roles and Heroism: Why Women are Underrepresented as Heroes

JESSICA M. STANFILL

Let's take a quiz.

For the following phrases, fill in the missing word:

1. If you want to offend someone you say: "You fight like a ___"
2. When asking who is in charge you say: "Who wears the ___ in this relationship?"
3. If you want someone to endure something you say: "Take it like a ___"
4. If someone does something bold you say: "That was a ___ move"

Shall I go on? If you answered "girl, pants, man, ballsy" you are a testament to the gendered society we live in—one where "girl" is synonymous with physical weakness, and male genitals are somehow interchangeable with virtues such as "courage."

It is no secret that in the hierarchical categorization of humans, men often find themselves at the top of the pecking order, with women at the bottom. Yes, society has advanced from the ways of the 40s and 50s, when overtly sexist sentiments flooded mainstream media, but the women of today still suffer from stereotypes, gender roles and marginalization; we, as a society, just disguise our sexism differently today than we did 70 years ago.

One way to observe the lack of growth in regard to public opinion on the capabilities of women is to take a look at the field of heroism. Between film, television, literature and the real world, women are counted out of the hero conversation more than they are counted in it. Is this because women are less likely to rise to the occasion and perform heroically than men? I don't believe so, no. Instead, I assert that women face a greater battle in being acknowledged as heroes than men for a very simple reason: we live in a sexist world.

The purpose of this chapter is to explore the history of how gender roles and stereotypes have served as boundaries to women in the realm of heroism, and how this phenomenon has, and continues to, impact female potential in a vast variety of fields. I will investigate the decades long trend of androcentric hero research, the distinction between heroine and hero, and how sexism and gender roles serve to dissuade women from behaving heroically. To close, I will examine the life and impact of two women -- JK Rowling and Kathrine Switzer -- who have pushed past the boundaries imposed on them by a patriarchal society and served as exemplars of heroism.

A HISTORY OF HEROISM SCIENCE

Heroism science is but a mere infant among psychological research fields. However, society's fascination with heroes is as old as humanity itself. Over the centuries, the study of the strengths and outward capacities of humanity has evolved, but nonetheless, a common thread connects the knights of the Arthurian era and the superheroes we celebrate today: for the majority of its history, heroism has largely been a boys' club.

The unspoken assumption that the term "hero" implies "male hero" was not always the norm. In the early days of creation myths of western cultures, deities were of both sexes (Becker & Eagly, 2004). During this period, many goddesses such as Isis, Ishtar, Demeter and Cybele were portrayed as the equals of gods and as possessing powerful forces of nature, fertility and creation (Monaghan, 1990). Most famous of these strong, independent figures perhaps is Athena, the goddess of war and wisdom, who was associated in ancient Greek culture with symbols such as armor, helmets and spears—a stark contrast to the commonly held view of the past several decades in which women have not been conceived as being capable of contributing to war and handling weapons (Efthimiou, 2017).

The association of women with strength, war, and by relation, with the term "hero" came to a screeching halt in the 1st century AD. The development of Christianity was the significant event that produced a shift in perceptions of heroism during this period. Under monotheism, there is no possibility of intertwining pantheons of male and female deities. So, when the Christian era entered center stage, the male gods took over and the goddesses, to the extent that they continued to exist, came to play subordinate roles until the cultural relevance of gods and goddesses phased out entirely (Efthimiou, 2017). And thus, with the introduction of the medieval ages, a new cultural association was established that firmly aligned heroism with masculinity. For decades on, the prototypical hero image emphasized divine characteristics that could only be embodied by men, who were in the image of God. This point is displayed most clearly through Max Weber's Great Man theory, in which he asserted that the worship of a hero is the transcendent admiration of a Great Man (Waters & Waters, 2015).

The most influential shift to heroism science that has solidified a patriarchal worldview within the field, however, cannot be claimed by savants of the ancient, medieval or modern periods. Rather, it is my belief that the sustained feminine suppression that is visible within the field today can be largely attributed to a single man who entered the scene in the post-modern era: Joseph Campbell.

In *The Hero with a Thousand Faces*, the classic study of how historic hero mythologies share similar plotlines across culture and time, Campbell (1949) documented the journey of a typically male hero. In Campbell's monomyth, in which an ordinary yet heroic figure leaves the comfort of home, immerses himself in the unfamiliar events of an outside world in which he has no real experience, fights and wins a decisive victory and, once he has done so, returns home with some essential boon or blessing, the idea that the hero must always be male is implicit. And unfortunately, Campbell did not venture to consider females in his original writings. His theory, therefore, only served to prolong the trend of "male" and "hero" being intertwined. And as fait or matter of circumstance would have it, Campbell's monomyth has experienced a particularly long shelf life, and just so happens to continue to permeate popular culture today.

The popularity of film and television series based around comic book superheroes, for example, can trace their origins straight to Campbell's monomyth. So, on this basis, the patriarchal trappings that surround the field of heroism science today can be at least partially attributed to Joseph Campbell. Campbell did not force into law any rule that mandated women should not be admired and recognized as heroic beings the same as men, but so long as he is considered the "father of heroism science" he will inevitably claim a certain degree of responsibility for the field's large disregard for female heroes.

HERO VS. HEROINE

Not only did Campbell neglect to factor in exemplars of females serving as heroes into his framework, but he actively spoke against the qualifications of women to go on the journey. Campbell based his mythic stages on history and the times he looked back to were some of the most sexist eras of mankind's past (Campbell, 2018). In this history women were either the subjects of men—mothers, daughters, lovers—or were the temptresses of men. Just consider the Disney princesses of the time—Cinderella and Snow White—as examples. These women were feminine icons who provided many a young girl with ideas about what it meant to be a girl, and they're entire existence was consumed mostly by the motivation of finding a husband. And these examples only represent a larger trend of female suppression that permeated the early 1900s, when women weren't allowed to fight or go on dangerous journeys and were expected to be subservient to their male counterparts (Guo, 2016).

This history is obvious in Campbell's framework, as he detailed only two roles for women: 1) the Goddess—which references the woman as the love interest or as some sort of maternal divinity or 2) the Temptress—which references the woman as a character that tempts the hero in a lusty fashion (Miyamoto, 2017). He even told Maureen Murdock, who would later go on to create a somewhat official "Heroine's Journey," that women didn't need to go on the journey (Murdock, 1990).

So, Campbell's vision, and by association the modern image of what a hero is, emulates the past. In an attempt to bring women into the hero conversation, Maureen Murdock created the heroine's journey (Murdock, 1990). This journey is not simply a female oriented version of Campbell's monomyth. Instead, it speaks to the specific challenges that women face in overcoming a male-dominated society.

In the 10-part heroine's journey, the day world is very specifically the male dominated world of the patriarchy based on chauvinism, where the man represents the power and the woman represents the sexuality (Stoffmuster, 2018). What happens in the heroine's journey is the woman has to use her masculine side and separate from the feminine in order to be successful in the male-dominated world. This journey therefore speaks to the fact that men who go on the hero's journey already have a certain degree of power, being that they are men. The heroine, on the other hand, battles not only the conflicts at hand within the story, but also deals with the prejudices associated with being a woman.

It seems clear that the only difference between a male hero and a female heroine, is that the heroine has to not only overcome whatever obstacle is in her way, but she also has to overcome the prejudices against her due to her gender. A true testament to change would therefore be the elimination of the use/need of the two distinct terms, heroine and hero. A world in which there need not be a distinction between heroine and hero would be a world where women didn't have to overcome a patriarchal society before embarking on their journey.

WHY WE NEED FEMALE HEROES

The 21st century has seen a number of blockbuster superhero action-adventure films. Batman, X-Men, Spiderman, Hulk, Ironman and a host of other "men" have flown, stomped, fallen and swung across screens in these Hollywood blockbusters. Although these plotlines are differentiated by different colored tights and capes, an age-old premise of superhero lore keynotes them all: someone out there needs to be protected, and only a big, strong man can do the job of protecting. The idea that women should neither need nor desire more protection than men remains a powerfully radical idea even in Western culture. We can imagine that men can fly, but not that women can and should be able to protect themselves...or dare I say, others who are in need of protecting (maybe even male others).

In response to these conclusions, one might question, "What's the big deal? They're just comic book stories." Well, hypothetical person with that question, the answer is this: science fiction, fantasy and superhero narratives provide important places for imagining different here-and-nows; for defamiliarizing social problems and exploring them in a context that offers fresh insights and radical visions of the future. That television and film in particular can imagine men flying, spinning webs, wielding nuclear power and manipulating time, but cannot imagine women who don't need a man's protection is a singularly disturbing and reactionary failure of the imagination.

To this, our hypothetical inquisitor might offer, "What about Wonder Woman and Bat Woman? Those are female heroes. What more do you want?" In response to this line of argument, I offer a simple conclusion: the fact that the female heroes we do have are gender reversed knock-offs of established male heroes, does not count as equality in terms of representation.

Perhaps at the beginning of what looks to be a period of dramatic cultural change in regard to the female image, cultural producers might begin to imagine and value forms of heroism that transcend the old, tired stereotype of the damsel in distress. Sociologist Jocelyn Hollander (2001) described the dominant trend of how gender is represented in mass-media as follows:

Women are taught to fear violence and to understand themselves as victims in need of protection in ways that men are not. To be a woman is to be constantly encouraged to understand one's physical self as endangered. To be a man is to understand one's self as powerful and not physically vulnerable. (p. 85)

In agreement with Hollander's stance, I challenge the media industry, particularly film and television, to take responsibility for the role it plays in perpetuating the solicitation of female characters as the ones needing protecting.

The shortage of female characters that serve as exemplars of Campbell's mono-myth in pop culture is concerning for a variety of reasons. Chiefly, the lack of female visibility in the realm of hero worship poses a particular issue for a key group in society: young girls. Arguably, no theory on heroism explains the primary cause for this concern better than the heroic leadership dynamic (HLD).

The HLD is a metaphor of heroism proposed by Allison and Goethals (2014) that centers around the idea that 1) people need heroes and 2) that one's life circumstances determine which specific heroes one needs. According to this theory, half of the human population (women) will at some point in their life need, or at least benefit from, a heroic female figure who has faced and conquered similar circumstances as she. Other theories of basic human needs back this point as well.

Erikson (1977) theorized that heroes are not only beneficial to children as models, but that they also provide children with a way to understand their culture and place in society. According to this line of understanding, the differences in how men and women (or boys and girls) behave is therefore a function of the typical roles that each is expected to play, as modeled by the dominant figures within each sex. Under the current societal norms, it is often the case that these dominant figures are those heralded as heroes. Consequently, young girls are presented with an over-abundance of male hero options and few to no female hero options.

Unfortunately, the women who receive the greatest amount of media attention today are the likes of The Kardashians and Real House Wives. These women tend to embody qualities that are defined by their woman-ness. They are sisters, mothers, girlfriends, wives, grandmothers, irritating secretaries; they seem to exist to be loved or unloved by the male heroes. And so young girls are presented with two primary options: idealize a social exemplar of female inferiority and submissiveness or find a male hero with whom they can only partially relate. Either way, we are doing a disservice to our young women by delivering to them a message that it is rare to be a heroic female—a message that is likely responsible for discouraging a great number of would be young heroes from pursuing such a status.

The impact of the lack of depth in the category of strong, capable female figures cannot be overstated. Previous research regarding young people's heroes suggest that most children have a person that they would name as their hero (Bromnick &

Swallow, 2010). This fact reemphasizes how important it is for the whole of society to be cognizant of what kind of heroes we put out there for children to idealize; essentially, every kid is going to have a hero, and they are going to pick whoever is available. And for young girls, that often means settling for heroes that aren't female to fulfill this void, or worse—idolizing inadequate female social figures.

So, while our society can claim triumphant advances on many fronts, the minimum degree of cultural evolution in terms of the image of what a woman can do, has resulted in 2018 still carrying many of the same trappings of a patriarchal society as 1918. As a final thought on this line of commentary, ask yourself this: how can we expect more female heroes to rise to the occasion if they don't have strong, successful examples to look up to? A hint: we can't.

THE HEROISM OF J.K. ROWLING

J.K. Rowling should be heralded in history as one of the most impactful figures of her generation (notice I didn't say "female figures"). While she should be acknowledged for brilliance and virtuousness independently of her gender, for the purpose of exemplifying the point of this chapter I will devote the following section to speaking to how she, as a woman, faced more obstacles than a man in a similar position would have in order to make it to where she is today.

For those of you who don't know, Rowling is the creator of the infamous Harry Potter series and is the United Kingdom's best-selling living author. Her seven-book series has sold more than 450 million copies and has the record for the best-selling book series of all time (Rowling, 2016). Rowling is an international icon, but her personal journey to heroic status was not glossy. Here is her story:

J.K. Rowling (actual name, Joanne) always knew she wanted to be a book author and has related to fans that she knew that was her purpose and calling in life as early as 6 years old. Those who had a say in her evolution as a writer, however, did not taught her as being destined for such a career. Her secondary school teacher, Steve Eddy, remembers Rowling as "not exceptional" but "one of a group of girls who were bright and good at English" (Parker, 2012). That's a rather lackluster review of one of the world's most acclaimed authors.

Despite a gaping lack of mentorship or support, Rowling kept at her craft. Life, however, would prove to challenge a swift course of development as a writer. Throughout her teenage years, Joanne's mother battled multiple sclerosis—a fact that has lead Rowling to recall her childhood as not particularly happy. In 1982, she took the entrance exams for Oxford but was not accepted and studied French at Exeter instead. She graduated in 1986 and worked a desk job for Amnesty International and had her first inspiration for Harry Potter in 1991 while traveling for work. This fanciful world was swiftly cast to the side, however, by the death of her mother that same year. Rowling was 25 when her mother died—a day that she remembers as the most traumatizing moment in her life.

After her mother died, Rowling moved to Portugal for a fresh start. She started dating a man name Jorge Arantes, became pregnant and moved into a small two-bedroom apartment with Arantes's mother. She miscarried. And in 1993, she and Arantes got pregnant again and she gave birth to her firstborn, Jessica, that summer. After Jessica was born, her marriage turned physically and emotionally abusive, and so, with a 13-month-old infant, Rowling returned to the UK. As a newly minted single mother with no job and a cramped apartment, Joanne fell into a deep depression and even considered suicide.

Two things kept her going: Jessica and the sparsely written manuscript of Harry Potter and the Philosopher's Stone that she had kept stowed away in a suitcase all those years. In the following months, Joanne lived on state benefits and spent much of her time writing in cafes with Jessica sleeping in a baby carrier next to her. The first installment of Harry Potter was published in 1997 by Bloomsburry, who requested she take the pen name "J.K." since women's names were found to be less appealing to audiences.

In summary, J.K. Rowling was tossed aside as an unspectacular member of a group of girls in grade school. She lost the most influential female figure in her life at the harsh young age of 25. She suffered a miscarriage and was then subsequently impregnated and abused by a man who she thought she could trust. She lived on disability because as a single mother, she was not an attractive potential employee. And finally, when she achieved the greatest project of her life, she couldn't publish it under her given name for fear that potential readers wouldn't buy a book written by a woman.

That's a particularly excessive amount of gender-oriented suffering for one person to endure before the age of 35. But in typical J.K. fashion, she refused to be anyone's damsel. She rescued herself.

Today, Joanne is the only person to have fallen off Forbes' list of billionaires because of excessive charitable giving. She stands for female empowerment, is an advocate for self-love and mental health, and has inspired an entire generation to love reading. Although Harry Potter came to a conclusion 11 years ago, she actively contributes to the benefit of society by serving as a social, moral and political inspiration to her fans. In every conceivable variation of the word, J.K. Rowling is a hero. She is also a female. And society would do well to make it less difficult for more women like her to influence the world and have a platform.

KATHRINE SWITZER

In any conversation on the topic of women in sports and gender equality, one would be hard pressed to go without mention of Kathrine Switzer. In 1967, Kathrine became the first woman to run the Boston Marathon (Switzer, 2017). The story of this feat, while it has a happy ending, only speaks to the misogynistic outlooks that women are often forced to overcome if they wish to be treated as capable beings in a male-dominated environment.

During her undergraduate career at the University of Syracuse, Kathrine trained unofficially with the men's cross-country team. Kathrine wasn't trying to prove anything by training with the men, but she had always been an athlete throughout her life, and she didn't intend on terminating that part of who she was because of lack of opportunity; there was no running team for women at Syracuse in the 60s, or anywhere else for that matter.

While at Syracuse, Kathrine decided she wanted to run the Boston Marathon. At the time that she made this decision, she didn't consider the detail that she was a girl—she was just a runner with a competitive spirit, and Boston was an infamous test for runners looking to explore their limits. When Arnie, the coach of the men's team, heard of this idea he quipped, "No woman can run the Boston Marathon" (p. 190). Eventually, Kathrine wore Arnie down to agree that if she could run the distance in practice, he would take her to Boston. Not only did Kathrine prove she could handle the 26-mile distance in practice, she put in an extra five-mile loop to total 31, "just to feel extra confident about Boston" (p. 192).

From her performance, Kathrine earned Arnie's respect and support for her running aspirations, but other men in her life, namely her boyfriend, were less than enthusiastic. Kathrine's boyfriend at the time was a 235-pound All-American football player who, upon hearing Kathrine's news announced that he would run Boston, too, and didn't need to train because "if a girl can run a marathon, I can run a marathon" (p. 193).

When Kathrine gathered the paperwork to register as a runner, there was no rule about gender listed in the bylaws for the marathon, so she sent in her registration form and signed it as she always signed her name: K.V. Switzer. On the day of the race, everything proceeded relatively uneventfully. At the starting lines, accompanied by Arnie, her chauvinistic boyfriend and another male runner from Syracuse, Kathrine was the only lipstick-wearing face in a sea of, well, non-lipstick wearing faces. But no one made much of a fuss about her. In fact, the other male runners were pleased to have a woman in their presence.

After the first few miles, however, the routine proceedings of the run quickly morphed into one of the most resilient displays of female strength in the history of sport. The following is an excerpt from Kathrine's autobiography:

Moments later, I heard the scraping noise of leather shoes coming up fast behind me. A big man with bared teeth was set to pounce and before I could react he grabbed my shoulder and flung me back screaming, "Get the hell out of my race and give me those numbers." Then he swiped down my front, trying to rip off my bib. Journalists rode alongside, thinking it was a prank and waiting for the moment when I'd give up. This made me even more resolved. In fact, it infuriated me. No matter what, I had to finish the race. If I didn't, people would say women couldn't do it. My mind was whirling, but that couldn't distract me from feeling the very big blisters in my arches that soon would burst. I could handle that; pain was nothing. It was part of what made you a hero, doing this, overcoming it, relegating pain to the incidental for a higher purpose. (p. 199)

Roughly four hours after the incident with the race official, Kathrine crossed the finish line. She didn't stop once. And, for those interested, the same couldn't be said of her super-star athlete boyfriend. By the end of the race, Kathrine was no longer just a kid who enjoyed running; she was a pillar of strength, an exemplar of what women could accomplish in the face of a mountain of voices which worked to minimize the extent of her capabilities.

In the years since her first marathon, Kathrine has tirelessly served the mission of empowering women. She campaigned to make women official competitors at the Boston Marathon and was eventually successful in 1972. She created the Avon International Running Circuit, a global series of woman's races that has grown to 400 races in 27 countries for over a million women. She was a major influencer in getting the women's marathon into the Olympic Games for the first time in 1984 in Los Angeles. She was inducted in the USA National Women's Hall of Fame for creating positive social change. And today, she continues to empower women through her foundation, 261 Fearless Inc., which serves to give women around the world the gifts of self-esteem, empowerment and fearlessness, through running.

Today, 58% of race participants in the U.S. are women. Just contemplate that statistic. In 1967, women represented 0% of participants. And the source of the exponential growth that the sport has seen in the past 50 years can all be traced back to a young college student who refused to stop moving forward when it seemed like the world was against her progress. I'd say that makes her a hero, and not only a hero for women, but for anyone who has ever been told they can't do something because of what is perceived of them from the outside.

CONCLUSION

The purpose of this chapter has been to illustrate that while men and women are equally capable of rising to the occasion and performing heroically when a situation calls for it, women face a remarkably greater challenge in being recognized by society as heroes—which is a central component in the actualization of heroism. The age-old trend of neglecting female inclusion into the realm of heroism has resulted in a modern society in which girls have more options of supermodels and reality television stars as female icons, than virtuous heroes. This lack of representation is a problem. And it is constantly perpetuated by the engrained sexism and restricting gender roles that influence, to a certain degree, every facet of life.

If we wish to advance beyond the reality of our present circumstances, in which a female being recognized with heroic status is a rarer phenomenon than getting struck by lightning, there are a few action steps we can take. First of all, we can get rid of the word "heroine." It is old and haggard and when searched for on the internet, brings up images of a highly addictive drug, rather than strong women. Let us recognize our women for being heroes because they merit that title independently of their sex. Secondly, let us infuse child media with images of strong women who don't need protecting and rescuing by a more powerful man. Sleeping Beauty is a classic tale, but it also teaches our young people that a good hero tale involves a limp girl lying in a bed, waiting for a boy to rescue her with a kiss...this is a classic that could use a facelift. Finally, let us celebrate the women who are out in the world performing as heroes in spite of the obstacles they have faced.

It is my strongly held belief that the world has a wealth of female heroes in the waiting—many of whom just need to be shown that it is possible to be both a woman and a hero. The responsibility, then, of those involved in heroism science, is to help these women realize what they can achieve, by highlighting the journeys of their fellow woman.

REFERENCES

Allison, S. T. (2015). The initiation of heroism science. Heroism Science, 1, 1-8.
Allison, S. T., Beggan, J. K., & Efthimiou, O. (2019). The art and science of heroism and heroic leadership. Lausanne, Switzerland: Frontiers.
Allison, S. T., & Goethals, G. R. (2014). "Now he belongs to the ages": The heroic leadership dynamic and deep narratives of greatness. In Goethals, G. R., et al. (Eds.), Conceptions of leadership: Enduring ideas and emerging insights. New York: Palgrave Macmillan.
Becker, S. W., & Eagly, A. H. (2004). The heroism of women and men. American Psychologist, 59(3), 163-178. http://dx.doi.org/10.1037/0003-066X.59.3.163
Bromnick, R. D., & Swallow, B. L. (2010). I like being who I am: A study of young people's ideals. Educational Studies, 25(2), 117-128. https://doi.org/10.1080/03055699997855
Campbell, J. (2008). The hero with a thousand faces (3rd ed.). Novato, CA: New World Library.

Campbell, O. (2018, July 12). The historical struggle to rid socialism of sexism. Smithsonian Magazine. Retrieved from https://www.smithsonianmag.com/history/historical-struggle rid-socialism-sexism 180969610/

Davis, J. L., Burnette, J. L., Allison, S. T., & Stone, H. (2011). Against the odds: Academic underdogs benefit from incremental theories. Social Psychology of Education, 14, 331-346.

Efthimiou, O. (2017). Heroic ecologies: embodied heroic leadership and sustainable futures. Sustainability Accounting, Management and Policy Journal, 8(4), 489-511. https://doi.org/10.1108/SAMPJ-08-2015-0074

Efthimiou, O., Allison, S. T., & Franco, Z. E. (Eds.) (2018). Heroism and wellbeing in the 21st Century: Applied and emerging perspectives. New York: Routledge.

Guo, J. (2016, January 25). Researchers have found a major problem with 'The Little Mermaid' and other Disney movies. The Washington Post. Retrieved from https://www. washingtonpost.com/news/wonk/wp/2016/01/25/researchers-have discovered-a-major-problem-with-the-little-mermaid-and-other-disney movies/?utm_term=.85799727723f

Hollander, J. A. (2001). Vulnerability and dangerousness: The construction of gender through conversation about violence. Gender & society, 15(1), 83-109. Retrieved from https://doi.org/10.1177/089124301015001005

Miyamoto, K. (2017, June 18). Why screenwriters should embrace the heroine's journey. Retrieved from https://screencraft.org/2017/06/18/how-screenwriters-can-embrace-the heroines-journey/

Monaghan, P. (1990). The book of goddesses and heroines. Woodbury, MN: Llewellyn Publications.

Munley, P. H. (1977). Erikson's theory of psychosocial development and career development. Journal of Vocational Behavior, 10(3), 261-269. Retrieved from   https://doi.org/10.1016/0001-8791(77)90062-8

Murdock, M. (1990). The heroine's journey: Woman's quest for wholeness. Boston, MA: Shambhala Publications.

Parker, I. (2012, October 1). Mugglemarch: J.K. Rowling writes a realist novel for adults. The New Yorker. Retrieved from https://www.newyorker.com/magazine/2012/10/01/mugglemarch

Rowling, J.M. (2016). J.K. Rowling. Retrieved from https://www.jkrowling.com/about/

Stoffmuster, V. (2018, September 23). Transformational storytelling: a conversation with Tom Schlesinger. Retrieved from https://stoffmuster.berlin/transformational-storytelling-a conversation-with-tom-schlesinger/

Switzer, K. (2017). Marathon woman. Lebanon, IN: Da Capo Press.

Waters, T., & Waters, D. (2015). Weber's rationalism and modern society: New translations on politics, bureaucracy, and social stratification. New York, NY: Palgrave MacMillan.

10

Coming from Behind Once Again: An Analysis of the Underdog Phenomenon

EMILY E. BRAUNEWELL

The path of the hero is rarely free of trials and tribulations. Iconic comparative mythologist Joseph Cambell (1949) was sure to emphasize the obstacles fictional heroes often face on what he called the hero's journey. Even in real life stories of heroism, we see the struggles a person frequently faces on the road to achieving hero status. However, despite the ubiquitous hardships involved in heroism, none weigh down the odds of the individual -- or individuals -- in question like those faced by a particular type of hero: the underdog.

Underdogs by definition are coming from circumstances that put their chances of achievement nearly at zero. More specifically, Vandello and colleagues (2017) defines an underdog as "disadvantaged parties facing advantaged opponents and unlikely to succeed" (Vandello, Goldschmeid, & Michniewicz, 2017). These disadvantaged circumstances can come in a wide variety of forms; some heroes come from low socioeconomic status, some are faced with significant physical or mental inferiorities, others may be forced to fight their way through socially oppressive scenarios. Underdog heroes are more common than we realize; characters in movies may be seen dragging themselves from hopeless upbringings, sports teams may face off against an undefeated competitor, or an underappreciated politician may be fighting for office.

Whatever the reason for their struggle, we love to root for the underdog, and the psychology behind choosing a hero that seems unlikely to succeed as opposed to a hero that will certainly achieve their goal has been difficult for researchers to untangle (Allison et al., 2019; Allison, Goethals, & Spyrou, 2019). There are also many conflicting themes and fragile framework of underdog appeal that adds to the complication of the phenomenon. Some individuals fear openly expressing their support of underdogs, for fear of being associated with a losing party (Vandello, Goldschmeid, & Michniewicz, 2017), or will only choose the underdog if it has minimal impact on their own well-being (Kim et al., 2008). However, despite these limitations, there are still an abundant number of underdogs—both fictional and in reality—that receive overwhelming support, and further understanding of why we support the underdog will aid psychologists in the in pursuit of a scientific understanding of heroism.
The Psychology of the Underdog Effect

Several theories have been proposed to better understand why underdogs are so popular among individuals. Evidence has shown that a prominent reason may be the way that we identify with underdog heroes. We see underdogs as versions of ourselves, as those that have to beat difficult odds to succeed. It is more difficult for us to picture ourselves as the superior challenger, who has no trials to overcome to achieve their goals. Rather, we align ourselves with the side that will have to fight harder to win. In identifying with the underdog, we allow ourselves to hope that we can one day also reach that same level of success despite obstacles that may obscure our path (Vandello et al., 2017).

A similar concept was examined by Kim et al., (2008). Their research on the reasons behind the support of underdogs elaborated specifically on the concept of the underdog's struggle. According to this theory, we are drawn to the underdog because we can empathize with the act of struggling, relating it to a time in our lives when we too had to fight to achieve what we wanted (Kim et al., 2008). This focus on struggle also holds implications for why we are attracted to underdog success stories, particularly those in leadership roles, because they are physical examples of the overcoming of said struggle. Thus, the perseverance that underdogs exhibit attracts a stronger level respect and likability for those that have overcome those trials (Allison, 2019; Allison & Burnette, 2009).

ENHANCING THE EMOTIONAL BALANCE

Our tendency to side with the underdog hero appears to press further than self-identification. It is possible that rooting for the underdog is a way to maintain the most efficient emotional response, despite the underdog's success or lack thereof. Frazier and Snyder (1991) observed evidence towards this factor in their study, particularly in sports. This paper suggests that there is logic behind backing the underdog. When cheering for a favorite or a "top dog", referring to the advantaged competitor (Allison & Burnette, 2009; Allison & Green, 2020), The prospect of them winning is expected. Consequently, when the favorite or top dog wins, the emotional thrill is mild. However, when they lose, the emotional impact is much more detrimental, as it harms the confidence that was invested into a party that was assured victory. On the other hand, if an individual invests in an underdog, the emotional risk is significantly less. As the expectation is for the weaker party to fall short, the emotional payoff is significantly greater, being that the underdog defeated the odds set against them for achieve success (Frazier & Snyder, 1991).

Research has also been conducted to more thoroughly evaluate that excitement that follows the emergence of an underdog. In other words, the emotional payoff side of the scale that comes forward as we choose who to follow. When an unknown athlete comes from seemingly out of nowhere and challenges the undefeated champion, or when a politician who fought from scarce resources shows the potential to rise against the dominant candidate, it provides an atmosphere that shakes up our expectations and excites us into rooting for the underdog. This concept was examined by Vandello et al. (2007). The "thrill of the unexpected" is enough to draw people towards underdogs, because it breaks the status quo (p. 342). We put our faith then into a competitor that will provide that thrill for us.

The way underdogs evoke our emotional responses is therefore another piece in the puzzle of why we support these heroes.

EVENING THE PLAYING FIELD

While the underdog has the ability to induce hope and excitement in us, there are possible explanations for the phenomenon that are less about personal enhancement and more about targeting the top dogs. Several studies have examined the idea that our attraction to the underdog may lie less in our desire to see them prevail, and more in the desire to see the advantaged party fail. An underdog becomes a representation of seeing the odds evened out, where the hopeless odds get to overtake those with abundant success. Some may refer to this as ensuring that scales of justice are equal (Vandello et al., 2007) or keeping the odds of a situation fair (Allison & Burnette, 2009). One study viewed this from the perspective of competition in business, and the way the underdog phenomenon may encourage individuals to support small businesses over mammoth corporations (McGinnis & Gentry, 2008). Results showed that people tend to seek out disadvantaged companies due to dislike for large corporations or inequity in capital, or, on the other hand due to an affection for the "little guy" (p. 198). This affection implies that individuals may actively try to avoid a company that they know is already rife with resources.

A more cynical explanation has also been the subject of speculation with psychologists. Some researchers have contemplated the role of what is known as schadenfreude, which can roughly be described as the pleasure that one feels at another's misfortune (Heider, 1958). Kim et al. (2008) compared schadenfreude to the underdog phenomenon. Experiencing the desire to see a top dog fail could possibly lead one to root for the competitor that has a slimmer chance of succeeding (p. 2553). Here there is less support for the underdog than hope that the more advantageous competitor will not succeed. Still, it provides possible insight into the phenomenon of the underdog, and what leads us to support them.

THE POSSIBILITY OF THE BANDWAGON

Researchers are toying with the idea that the support of underdogs, what they are specifically calling the underdog effect, could coincide with that of another phenomenon, called the bandwagon effect. While the underdog effect refers to the support of an individual or group that has little to no chance of success (Vandello, Goldschmeid, & Michniewicz, 2017), the bandwagon effect refers to a person's tendency to adopt a trend or behavior because they see others doing it (Cherry, 2017). Some psychologists theorize that individuals may choose to support an underdog through the bandwagon effect. That is, they see that others are beginning to support an underdog hero, and therefore choose to support them as well. A study on this possibility was assessed in regard to voting, and whether a person could be swayed to vote for an underdog politician because others are beginning to (Fleitas, 1971). The results did show evidence that voters could be persuaded to switch their vote to an underdog candidate if one candidate is painted as more domineering than the other (p. 438). However, this phenomenon needs more research before it can be confirmed as a viable way to predict underdog support.

TALES OF THE UNDERDOG: CASE STUDIES

While the reasons we support them are still obscure, the story of the underdog hero frequently reoccurs, both in fiction and in reality. It is difficult to go long without hearing of someone who overcame the odds or surpassed the powerhouse and achieved what seemed impossible. The following sections will track stories of those who overcame significant obstacles to reach their goals and can now claim the title of underdog hero.

Athletics are one of the most common places for an underdog to emerge. In this case, the struggle does not lie only on the field, but in the social contexts both inside and outside the team at stake. Thus, the story of the T.C Williams Titans, a high school football team fighting against not just rival teams, but the racial injustices of the south, has become an iconic underdog film, titled Remember the Titans. Although the movie was indeed based on a true story, this analysis will focus on the popular film version and its relation to the underdog phenomenon.

The Titan's Story

In Alexandria, Virginia, in 1971, racial tension was at a peak. The city's residents, both black and white, could feel this tension throughout their whole lives, even at the level of high school athletics. So, when a law-change initiated integration of the black and white school districts, the result was far from peaceful.

Bill Yoast, a successful white football coach and nominee for the Virginia High School Hall of Fame, quickly realizes the challenges at hand when the head coaching job at the newly integrated T.C. Williams High School will be given to Herman Boone, a successful black football coach from North Carolina, and the city—specifically the players—are left up in arms. However, he is quick to learn that his challenges will be nothing compared to those of Boone, and those of his new team.

Upon arrival to their first week at training camp, Boone does not back down from the clear racial divide that is already in place, asserting his style as an unwavering "dictator" and forcing the reluctant black and white players to intermingle. Thus, Yoast and Boone face their first racial barriers within their own team, before they even reach the school year. It takes several weeks of camp before they are able to push past the discrimination and create chemistry among their players. This new-found comradery helps to smooth over the issues within the team, but the true challenges become apparent once they face the outside world.

The Titans must go from conquering the obstacles inside themselves, to conquering the obstacles provided by the people around them. Students and members of the community fight to try and get Boone fired, appalled that a white man lost his job to a black one. This discrimination leads to a must-win situation for the Titans; if they lose a single game, then Boone will be fired as head coach. Thus, the Titans begin their season at a severe disadvantage. With little support from their community thanks to racism and oppression, and the athletic threat of all-white teams who have never faced these kinds of set-backs, this team has become the underdogs.

They begin strongly, but an injury to the starting quarterback and racial pressure from the outside world begins to take its toll on the Titans. After local white men throw a brick through Boone's window, threatening both him and his family, the tension reaches an all-time high. Games are cut close, teammates begin to brawl, and it seems as though this team will fall apart at the seams. However, the team gets together and decides that they want more from themselves than players who will crumble at the first sign of trouble; they want a family who will defeat the odds that have been set against them. So, Coach Boone, Coach Yoast, and the Titans continue to fight their way through the season, winning game after game, and overcoming the tremendous amounts of discrimination in their path.

Just when the Titans believe that they had overcome their greatest trials and were on their way to a perfect season, a tragedy strikes that leaves the Titans once again questioning their chances. Gerry "Superman" Bertier, the team's captain, is severely injured in a car accident just before the championship game, paralyzing him from the waist down. The team, devastated by the loss of their star teammate and the trauma to their friend, begin to fear that this is one hurdle that they just cannot overcome. They face a powerhouse team and a brutal loss, along with the continued social pressures closing in from the outside. Still, they choose to face this last challenge with grace, as they have since the beginning.

The Titans initially struggle, trailing George C. Marshall High until the second half. It isn't until a last-minute fumble by Marshall and a creative play from Boone, with the use of their still injured quarterback, that the Titans are able to push past that final obstacle and secure the title of State Champions—with a perfect season to go with it.

This team faced countless trials throughout their season—trials that most people did not believe they could overcome—and managed to beat the odds to achieve more than just a trophy; they showed those around them that they were stronger than the discrimination and doubt, and what it meant to be a true underdog hero (Bruckheimer, Oman, & Yakin, 2000).

Titans as Underdogs

The most notable factor that makes the story of the Remember the Titans classic underdog tale is that of disadvantaged odds. This team had more to overcome than simply a competitor on the field; the main disadvantage came from the social pressures that went on around them. The community surrounding the team did not initially support the integration of black and white students, and the racial tensions affected the players inside and out. Not only did they have to try and settle conflict among themselves, but they had to try and fight against those around them that claimed they should not be allowed to compete with one another. Additionally, the issue of race forced the team into a must-win scenario, which added significant pressure to both the coaches and the players in every game they approached. Meanwhile, the issue of race was not experienced by the other teams that the Titans would be facing, placing their competitors at a significant advantage.

Aside from race, the Titans then had to face both the physical loss and emotional effect of losing a teammate to a severe injury. Without the presence of their captain and leader, a player who helped to bring the team as far as they had—both on the field and within their team culture—the rest of the players were thrown an unexpected variable at the last minute. While the team could have let this bring them down, they continued to fight for the title.

The theme of the community is what is interesting regarding Remember the Titans. In the beginning of the film, most of the city rejects the integrated team, claiming that Yoast should have remained coach and that black and white players were never meant to be together. However, over the course of the film, you can see that the immediate community around T.C. Williams High School does begin to recognize that the team is doing wonderful things. Thus, people begin to root for the underdog. The fans are excited by the unexpected outcome of a successful, integrated team, and are inspired to see a team overcome such brutal odds to take on the championship title.

Still, what is striking is that many of the fans are still reluctant to openly support the Titans, due to the intense racial tensions that are occurring. As mentioned earlier, a prominent phenomenon in the support of underdogs is the tendency to express support, for fear of being associated with a party that will likely prove unsuccessful (Vandello, Goldschmeid, & Michniewicz, 2017). Gerry Bertier's girlfriend and mother, for example, are hesitant to openly accept the team for what it is. While the team is inducing these feelings of hope and defeating these seemingly impossible odds, those around them still fear the retaliation of a community struck down by discrimination. These, and many other reasons, allow Remember the Titans to be labeled as one of the most inspirational underdog stories that has been told. For both athletes and non-athletes alike, due to the way the team fiercely overcomes the racial and physical barriers that stand in their way.

From Homeless to Hero: Christopher Gardner's Story

The athletic field is not the only place where an underdog hero can arise. Sometimes it happens in the professional field, when a person who had no resources and no hope rises above the odds to find success. This is the case for real-life underdog Chris Gardner, whose life was portrayed in a cinematic adaptation titled The Pursuit of Happyness in 2006. Gardner's life was a true "rags to riches" story, and the way that he achieved success and continues to inspire people with his determination makes him a perfect candidate for the title of underdog.

Christopher Gardner was born in Milwaukee in 1954. His upbringing was anything but easy; he and his sisters were raised by their mother and his stepfather. Gardner frequently watched his mother suffer abuse from his stepfather, taking much abuse himself, for the majority of his childhood and adolescence. Despite this abuse though, his mother never stopped telling Gardner that he could do whatever he set his mind to.
Gardner joined the United States Navy upon graduation from high school, and then shortly after his discharge from service he took a job as a lab assistant in San Francisco. This job served him well, and it seemed that he would be able to move on from his brutal childhood, until he became involved with a woman named Jackie Medina. The pair had a son together named Christopher Jr., and Gardner was forced to quit his job to try and find a career that could support his new child.

A critical moment in Gardner's life was when he approached a man who was parking his Ferrari in a parking garage. Gardner asked the man—named Bob Bridges—what he did for a living. Bridges decided to take Gardner to lunch, and this Gardner was introduced to the basics of the stock market. Gardner pursued this opportunity, landing a spot in a training program with E.F. Hutton that he believed would help him finally get his feet off the ground financially.

Despite his entrance in the program, Gardner's troubles far from disappeared. When the manager of the program was fired, he was left once again searching for options. He managed to befriend a broker that landed him an interview with Dean Witter Reynolds, but he continued to struggle. As a result, Jackie took Christopher Jr. and left after an aggressive argument between the couple that had Gardner arrested and taken to jail for 10 days.

Upon release from jail, Gardner was far from prepared from his interview. Dressed in stained shoes and a Members Only jacket, he was honest about his situation to the interviewer. As a man who had been beaten down his entire life, often having to fight to survive, Gardner still did not back down from the challenge. His charisma and natural intelligence wooed the interviewer, who saw the underdog's potential, and Gardner managed to find himself admitted to the Dean Witter Reynolds training program. Here, he was able to make a small salary and, after several months, saw Jackie and his son returned. Jackie believed that Christopher Jr. would be better off with his father.

However, the apartment where Gardner was living did not allow children. Gardner and his son were then forced to leave and find a new place to live. Homeless and alone with his son, Gardner had reached an all-time low. He was always on the hunt for a place to stay with his child; bathroom floors, churches, soup kitchens, to name a few. Yet, he continued to work and work at his training program, becoming one of the most successful trainees involved. When he was finally given his entrance exam, he scored an 88%, and was hired as an employee by Dean Witter, where his growth as a stock broker began.

After stints with companies in New York, Gardner decided to move to Chicago. There, he was able to open his own company, Gardner Rich & Company. By 1988, Gardner had surpassed any goals he could have imagined for himself; he was a self-made millionaire, now with two children, Jr. and Jacintha. Today, Gardner is worth $60 million. He has a new company by the name of Gardner International Holdings, and is now a motivational speaker to inspire those around them to never stop fighting for their dreams (Ewing, 2017).

Chris Gardner's continues to be treasured as a well-known underdog hero. The way that his journey from abuse to homelessness to millionaire-status touches individuals worldwide allows psychologists to further understand the underdog phenomenon. Gardner had to overcome countless obstacles to get to where he is today. He started life with few role models other than his mother and suffered physical and emotional trauma via his stepfather for most of his youth. His financial disadvantages throughout the rest of his life then led to difficulties in creating a stable life for himself and for his son. As well as this, the majority of those interviewing for the positions in stock broker firms likely had the previous education to prepare them, and at least the money to provide adequate clothing for an interview.

Gardner was acting on information gathered at lunch and had to fight to prove his qualifications despite his appearance. He also had the weight of his son's health on his shoulders through it all. Yet Gardner managed to achieve his success despite all of this going against him. Gardner also had several people take a chance on him, despite his underdog status. People that had chosen to root for the underdog. Bob Bridges, Martyn and the interviewer of Dean Witter Reynolds, for example. He also continues to inspire and instill hope among those that can identify with his struggle, through his motivation. Individuals love Gardner's story because they can see a man who, despite countless disadvantages, went against any doubt or top dog in his path and achieved more than he could ever have hoped to.

CONCLUSION

The underdog remains a complex phenomenon in hero psychology. Why we choose to root for a party with seemingly no chances of success proves difficult to understand. However, the lack of probability for underdog success does not lessen the excitement that individuals feel when someone that never should have succeeded defeats impossible odds. Whether it is our identification with their struggle, the emotional payoff of seeing the "little guy" win, or the desire to see the top dog fall, the underdog hero remains a ubiquitous story across cultures.

Future research and understanding of this phenomenon can help psychologists to study the reasons we may be drawn to or may shy away from support of these heroes. This understanding could create implications for what may prompt us to support or ignore any kind of hero and allow researchers to untangle the mystery of what makes an individual or group a hero to begin with. Moreover, as underdog heroes are often the most creative heroes (Bennett, Efthimiou, & Allison, 2020), it is imperative that societies foster avenues through which underdogs can achieve their goals and disseminate their contributions.

REFERENCES

Allison, S. T. (2019). Heroic consciousness. Heroism Science, 4, 1-43.

Allison, S. T., & Burnette, J. (2009). Fairness and preference for underdogs and top dogs. In R. Kramer, A. Tenbrunsel, & M. Bazerman, (Eds), Social Decision Making: Social Dilemmas, Social Values, and Ethical Judgments. New York: Psychology Press.

Allison, S. T., Eylon, D., Beggan, J.K., & Bachelder, J. (2009). The demise of leadership: Positivity and negativity in evaluations of dead leaders. The Leadership Quarterly, 20, 115-129.

Allison, S. T., Goethals, G. R., & Spyrou, S. P. (2019). Donald Trump as the archetypal puer aeternus: The psychology of mature and immature leadership. In K. Bezio & G. R. Goethals (Eds.), Leadership and populism. Northampton, MA: Edward Elgar.

Allison, S. T., Goethals, G. R., Marrinan, A. R., Parker, O. M., Spyrou, S. P., Stein, M. (2019). The metamorphosis of the hero: Principles, processes, and purpose. Frontiers in Psychology.

Allison, S. T., & Green, J. D. (2021). Nostalgia and heroism: Theoretical convergence of memory, motivation, and function. Frontiers in Psychology.

Bennett, D., Efthimiou, O., & Allison, S. T. (2020). The role of heroic creativity and leadership in creative work. In A. de Dios & L. Kong (Eds.), Handbook on the geographies of creativity. Cheltenham, UK: Edward Elgar.

Bruckheimer, J. (Producer), Oman, C. (Producer), & Yakin, B. (Director). (2000). Remember the Titans [Motion Picture]. United States: Walt Disney Pictures.

Campbell, J., Cousineau, P., & Brown, S. L. (1990). The hero's journey: The world of Joseph Campbell: Joseph Campbell on his life and work. San Francisco: Harper & Row.

Cherry, K. (2018, September). Bandwagon effect as a cognitive bias. Retrieved from https://www.verywellmind.com

Ewing, D. (2017, October 29th). Chris Gardner: The True Story of the Pursuit of Happyness. Retrieved from http://www.ninjajournalist.com.

Fleitas, D. W. (1971). Bandwagon and underdog effects in minimal information elections. American Political Science Association. 65(2). 434-438.

Frazier, J. A., & Snyder, E. E, (1991). The underdog concept in sport. Sociology of Sport Journal. 8. 380-388.

Heider, F. (1958). The psychology of interpersonal relations. New York: John Wiley & Sons

Kim, J., Allison, S. T., Eylon, D., Goethals, G., Markus, M., McGuire, H., & Hindle, S. (2008). Rooting for (and then Abandoning) the Underdog. Journal of Applied Social Psychology, 38, 2550-2573.

Vandello, J. A., Goldschmied, N., & Michniewicz, K. (2017). Underdogs as heroes. In S. T. Allison, G. R. Goethals, & R. M. Kramer (Eds.), Handbook of heroism and heroic leadership (pp. 339-355). New York, NY: Routledge.

Vandello, J. A., Goldschmied, N., & Richards, D. A. R. (2007). The Appeal of the underdog. Personality and Psychology Bulletin. 33(12). 1603-1616.

Section 4: Applications of Heroism

11

Heroism and Hofstede's Dimensions: A Cross-Cultural Analysis

ALEXA M. BERTRAND

Freedom is a right that many are denied, even now as we enter the decade of the 2020s. Freedom is an essential human right that many have struggled, fought, and died to preserve. Mahatma Gandhi and George Washington are no exception to this effort. In the years when the United States and India were under British rule, these men stood up for the rights of their countries and defended them tooth and nail. Many people owe their qualities of life to these men and few may acknowledge it. This research aims to shed light on what these men fought for, and how they became some of the world's most recognized and admired heroes.

HOFSTEDE'S DIMENSIONS

In the early 1970s, Geert Hofstede rounded up several data he had been compounding over the last five years in one of the most insightful and influential cross-cultural studies to date. Hofstede drew data from 116,000 IBM employees around the world in 72 countries to analyze their workplace behavior and how they would like to interact with one another as well as their superiors. Primarily, Hofstede wanted to grasp "the way people in different countries perceive and interpret their world" (Hofstede, 1983). Hofstede was one of the first to conduct such a study aiming to shed light on differences between cultures and bring attention to value systems for theorists and researchers to take into account when collecting data.

Prior to Hofstede's work, statistically significant differences among populations of different origins would be accounted for as a "cultural variable" with no specific reasoning (Minkov & Hofstede, 2011). Hofstede's work allowed the world to see the small intricacies of those populations that would cause these statistically significant results. Ultimately, Hofstede compiled his data to represent statistics of 50 countries differing across four cultural dimensions. The dimensions that distinctly came to view following close data analysis included: Power Distance Index, Individualism Index, Masculinity Index, and Uncertainty Avoidance Index (Hofstede, 1983).

In the field of heroism science, few scholars have studied the impact that culture has on the way societies in different geographic locations may perceive heroes (Allison, Goethals, & Kramer, 2017). Aspects that may make someone heroic in the United States may differ quite a bit from those that would predict heroes elsewhere. In a study concerning heroic perceptions of historical figures across 37 countries, several alarming data points arose. Muslim participants evaluated Osama bin Laden and Saddam Hussein significantly more positively than all participants of other backgrounds. However, all participants agreed that scientists Isaac Newton and Albert Einstein were remarkable heroes (Hanke et al., 2015). These data suggest that culture, specifically religious affiliation, may be a significant determinant in how individuals may be able to perceive arguably some of the world's most hated villains in a potentially positive manner. Conversely, extreme accolades in academia may simply be universally perceived as heroic. This study stresses the importance that culture may serve in a society deeming someone a hero.

In reference to the previous study mentioned, it may be interesting to analyze how cultures perceive heroes in reference to Allison and Goethals' (2011) proposed Great Eight traits of heroism. Perhaps these eight traits may vary across cultures, with some remaining similar and some being completely different. The eight traits describing heroes culminated in this study include: intelligent, strong, reliable, resilient, caring, charismatic, selfless, and inspiring (Allison, Goethals, & Kramer, 2017). In relation to Hofstede's study, these traits of heroism may be fundamentally related to the cultural dimensions that Hofstede has determined per country.

In this chapter, we will first discuss Hofstede's four dimensions and the relationship that each holds with heroism. Then, we will look closely at two exemplars of heroism from vastly different cultures, George Washington and Mahatma Gandhi, to explore how and why they are seen as heroes today within their own cultures. In looking at these two heroes, we will discuss how their personal and situational qualities may predict the making of other heroes within their societies. Lastly, we will explore the heroism of other cultures that may be intriguing to analyze using Hofstede's dimensions and areas of future research.

POWER DISTANCE INDEX

Power distance refers to social inequality, particularly in relation to authority figures (Minkov & Hofstede, 2011). A high power distance indicates that a society is highly stratified with a large degree of deference given to those of higher positions, while a low power distance indicates a society that is more equally leveled with subordinates maintaining a closer level of input to those of higher positions. High power distance cultures are often seen in those countries that still have some sort of caste system or extremely wide gaps between social classes. Low power distance is seen in more progressive countries where all opinions are perceived as valuable and society is less structured into classes. For example, Austria and Denmark have power distances of 11 and 18, respectively, ranking as some of the lowest power distances, while India has a power distance of 77, ranking as one of the highest (Hofstede, National Cultures in Four Dimensions: A Research-Based Theory of Cultural Differences among Nations, 1983).

Examples of power distance can often be seen in education, which as a child can significantly contribute to one's personal identity and formation of values. In countries of higher power distance, students are often encouraged to speak up and even challenge a teacher, in addition to education being student-centered and encouraging positive growth in a child's behavior. In countries of lower power distance, students must show the utmost respect to teachers and are rarely allowed to voice their opinions (Hofstede, 1986). Therefore, this measurement of culture may be central to the perception of heroes in the degree that it plays in the development of the self in the relation to society. Heroes in cultures of low power distance may seem more relatable, further making the ordinary person believe that hero status is achievable, while the opposite may be seen for heroes in cultures of high power distance.

INDIVIDUALISM INDEX

Individualism refers to the "relationship between the individual and the group" (Minkov & Hofstede, 2011). In other words, individualism speaks to the degree that an individual is free to act on his own free will and make decisions that may only benefit himself. A high level of individualism indicates a society where the benefits of the individual are taken into consideration before that of the group, in addition to loose ties to society as a whole with the freedom to move from in-group to in-group. A low level of individualism, otherwise known as collectivism, refers to a society where the best interest of the group is of higher importance than one's own self interest, and an individual is permanently tied to in-groups that expect ultimate loyalty (Hofstede, 1986). For example, countries of Latin America and East Asia are seen to have some of the lowest individualism scores with Guatemala and Indonesia ranking at 6 and 14, respectively, while the United States has the highest level of individualism at 91.

Perhaps the most blatant example of individualism relating to heroism is the concept of the "self-made man" or woman. Western culture has seen this sort of ideal across mass media, particularly in film and literature, as being wildly popular. These characters, either fictional or real, "transform themselves and their social situation through personal initiative" (Traube, 1989). In a study examining the differences and perceptions of the Disney version of Mulan in America, and the Chinese version of Mulan in China, significant disparities were found.

Primarily, the Disney version displays "a young lady coming of age…trying to find herself", a quote from Peter Schneider, director of films for Disney. Conversely, the story of Mulan in China is attributed more towards a young girl attempting to exhibit her patriotism to her country. Following viewing the their respective versions, American participants expressed thoughts and feelings of individualism, while Chinese participants expressed collectivism (Mo, 2015). This example shows how the individualism index not only applies to culture, but is also widespread through media and is central to a society's concept of heroism and the purposes for doing heroic deeds.

Masculinity, in Hofstede's original terms, refers to the social implications of being born as a boy or girl (Minkov & Hofstede, 2011). In later years, Hofstede has expanded this definition to include society's tendency to encourage assertiveness and self-reliance, rather than nurture and responsibility (Hofstede, 1983). Therefore, societies ranking with higher levels of masculinity tend to exhibit intense and firm leadership with fewer women in positions of power than countries with lower levels of masculinity, otherwise known as femininity. For example, Sweden is ranked the lowest in masculinity with a ranking of 5, while countries of Eastern Asia and countries recently occupied by Nazi Germany are ranked the highest with Japan and Austria ranked as the top two positions at 95 and 79, respectively.

Society often may make heroes out of powerful and innovative politicians or business leaders. In countries identified as more feminine, female heroes will tend to be more frequent as they have easier access to positions of power, allowing them to make some of these social or economic changes that may be perceived as heroic in comparison to countries that rank higher in masculinity. To give a little bit of perspective, in 2017, Sweden's governmental body was comprised of 43.6% women, while that of Japan was comprised of 9.3% ("Proportion of seats held," 2017). This staggering difference in percentage indicates that it would be much more difficult for women of Japan to make social change than women of Sweden, and could possibly be extrapolated to other dimensions of society. Therefore, the chances of women becoming heroes in Eastern Asian countries is drastically reduced in comparison to more progressive societies that have enjoyed some history of promoting gender equality.

Uncertainty avoidance refers to "the extent to which members of a culture feel threatened by ambiguous or unknown situations" (Minkov & Hofstede, 2011). This cultural dimension is perhaps the most centrally related to the idea of heroism, since risk is a key aspect to the definition of heroism (Allison, Goethals, & Kramer, 2017). Countries that have a higher ranking for uncertainty avoidance tend to discourage risk-taking behaviors and promote safety at all costs, while those with lower rankings tend to encourage risky decision-making and some may even encourage potential threats to one's safety to serve the greater good. Some examples include: Singapore and Denmark with scores of 8 and 23, respectively, while Guatemala and Uruguay have scores of 101 and 100, respectively. Although the reasoning for these countries having these scores seems convoluted, there is a basis.

With regard to an evolutionary perspective of heroism, Kafashan's kin selection theory may explain why countries of Latin America seem to rank the highest on uncertainty avoidance. Kin selection theory suggests that heroism often occurs when trying to protect one's kin to preserve their genetic contribution to society (Kafashan, Sparks, Rotella, & Barclay, 2015). The family unit in Latin America is arguably one of the strongest worldwide.

A study of the organization of Latin culture states that "families watch out for their members in return for loyalty." Outside of the family, Latin Americans tend to have a sense of distrust to all others who have not displayed undying loyalty (Osland, De Franco, & Osland, 2007). This insight suggests that Latin Americans are unlikely to engage in heroic behavior unless it is on behalf of their kin, therefore expressing high uncertainty avoidance. In addressing the other two rankings, Western European cultures tend to express firmness in business, as do countries of Eastern Asia, in addition to their profound sense of patriotism (Mo, 2015). These factors are all relevant in whether one will accept the risk of performing a heroic action.

In the next section, we will look more closely at Hofstede's dimensions in relation to the United States and India, which vary quite significantly. We will use George Washington and Mahatma Gandhi as examples to apply these dimensions and draw conclusions on the implications that Hofstede's dimensions have in the perception of heroism within the context of these two countries.

The United States scores relatively low on Power Distance with a score of 40. The United States scores the highest of all 50 countries on Individualism with a score of 91. Slightly above average, the United States scores a 62 on Masculinity. Lastly, the United States scores in the mid-range of Uncertainty Avoidance with a 46.

The Case of George Washington

George Washington was born into a wealthy family in Virginia that was highly invested in the tobacco industry. His family had many connections and provided him with access to schooling. Upon the death of his father, his brother married into a very wealthy family, which afforded Washington the ability to learn complex subjects and pursue a career in surveying, otherwise known as map-making. Washington was a very bright young man, ultimately contributing to his strategic decision-making throughout his involvement with the birth of the United States as an independent nation.

George Washington's debut of heroism was during his commitment to his country in the French and Indian War. He left the war as a colonel in the Virginia military and made quite a name for himself. Shortly after, Washington was elected to the Virginia colonial legislature. He worked his way up to serve on the First Continental Congress and remained a vital part of the legislative group opposing the British in the American Revolution. During a congressional meeting in 1775, Washington was elected First General of the Continental Army. In a display of his humility, he refused pay for this position throughout the extent of the war.

Washington's initial efforts in the Revolution were met with great success. The army won several key battles under his leadership, such as the Battles of Trenton, Princeton, and notably, Saratoga. Following the Battle of Saratoga in 1777, Washington leveraged his connections with French officials to gain the support of the French army. Throughout the next few years, his soldiers experienced many hardships caused by illness, but Washington willed his men to fight through the discouragement of quickly dwindling numbers of soldiers in their military.

In 1781, Washington and his men triumphantly defeated the British in the Battle of Yorktown, which resulted in the Treaty of Paris, recognizing the United States as an independent nation. Following the conclusion of the war, Washington assumed retirement and returned to his home in Virginia, much to the dismay of the public who expected him to become the leader of the newly formed nation. Upon the ratification of the Constitution in 1789, Washington was unanimously elected the first President of the United States. Washington's leadership as president reflected bipartisan values in constantly reasoning between the poor and rich economically. He served two terms as president and upon retiring, emphasized neutrality among political parties to serve the American people as best as possible (Huss, 2013).

As the leader of both the military and United States government, Washington displayed lower than average power distance by continually being directly involved in war even with the immense responsibility of serving as the nation's leader. Today, American leaders still reflect this dynamic with citizens. It is not uncommon to see an American president, senators, or representatives engaging with communities either through rallies, charitable efforts, and even social media. President Trump has notably used Twitter to engage with the public unlike any other government leader to date. "Mr. Trump's use of Twitter marked the culmination of two decades of change in the way politicians communicated with the public. That style has become more personal, more instantaneous" (Buncombe, 2018). This proximity between a leader with the American public shows how a low power distance has remained an integral part of American society from the era of George Washington to now.

Reflecting the American individualism score of 91, Washington characterized the American yearning for separation from British rule in leading the Revolution while also taking on this leadership position on his own. Washington's first term as President lacked much of the structure that American government has today. There were not as many Cabinet or departmental positions as are seen in the current government. Therefore, Washington had to display immense individualism to make positive decisions for the American people without much other support. In today's society, individualism is central to American culture. The First

Amendment of the Constitution guarantees freedom of speech, religion, press, and assembly to all Americans. "The subjective individualism of the First Amendment makes American society an open society" (Sanz, 2014). This openness of society allows Americans to explore individual identity and feel comfortable expressing that identity.

Washington's masculinity was particularly visible in constant negotiations with subordinates in the military as well as with his friends who had varying political views serving as his sole support system during his presidency (Huss, 2013). Washington had to maintain a fierce and assertive outlook as a leader so others would not cloud his judgment or potentially get in his way. In American society today, masculinity can often be seen in many business leaders and office cultures. Specifically, in business, Americans notably experience high levels of stress and are prone to mask weakness at all costs. Additionally, Americans often stray away from cooperation and when there are conflicts, prefer to address them head on (Fan & Zigang, 2004). This sort of assertive and confrontational behavior speaks to the higher than average masculinity score the United States attained in Hofstede's study.

Washington exhibited moderate uncertainty avoidance both in the war and as President. Knowing that the American military was less equipped than that of the British, Washington strategically calculated plans of attack. A noteworthy example is when Washington led his men across the Delaware during the night and across snow to ambush the British in the Battle of Trenton (Huss, 2013). Additionally, in knowing that the public strongly favored Washington to serve as President following the war, he expressed initial hesitance in taking on this role by retiring to his home only to be convinced into taking on the position.

Uncertainty avoidance can commonly be seen in American culture today in consumer purchases both in stores and online. American companies often provide a historical outlook on a company for reputable purposes, in addition to free help lines, frequently asked questions, customer reviews and more (Singh & Baack, 2017). Americans like to have some background knowledge before making purchasing decisions, however, many Americans also make impulse purchases. This tendency to want a small bit of information before making decisions reflects a medium uncertainty avoidance in American culture.

Hofstede and The Great Eight

The Great Eight traits of heroism are typically what is used now to describe the central features of a hero (Allison, Goethals, & Kramer, 2017). In referencing Hofstede's cultural dimensions and how they play into American heroism, we can attempt to find relations between each dimension and traits within the Great Eight. I believe that power distance is related closely with the intelligent and inspirational qualities of a hero. Those who are extremely intelligent and inspiring, as was Washington, seem almost on a higher level than the rest of society, therefore creating this idea of power distance. Americans often perceive heroes as being larger than life, especially with how they are received by society following their heroic deeds. This sort of societal response can almost elevate a hero from their once equal position, as reflected in the low score of the United States, to a higher-than-average power level, thus inducing this sense of power distance.

In relation to individualism, the Great Eight traits seem to stress a sense of collectivism. Perhaps this relationship contributes to why Americans perceive an individual as hero, since they are going against the norm of American culture. The traits I particularly see as relating to collectivism include the ideas of reliability, care, and selflessness, all exhibited by Washington. Americans are often preoccupied with their own affairs, which may contribute to the American perception of heroism. Those who sacrifice their individualism for others are few, therefore enhancing their sense of heroism to the American public.

I believe that masculinity is most closely related with the strength, resilience, and charismatic aspects of the Great Eight. Typical heroic figures of American culture are those who are not afraid to stand up to opposition and show that they are fierce. Washington clearly displays these traits in his opposition of the British through times of success and failure, as well as being elected to serve as the United States' first President. Throughout American pop culture and media, heroes who display a vast sense of masculinity are typically those that receive such high praise.

Lastly, I believe that uncertainty avoidance may only be related to intelligence. Those who have a high level of intelligence are able to critically analyze situations and make appropriate judgment calls concerning risk. Although Americans tend to avoid risk, perhaps what makes heroes so special in American culture is their

ability to take on risks even in the fear of the unknown. Washington strategically used his incredible intelligence to beat the British and liberate America. Kohen et al. (2017) alludes to the idea that many heroes often have some sort of special training that may even reduce their risk in situations requiring a hero, directly relating to the concept of uncertainty avoidance. Washington's previous experience in the military and with legislative bodies primed him to be exemplary in leading the American Revolution and serving as the first President. Many other American heroes have replicated this idea of heroism stemming from some special ability learned prior to their exhibition of their heroism.
India

INDIA AND HOFSTEDE'S DIMENSIONS

India has a high level of power distance, scoring at 77. In comparison to the United States, India has a much lower level of individualism, coming in as more of a collectivistic nation with a score of 48. Additionally, India has a slightly above average level of masculinity scoring at 56. India scores at a level of 40 for uncertainty avoidance, ranking as one of the countries with the lowest ranking.

Mahatma Gandhi

Mahatma Gandhi was born into a family that had very few material possessions and not much access to schooling. His father was the chief minister of their small principality, and his mother was very much absorbed in their Hindu-based religion. Gandhi went through a period of time in adolescence of rebellion only to be followed by a deep commitment of self-improvement. He found a way to get into college with a background of very little primary education and pursued a degree in law in England.

Upon returning to India, he found very little work and was forced to pursue a career in South Africa, also a colony of Britain at the time, where he was met with a lot of discrimination. Gandhi fought for the civil rights of Indians in South Africa and was met with a lot of opposition, sometimes even being physically beaten. He was absorbed in religious studies and ultimately took a mantra of "nonpossession" and "equability" (Nanda, 2018). Gandhi returned to India in January of 1915, where he gained traction as a political leader. As the British imposed ever increasing repression on Indian citizens, Gandhi championed nonviolent protests against the British and was arrested. He remained in jail for two years and upon his release, found India to have taken many steps backward in its progression. In protest, he went on his renowned three-week fast and was ultimately named the president of the Congress party.

Gandhi led the well-known Salt March, defending the poor who had been imposed with a large tax increase on salt, with almost 100,000 people involved. Gandhi's efforts were centered around the desegregation of the Indian population and the "untouchables", those of the lowest caste (Nanda, 2018). Upon the start of World War II, the British aimed to reconcile with the Indians and allow them an independent state, so long as the Hindus and Muslims were separated, to Gandhi's dismay. This reconciliation resulted in the creation of India and Pakistan in August of 1947. He lived out the rest of his life opposing the animosity between Hindus and Muslims until he was assassinated on January 30, 1948 (Nanda, 2018).

Hofstede and Mahatma Gandhi

Gandhi was born into a middle class family and slowly rose through the caste system to become one of the most powerful political leaders in India. The power distance in India was depicted clearly in the British's attempts to segregate and dehumanize the poor, known as the "untouchables" (Nanda, 2018). Gandhi made it his life's work to fight against this extreme degree of power distance. In India today, power distance is exemplified by how an individual responds to another's accessories. For example, a rural cyclist will dismount his bike to stand attention to a passing Jeep, which is a symbol of a government official. Additionally, one who wears a white khadi, typical dress of an Indian "VIP", demands immediate obedience and preferential treatment wherever he may go. Through these behaviors, one can easily see that high power distance dominates Indian culture even today (Raghunathan, 2011).

Similar to India's relative score of collectivism, Gandhi fought for the rights of the "untouchables" most notably through the Salt March, which would not serve him or the members of his caste in any way. Gandhi aimed to better society as a whole rather than simply just himself on an individual level. Collectivism in Indian culture is most notably seen in family dynamics. Families often live together among three or even four generations, and each family member's decisions are usually made together as a family in the hopes of benefitting the whole family. These decisions often center around career choices, religious preferences, and even marriage (Chadda & Deb, 2013).

Slightly more feminine than Washington, Gandhi pursued his political and social agenda through nonviolent ways and always discouraged violence. He was a man of a peaceful nature and encouraged the reconciliation of differences between two opposing parties. Among Indian workplaces, this sense of a medium degree of masculinity can be seen. Businessmen of India have consistently showed more interest in quality of life and personal relationships, while women have slowly been beginning to grow in numbers in top management positions of Indian firms (Ganesh & Ganesh, 2014). This change in a trend towards gender equality, shows that Indian culture is moving more progressively towards femininity rather than high masculinity, as in the United States.

Most notably, Gandhi displayed lower than average uncertainty avoidance with his incredible will to take risks. India was severely unequipped to face the heavily armed British in the hopes of gaining independence, yet Gandhi was not phased. He met the opposition with great strength and always stood his ground. India's risk-taking behavior can clearly be seen in it's deep desire to grow economically. Indian banks maintain high competition and are constantly engaging in risky behavior to provide those seeking loans with funds to promote economic growth (Sarkar & Sensarma, 2016). India has notably taken on business from multiple multinational companies and welcomed them into the economy without hesitation. The country is eager to expand its economy and compete as a world leader, therefore promoting risk-taking, or low uncertainty avoidance.

Hofstede and The Great Eight

Relative to the discussion in the section covering the United States, I believe that some of the relationships between the Great Eight and Hofstede's dimensions remain the same, while others differ in the Indian context. I do believe that the intelligent and inspirational traits of a hero relate to power distance in India, however, I would also venture to add the strength aspect. In Indian culture, those of lower castes appear to be weak. I would venture to say that those of higher castes, or of higher power in this context, are seen to be very strong and powerful. Gandhi represented these three traits in relation to power distance. He was very bright, inspirational to most members of the Indian community, and displayed immense mental strength through constant fasting and standing up to formidable opposition. In extrapolating this idea to Indian heroism, I believe that it may be harder for those of lower castes to achieve a degree of heroism as many may feel discouraged by a lack of credibility. Being of a higher caste may be a strong predictor of heroism in Indian culture.

Contrary to the individualist nature of the United States, I believe the collectivist nature of India lends itself more to the reliable, caring, and selfless traits of the Great Eight. Gandhi exemplified all of these traits to their highest extent. He did not have to fight for the poor, as he was not a member of that caste, yet he felt strongly about equality for all. He represented the pinnacle of the collectivist nature of India. I feel that Indian heroism is centered around the necessity to live up to the Indian expectation of a collectivistic nature on a larger scale. Heroism in India resides on the basis of doing more for others besides simply one's family and extended family.

Additionally, the slight femininity of India is also related to the same three traits of collectivism. Gandhi represented a nurturing nature, specifically in choosing to reside in villages of the poor and constantly providing nursing to his sick father and wife in their late lives (Nanda, 2018). Those who admire Gandhi specifically speak of his kind and gentle nature. However, he also maintained a degree of masculinity, refusing to back down from the enormous challenge of gaining Indian independence. I believe that heroism in India may also be based on a perfect mixture of assertiveness and placidity.

Lastly, to address India's low uncertainty avoidance, I believe the trait of resiliency is highly related. Since Indians are prone to taking risk, they must possess the ability to arise from failures quickly and remain steadfast to their goals. Gandhi exhibited this quality throughout his multiple arrests, only to return to the political sphere and continue on in his fight for freedom for all. I do not believe that all people can possess this quality. Perhaps what makes an Indian hero so otherworldly is his ability to continue reaching towards a goal, even in the face of many obstacles that may seem difficult to overcome.

In challenging the Great Eight in an Indian context, I believe charisma is an after-effect of displays of heroism. Gandhi did not have a strong following at the beginning of his plight. He gained this following through his publicized struggles. He had to convince society to believe in his cause and join the movement. Additionally, I believe that in Indian culture, the trait of humility is central to the Great Eight. Gandhi lived by a mantra of not owning any material possessions and would return any funds he received to the benefit of others. Humility, I believe, is central to the collectivistic and feminine aspects of Indian heroism. This practice is ultimately what made him so admirable as not only a leader, but a hero.

CONCLUSION

The research on India and the United States provides valuable insights in cultural differences predicting and producing heroism. Although fighting for closely the same cause, there are vast differences between the behaviors that George Washington took and those that Mahatma Gandhi took in achieving fruition. I believe that these differences are fundamental examples of how cultures may differ in their production and reverence of heroes. In these in-depth case analyses, I have shed light on the importance of Hofstede's cultural dimensions in the cultures of these two nations and how they relate to heroism. As a result of these dimensions, the Great Eight may be subjected to potential changes cross-culturally.

I argue that the progression of heroism science would benefit strongly from the application of Hofstede's dimensions and deep analysis of heroes in other cultural contexts. I would be particularly interested in addressing heroism in countries that have a perplexing mixture of scores across Hofstede's dimensions. One area of possible future research would be the study of heroism in Latin America. The contrast between low scores of individualism and high scores of masculinity is intriguing in exploring the development of heroes. For example, Venezuela has a score of 12 for individualism, while having a score of 73 for masculinity (Hofstede, 1983).

Furthermore, it may be interesting to address cultures where Hofstede's dimensions seem to no longer apply. In the 1983 study performed by Hofstede, Yugoslavia was named one of the 50 countries (Hofstede, 1983). I would be very interested to examine how the divide between this conglomerate of nations has affected these cultural dimensions, or if it has at all. It may also be interesting to analyze these dimensions within countries Hofstede did not analyze. A particular region that comes to mind is Eastern Europe with its recent economic boom and progression into the world economy.

This research has just opened the door to possibilities of cross-cultural analyses in heroism science. I believe there is much work to be done in this area, particularly in countries that have growing populations and are progressing developmentally. Future research should look towards extrapolating the Great Eight and definitions of heroism cross-culturally to see if there are any disparities. Perceptions of heroism differ from person to person, naturally they would differ across cultures. Cultural differences affect psychology in profound ways, it is of much value to see how they affect heroism science.

REFERENCES

Allison, S. T., & Goethals, G. R. (2011). Heroes: What they do and why we need them. New York: Oxford University Press.

Allison, S. T., Goethals, G. R., & Kramer, R. M. (Eds.) (2017). Handbook of heroism and heroic leadership. New York: Routledge.

Allison, S. T., Goethals, G. R., & Kramer, R. M. (2017). Setting the scene the rise and coalescence of heroism science. In S. T. Allison, G. R. Goethals, & R. M. Kramer (Eds.), Handbook of heroism and heroic leadership. New York: Routledge.

Allison, S. T., Goethals, G. R., Marrinan, A. R., Parker, O. M., Spyrou, S. P., Stein, M. (2019). The metamorphosis of the hero: Principles, processes, and purpose. Frontiers in Psychology.

Buncombe, A. (2018, January 17). Donald trump one year on: How the twitter president changed social media and the country's top office. Retrieved from https://www.independent.co.uk/news/world/americas/us-politics/the-twitter-president-   how-potus-changed-social-media-and-the-presidency-a8164161.html

Chadda, R. K., & Deb, K. S. (2013). Indian family systems, collectivistic society and psychotherapy. Indian J Psychiatry, 55(2), 299-309.

Fan, P., & Zigang, Z. (2004). Cross-cultural challenges when doing business in china. Singapore Management Review, 26(1), 81-90.

Ganesh, S., & Ganesh, M. P. (2014). Effects of masculinity-femininity on quality of work life understanding the moderating roles of gender and social support. Gender in Management, 29(4), 229-253.

Goethals, G. R., & Allison, S. T. (2014). Kings and charisma, Lincoln and leadership: An evolutionary perspective. In Goethals, G. R., et al. (Eds.), Conceptions of leadership: Enduring ideas and emerging insights. New York: Palgrave Macmillan.

Hanke, K., Liu, J. H., Sibley, C. G., Paez, D., Gaines Jr., S. O., Moloney, G., et al. (2015). "Heroes" and "villains" of world history across cultures. PLOS ONE, 1-21.

Hofstede, G. (1986). Cultural difference in teaching and learning. International Journal of Intercultural Relations, 10, 301-320.

Hofstede, G. (1983). National cultures in four dimensions: A research-based theory of cultural differences among nations. International Studies of Management & Organization, 13(1/2), 46-74.

Hoyt, C. L., Allison, S. T., Barnowski, A., & Sultan, A. (2020). Lay theories of heroism and leadership: The role of gender, communion, and agency. Social Psychology.

Huss, D. (2013). George washington (1732–1799). Retrieved from http://www.crfcelebrateamerica.org/index.php/holiday-heroes/89-george-washington

Kafashan, S., Sparks, A., Rotella, A., & Barclay, P. (2015). Why heroism exists evolutionary perspectives on extreme helping. In S. T. Allison, G. R. Goethals, & R. M. Kramer (Eds.), Handbook of heroism and heroic leadership. New York: Routledge.

Kohen, A., Langdon, M., & Riches, B. R. (2017). The making of a hero: Cultivating empathy, altruism, and heroic imagination. Journal of Humanistic Psychology, 1-17.

Minkov, M., & Hofstede, G. (2011). The evolution of hofstede's doctrine. Cross Cultural Management, 18(1), 10-20.

Mo, W. (2015). A cross-cultural analysis of disney mulan film and chinese mulan drama impacts on chinese audience's attitude (Master's Thesis). Retrieved from http://dspace.bu.ac.th/bitstream/123456789/1740/1/Wenmin.mo.pdf

Nanda, B. (2018, October 26). Mahatma gandhi. Retrieved from https://www.britannica.com/biography/Mahatma-Gandhi

Osland, J. S., De Franco, S., & Osland, A. (2007). Organizational implications of latin american culture: Lessons for the expatriate manager. Economia e Gestão, 7(14), 109-120.

Proportion of seats held by women in national parliaments (%). (2017). Retrieved from https://data.worldbank.org/indicator/SG.GEN.PARL.ZS

Raghunathan, V. (2011, June 25). Power distance index and corruption. Retrieved from https://economictimes.indiatimes.com/opinion/et-commentary/power-distance-index-and-corruption/articleshow/8985180.cms

Sanz, E. (2014). The first amendment and cultural creation. Retrieved from https://law.yale.edu/system/files/area/center/isp/documents/esteve_sanz_-_the_first_amendment_and_cultural_creation_-_fesc.pdf

Sarkar, S., & Sensarma, R. (2016). The relationship between competition and risk-taking behaviour of indian banks. Journal of Financial and Economic Policy, 8(1), 95-119.

Singh, N., & Baack, D. W. (2017). Web site adaptation: A cross-cultural comparison of u.s. and mexican web sites. Journal of Computer-Mediated Communication, 9(4).

Traube, E. G. (1989). Secrets of success in postmodern society. Cultural Anthropology, 273-300.

12

Heroic Transformation of Setting: The Relationship between the Hero and Her Environment

SHARON H. SHIN

Becoming a hero is a paradox.
To be a hero in your society, you must first leave it.
You must be willing to separate yourself from the place you love
To advance it.
Growing apart to be better together.
You will need to become independent from your society,
Letting go of many of the ideas and beliefs you've learned from it.
Distancing yourself from everything you once believed and embraced.
To be a hero, you will change in ways you've never expected.
You'll have adventures and thrills in your new environment
That you'll remember for the rest of your life.
You'll feel emotions you've never felt before.
You'll face the fears that agonize and pain you.

And you will become better than ever.
In the end, you'll appreciate your journey because you've gained the ability
To save and transform your society back home.
But when you come back, you'll realize that your perception of home has changed.
Is home the place you've known and loved your whole life?
Or is it the place where you've grown and learned to become your best self?
Your heart longs for home.
But where your heart longs for is unclear.

Heroic transformation is central to heroism because it marks the hero's coming of age, fosters emotional healing, cultivates social unity, and advances their society (Allison & Goethals, 2017). The transformation prepares the hero to ultimately return home to impart their knowledge and wisdom with their society, pushing them to grow just as the hero did. To continue advancing, societies require brave and passionate heroes who are willing to go through a transformation.

The three aspects of the hero's transformation are the transformation of setting, transformation of self, and transformation of society. By first experiencing a new setting, the hero is able to transform themselves, and by transforming themselves, they, in turn, are able to transform their society. Each step is important and produces the next. Without one, the other steps in the transformation process cannot happen (Allison & Goethals, 2017; Allison, Goethals, & Kramer, 2017).

In this chapter, we will be focusing on the transformation of setting, the first and foundational step of the hero's journey (Allison & Goethals, 2017). The change in setting occurs when the individual leaves their home and finds themselves in a new environment (Allison, Goethals, & Spyrou, 2019). The novel setting is fascinating, awe striking, and challenges the hero to step out of their comfort zones and grow. Though there are many ways a transformation of setting can lead to self-change, we will be focusing on a select few, and how these factors shape the individual to grow, learn, and ultimately become a hero.

Being in a new setting challenges the hero to consider ways of thinking they've never considered before. In a new place far away from home, they must be willing to make the effort to shift their perspectives to adapt and persevere in their new environment. This step is critical to the hero's journey because it leads them to the face the fact that their way of thinking is not universal and superior. By being exposed to newfound ideas and beliefs in their new environment, they begin to understand that there are other perspectives out there in the world that are valid and worth integrating into their own lives. Upon this realization that the world is full of reasonable world views they've not thought of before, the hero is challenged to consider the reasonability of their own world view. This stage challenges the foundations of the hero's beliefs, shaking the hero to their core, testing which beliefs and ideas the hero is willing to leave behind and which the hero stays loyal to.

Thus, the change in setting is the first point in the hero's journey where they begin to transform mentally. With an inundation of new information surrounding them, they are tasked with the test of growing in a setting where everything is unfamiliar and strange. They are challenged to embrace a cosmopolitan mindset in their new setting where they can entertain, understand, and accept new ideas not previously held by their previous society. Engulfed with ideas that progress and challenge them, the hero learns to embrace and adopt different perspectives. In a new setting, the hero can implement new ideas, beliefs, and perspectives into their life that will ultimately advance their home society.

THE GREATNESS OF GINSBURG

Ruth Bader Ginsburg, America's second female Supreme Court Justice embodies this shift in perspectives through her experience of a change in setting. As a female growing up in a time without gender equality, she was discouraged from deviating from the societal norm for women and was actively barred from career opportunities due to her gender. As one of nine females in her class at Harvard Law School, she was openly criticized and shamed for taking a spot in the class meant for a man (Lepore, 2018).

As disgruntled as she was with the gender norms in the USA, her transformation of self did not occur until she experienced a change in setting upon her visit to Sweden. While working in Sweden on a book about civil procedures, she noticed that "between 20 and 25 percent of the law students in Sweden were women" (Galanes, 2015). Additionally, Ginsburg noted that while it was nonexistent in the United States, in Sweden, there were "women on the bench" (Galanes, 2015). While she was discriminated against and actively put down for her gender while pursuing a career in law in the United States, Ruth realized this inequality did not exist in other countries. She realized that it was possible for a country to embrace gender equality. There existed a world where women were supported and respected for being independent and pursuing their own careers.

Her trip to Sweden was the beginning of her hero's journey- she was introduced to new perspectives on gender roles, and she began to take note that women in other countries were being treated with equality and respect. Since then, Ruth Bader Ginsburg has been a champion for equal rights and opportunities for both men and women. By going to Sweden, Ruth was introduced to a new way of life that inspired her in how she viewed law. To Ginsburg, law was no longer something that was specifically catered to men. Rather, law was an area that offered her the ability to transform and progress the rights and opportunities women had.

In a new place, if a hero cannot be to be open-minded in their perspectives, they ultimately will not be able to become a hero. Subsequently, if they cannot come to appreciate new ideas and perspectives, they cannot effect change in their societies back home. A transformation in setting is critical to the hero's journey because it introduces new ideas, beliefs, and perspectives that captivate and challenge the hero. Without an appreciation of the newfound perspectives and beliefs in their new setting, the hero is limited in their abilities to grow and transform themselves.

In addition to experiencing a mental transformation in a new setting, the hero experiences a physical one as well. By being in a new setting, they can experience new ventures they would not have been able to in their own society. They can try new things, see new sights, and be engulfed in feelings of amazement and wonder. As these new adventures are often exciting and thrilling, the hero becomes more willing to step out of their comfort zones to try new things, a key component to the hero's journey. By opening up to the unknown and widening their scope of willingness, the hero learns to embrace events that challenge and stimulate them. This eagerness, in turn, leads to the development of new heroic qualities such as being daring, being calm under pressure, and having confidence in their abilities and skills. If the hero can step out of their comfort zone to try new things, they may, as a result, also be more likely to step out of their comfort zone to help someone in need.

A key event the hero will face in their new setting while having new experiences is the necessity for self-reflection. As they will be inundated with hidden meanings, details, and symbols, they will need time to consolidate the information they are receiving. As these events may lead to contradictions and bouts of confusion, the hero will experience inner conflicts and turmoil they will need to address. To avoid having moments of cognitive dissonance, the hero will need to take a step back and allow themselves to process their emotions and thoughts (Allison, Beggan, & Efthimiou, 2019; Allison & Goethals, 2017). Through self-reflection methods, such as mindful meditation, the hero will be able to understand and make sense of their new knowledge, ultimately being able to "act in accord with their moral ideals" (Jones, 2017, p. 3). By being open about the feelings and experiences they are having, the hero is able to be vulnerable about their struggles and accept growth.

As thrilling as many of the experiences they will face will be, there will also be trials and tribulations that the hero will struggle through. When they are faced with encountering some of their greatest fears, the hero will need to address and confront the areas of their lives that they've avoided and suppressed. The trials that they face will require them to be open and willing to face their fears, challenging them to look deep within themselves to find a strength they did not know was there. Through the practice of self-reflection and connecting to their inner self, the hero will be able to find their inner courage to rise above what terrifies them.

THE REMARKABLE REMY FROM RATATOUILLE

An example of a hero who undergoes new experiences is Remy from the Disney movie, Ratatouille (Lewis & Bird, 2007). As a rat who aspires to be a chef, he is exhilarated when he realizes he is in Paris. In fact, a key moment in the movie is when he climbs up onto the roof and is immersed in feelings of awe and wonder when he sees the Eiffel Tower and the skyline of Paris. As Remy is full of joy as he admires the bright lights and beautiful city, he notices that he is above his role model, Gusteau's, restaurant. This realization and overwhelming excitement about being in a new environment encourages Remy to go inside the restaurant and explore, a feat he would not have done previously.

Along with giving Remy the courage to go inside the restaurant, the change in setting also gives Remy the opportunity to cook in Gusteau's restaurant. Given the resources and the means to cook dishes he's always wanted to make, he is able to hone his cooking skills, practicing new techniques and flavor combinations. His dishes are met with raving reviews and help mend the diminishing reputation of Gusteau's restaurant. However, despite his gifts and skills, Remy is plagued throughout his journey by his fear that, as a rat, he will never be able to be taken seriously by the high-status cooking community (Lewis & Bird, 2007).

At the end of the movie, when Remy is exposed, he experiences his greatest fear: every employee in the restaurant was disappointed and quit because they did not want to be associated with a rat. They did not believe in his ability to succeed and dismissed him because he wasn't a human. Despite Remy's gift in cooking, his status as a rat prevented the employees from treating him with respect and consideration (Lewis & Bird, 2007).

However, in the moment when he is offered the decision of leaving to go back home to his family or to stay and finish the task of cooking for Paris' harshest food critic, Ego, Remy takes up the challenge and chooses the latter. Throughout the movie, we see him connecting to his deeper self, such as when he talks to the imaginary Gusteau in his mind about his fears about being exposed and rejected by humans (Lewis & Bird, 2007). With a guide to his inner thoughts, we see that though he is afraid that he will be belittled for being a rat, he comes to the point where he is willing to try despite his fears. Through learning new techniques in the kitchen and perfecting recipes, Remy learned to find his worth in himself instead of from others.

As Remy experienced, a change in setting allows for experiences the hero would not have had back in their homes. However, this change comes with the catch that they will need to face the fears they were able to avoid before. A change in setting is inundated with new feelings, sensations, and emotions that need to be processed. Through connecting to their deeper self through methods of self-reflection, the hero is ultimately able to conquer their fears and move forward in their lives.

THE COURAGEOUS CARL WILKENS

In a new setting, the hero will encounter people who are different from them. Whether it is ethnicity, cultural beliefs, or religion, there will always be a factor that will divide the hero from their new community. While it has become normalized in our society to accept these barriers, the hero must be willing to reject this societal norm and aim to break down these barriers. Through spending time with, listening to, and understanding the "other," the hero is able to connect to and feel in community with their newfound group.

An example of a hero who overcame the boundaries between themselves and their new community is Carl Wilkens. Wilkens stayed behind in Rwanda during the 1994 Genocide to ensure the well-being of his two employees. With the US closing their embassy in the country and all the other Americans leaving, Wilkens risked his life at a time where everyone else chose to flee for safety. In fact, after the border closed, Wilkens was the only American to stay in Rwanda. In addition to risking his life by being potentially persecuted in the genocide, Wilkens also further endangered himself by helping and sheltering refugees (Kohen, Langdon, & Riches, 2017, p. 5).

When he was later asked about why he decided to stay, he shared that he was fearful and regretted his decision at times. Wilkens shared that he felt that he made a mistake for endangering his life when he had a family back home that he loved and cared about. However, when he thought about his two employees, his fears disappeared, and he was reminded of why he decided to stay (Kohen et al., 2017, p. 6).

In his thought process, it is evident that though initially he felt inclined to divide himself from the Rwandans, he actively changed his mind set to make that division went away. This decision to stay highlights Wilkens' courage and lack of distinction between himself and the Rwandan community. To him, people were people who needed protection during a time of tribulation. There was no "we" vs. "them". It was people who were being persecuted, and people who had the means and abilities to help.

While the Americans leaving understood that the people of Rwanda were in danger, they did not fully connect to their community to feel obliged to stay. Unfortunately, this attitude is human nature. We are more likely to help people who are like us than people who are not (Kafashan, Sparks, Rotella, & Barclay, 2017, p. 38). As it is a natural tendency to draw lines, it is heroic and brave when an individual is willing to help regardless of these lines.

This phenomenon is also observed in Ratatouille. With Remy being a rat and Alfredo Linguini being a human, there were many initial struggles. First, since rats are the main vermin in the kitchen, Linguini struggled to accept Remy as a chef. Remy, in turn, also struggled to trust Linguini because Remy was told all his life about how cruel humans were. However, despite the initial stereotypes they used to judge one another, the pair eventually realized the stereotypes were false, and they began to appreciate one another's inner qualities

Through communication and acceptance, the pair were able to overcome the barriers of "us" and "them". In a world where they were discouraged from associating with one another, they broke down barriers to build a friendship. Even though they should have been mortal enemies, the change in setting for Remy led them to develop a friendship they would not have otherwise had. Between them, there was no "us" and "them." Regardless of species, stereotypes, and initial hesitations, they chose to be friends who cared about and supported one another (Lewis & Bird, 2007).

OPENNESS TO TRANSFORMATION

Being in a new setting paves the way for the hero to be more open to transformation. In a new place, they will have to learn to be independent and autonomous. Through this change, they are more likely to make decisions on their own behalf and not be swayed by others. Furthermore, as they are independent from their society back home, the hero may feel more comfortable making decisions based on their own inclinations rather than making decisions society wants them to make. By being in a new society, the hero is no longer obligated to follow their previous society's expectations. They can act however they want, say whatever they want, and do whatever they want without the consequences that they would have faced back home. With a newfound appreciation to deviate from the norm, the hero can explore new limits that they were once banned from crossing. This newfound freedom leads to a transformation of self because the hero is no longer bound by what their society dictates is right and wrong. They are able to develop their own values independently from society.

There are both purposeful and accidental impediments by society to deter individuals from becoming heroes. Whether it is on purpose or not, it is evident that the social environment is a powerful motivator for individuals to act in ways that they would not have otherwise (Parks, 2017). Therefore, by being in a new environment that does not enforce the values of the previous society, the individual may be more likely to stray from their previous society's expectations. A transformation in setting may encourage the hero to explore their options in their behaviors and actions, leading them to become more comfortable with doing acts of heroism that were once suppressed by society.

Furthermore, a transformation in setting may not only dissolve the pressures of the hero's previous society, but it may also promote acts that are heroic. For example, the new environment may challenge the hero to behave in ways that are in more line with heroism. Therefore, upon arriving back home, the hero may exhibit the behaviors that they learned in their new setting. The power of a social environment is evident in how it can suppress acts of heroism. However, in the opposite way, a social environment can also promote acts of heroism. Though the social environment may be harmful to heroism at times, it is possible that being in a new environment can be helpful to the development of heroism.

Ruth Bader Ginsburg experienced the power of a social environment and subsequently exhibited changes from when she came back from Sweden. Though she used to fall in line with what society ordered females to do, after her trip, she began to deviate from the norm. By being in Sweden, a country where the gender norms of the USA were not enforced, Ginsburg felt more comfortable opening up to and exploring the areas of gender rights. As she was in a new environment with no social consequences for being a woman, she was encouraged to become bolder and more grounded in her beliefs about women's rights (Galanes, 2015).

In her time in Sweden, Ginsburg interacted with women who were lawyers and even saw a woman in court working while she was eight months pregnant. This experience may have led to an epiphany for Ginsburg because it reminded her of her own experience when she purposefully hid the fact that she was pregnant from the university that she worked at because she was afraid of being fired from her position as a professor. While it was an offense that constituted job termination in the USA, being pregnant while working was something Sweden encouraged and protected (Lepore, 2018). The duality of being a woman who was appreciated both at home and in the workforce solidified Ginsburg's beliefs of the necessity of gender equality.

Therefore, by experiencing a social environment where women were equal to men in their rights and protections, Ruth was able to return home with courage and passion to transform gender rights. Though she was previously hesitant to speak up against the crowd due to being afraid to make waves, Ginsburg began to actively champion for equal rights after her transformation of setting. By experiencing a new norm, Ginsburg was able to shift from her previous society's perspective to the perspective that she wanted to embrace. In her new setting, Ginsburg found her courage to speak out against the crowd.

HOW THE SETTING DETERMINES HEROISM

As the first step in the hero's transformation, the transformation of setting determines whether the individual will become a hero or not. The setting is where they will be taught life lessons, inspired, and motivated to grow. They will be encouraged to embrace the new principles they learn in their new setting, implementing these notions into their life. They will have the choice of whether to grow or whether to stay stagnant: the choice of being egocentric and consider their own needs, or sociocentric and consider their society's needs (Allison, 2019; Allison & Goethals, 2017). The setting is also where they will learn the most about themselves and their society back home. It will be the place where the individual realizes that both they and their society are broken in some way, and that they both require transformation. In the new setting, the individual will be confronted with the notion that a change is necessary and essential for advancement. It will be up to them to accept the hard truth that they will need to personally transform to advance their society. It will be a difficult and often remorseful feat- accepting that the society one grew up in is imperfect, and they are the only one who can do something about it.

The setting will also challenge the hero by bringing out their biggest fears and hurdles. In the moment, the individual will have two choices: running from or running towards the fear. By running towards their fear, they will ultimately be able to confront their fears, overcome them, and grow to be a stronger person. However, by running away, they may lose their chance at heroism. As a hero is someone who enhances, models morals to, and protects others, it is important that they learn to stand their ground when they are afraid (Kinsella, Ritchie, & Igou, 2017, p. 26). It is crucial that they can conquer their fears before helping and protecting others from theirs.

To enhance others, the individual must be able to enhance the areas where they need personal development. To model morals to others, they must be able to first stick to their own morals and follow them wherever they lead. To protect others, the hero must reach a level of selflessness where they value the lives of others equally to their own life. The setting in the hero's journey is juxtaposing because it will simultaneously be where they have the best and worst moments in their life.

CONCLUSION

The setting is where the hero's journey begins. It is the place where the individual must adapt from an individualistic perspective to a group-oriented perspective. As a hero, they must sacrifice their wants to benefit the entire group. They must be willing to set an example by being the first to put their lives and reputations on the line for what they believe in (Decter-Frain, Vanstone, & Frimer, 2017, p. 129). The ultimate marker of an individual becoming a hero is them returning to their society back home with a new way of thinking. With this change in perspective, they will be able to notice the cracks in society others have not seen, give ideas to problems others have not thought of, and advance society forward with their newfound knowledge and life experiences.

Heroic transformation involves a bit of a juxtaposition. By leaving their old traits behind in their new setting and bringing back their skills, beliefs, and perspectives home, the hero simultaneously exists in two planes. They exist as their old selves in their new society, and they exist as their new selves in their old society. Though it sounds lonely, this simultaneous existence may be a good thing. By existing in multiple places, the hero can connect to various societies around the world. They no longer belong to one place. Rather, they belong to the world, ready to help and transform where help is needed.

REFERENCES

Allison, S. T. (Ed.) (2019). Heroic transformation: How heroes change themselves and the world. Richmond: Palsgrove.

Allison, S. T., Beggan, J. K., & Efthimiou, O. (2019). The art and science of heroism and heroic leadership. Lausanne, Switzerland: Frontiers.

Allison, S. T., & Goethals, G. R. (2017). The hero's transformation. In S. T. Allison, G. R. Goethals, & R. M. Kramer (Eds.), Handbook of heroism and heroic leadership. New York: Routledge.

Allison, S. T., Goethals, G. R., & Kramer, R. M. (Eds.) (2017). Handbook of heroism and heroic leadership. New York: Routledge.

Allison, S. T., Goethals, G. R., & Kramer, R. M. (2017). Setting the scene: The rise and coalescence of heroism science. In S. T. Allison, G. R. Goethals, & R. M. Kramer (Eds.), Handbook of heroism and heroic leadership. New York: Routledge.

Allison, S. T., Goethals, G. R., & Spyrou, S. P. (2019). Donald Trump as the archetypal puer aeternus: The psychology of mature and immature leadership. In K. Bezio & G. R. Goethals (Eds.), Leadership and populism. Northampton, MA: Edward Elgar.

Beggan, J. K., & Allison, S. T. (Eds.) (2018). Leadership and sexuality: Power, principles, and processes. Northampton, MA: Edward Elgar.

Decter-Frain, A., Vanstone, R., & Frimer, J.A. (2017). Why and how groups create moral heroes. In S. T. Allison, G. R. Goethals, & R. M. Kramer (Eds.), Handbook of heroism and heroic leadership. New York: Routledge.

Galanes, P. (2015, November 14). Ruth Bader Ginsburg and Gloria Steinem on the Unending Fight for Women's Rights. The New York Times. Retrieved from https://www.nytimes.com/2015/11/15/fashion/ruth-bader-ginsburg-and-gloria-steinem-on-the-unending-fight-for-womens-rights.html

Goethals, G. R., & Allison, S. T. (2019). The romance of heroism and heroic leadership: Ambiguity, attribution, and apotheosis. West Yorkshire: Emerald.

Hoyt, C. L., Allison, S. T., Barnowski, A., & Sultan, A. (2020). Lay theories of heroism and leadership: The role of gender, communion, and agency. Social Psychology.

Jones, P. (2017). Mindfulness-based heroism: Creating enlightened heroes. Journal of Humanistic Psychology, 58(5), 1-24.

Kohen, A., Langdon, M., & Riches, B.R. (2017). The making of a hero: Cultivating empathy, altruism, and heroic imagination. *Journal of Humanistic Psychology*, 1-17.

Kafashan, S., Sparks, A., Rotella, A., & Barclay, P. (2017). Why heroism exists: Evolutionary perspectives on extreme helping. In S. T. Allison, G. R. Goethals, & R. M. Kramer (Eds.), *Handbook of heroism and heroic leadership.* New York: Routledge.

Kinsella, E.L., Ritchie, T.D., & Igou, E.R. (2017). Attributes and applications of heroes: A brief history of lay and academic perspectives. In S. T. Allison, G. R. Goethals, & R. M. Kramer (Eds.), *Handbook of heroism and heroic leadership.* New York: Routledge.

Lepore, J. (2018, October 8). Ruth Bader Ginsburg's unlikely path to the Supreme Court. *The New Yorker.* Retrieved from https://www.newyorker.com/magazine/2018/10/08/ruth-bader-ginsburgs-unlikely-path-to-the-supreme-court

Lewis, B. (Producer), & Bird, B. (Director). (2007). *Ratatouille* [Motion picture]. United States: Buena Vista Pictures.

Parks, C.D. (2017). Accidental and purposeful impediments to heroism. In S. T. Allison, G. R. Goethals, & R. M. Kramer (Eds.), *Handbook of heroism and heroic leadership.* New York: Routledge.

13

HEROIC PURSUITS OF SCIENTIFIC KNOWLEDGE

E. H. HA

What is science? We define it as knowledge or a system of knowledge covering general truths or the operation of general laws especially as obtained and tested through the scientific method (Merriam-Webster, 2019a). What is the scientific method? It refers to principles and procedures for the systematic pursuit of knowledge involving the recognition and formulation of a problem, the collection of data through observation and experimentation, and the formulation and testing of hypotheses (Merriam-Webster, 2019b). At what point is observational evidence considered to be sufficient enough to cross over to becoming a theory? Can we really know the scientific truth about the world when it is impossible to observe every aspect of the world? How and when do we know the officially abandon one theory in favor of another one? Is there really a one "correct" way of doing science?

As one can see, the relativity of the definition of the term "science" can be difficult to determine and is still up for debate on how to perform "good" science in the pursuit of knowledge. "Science" comes from the Latin word Scientia, which is referred to the results of logical demonstrations that revealed general and necessary truths (Godfrey-Smith, 2008). Before we had the specific disciplines of science that we know of today, science in the 17th century was called "natural philosophy" (i.e. physics, astronomy, other inquiries into the causes of things) or "natural history" (i.e. botany, zoology, and other descriptions of the contents of the world).

Over time, science developed the need for observation and experimentation and the current understanding of the term "science" are products of the 19th century. Science is something that descends from specific people and places (i.e. Copernicus, Kepler, Galileo, Descartes, etc.), including the scientific field itself. Given the unwieldy beast that is the philosophy of science, many philosophers of science have and are currently still trying to debating on how to go about what is the best way to go about science. One of many science philosophers who have tried to answer this question is Thomas Kuhn (1962) with his book *The Structure of Scientific Revolutions*, which arguably has changed the entire field of science and was crafted in a uniquely heroic way.

Philosopher of science Karl Popper, an academic rival of Kuhn, proposed that a good scientist is someone who can come up with imaginative, creative, risky ideas and is willing to subject these imaginative ideas to rigorous critical testing (Godfrey-Smith, 2008). One pertinent risky example of this is Philip Zimbardo's Stanford Prison experiment, which served as a substantial beginning for social and moral psychology. Though Zimbardo was painted in a negative light due to the consequences of the study, Zimbardo was arguably heroic in certain lights as well. Throughout this chapter, I will elaborate on the heroic themes that Thomas Kuhn and Philip Zimbardo have embodied in pursuit of the Truth in the grand scheme of scientific knowledge by using the social influence-based taxonomy of heroes (Allison & Goethals, 2013; Goethals & Allison, 2012; Allison & Green, 2020).

THOMAS KUHN: DEFINING SCIENTIFIC PROGRESS

Thomas Kuhn was an American historian of science whose 1962 book, *The Structure of Scientific Revolutions,* was arguably one of the most influential works of history and philosophy written in the 20th century (Britannica, 2018). Since its publication, the view of science by philosophers, historians, and sociologist has drastically changed and shattered traditional myths about how scientific behavior has little to do with traditional philosophical theories of rationality and knowledge (Godfrey-Smith, 2008).

Kuhn (1962) made claims on how science operates and drew philosophical conclusions form these claims. Though it was controversial and influential, Kuhn showed how interesting it is to mix history and psychology of science with questions about evidence and justification (Godfrey-Smith, 2008). In other words, though scientists and some philosophers like Popper emphasize that the rigidity of science is what makes scientific progress successful, Kuhn argues the arbitrary, personal natural of factors that often influence scientific decisions are actually key to science's success. Without flexibility, scientific research would not have proceeded as effectively as it has done so far. Kuhn also popularized the term "paradigm", which he talks about in a broad and narrow sense. A paradigm is a whole way of doing science in some particular field, or a whole package of claims about the world with methods for gathering and analyzing data. Kuhn also wrote that not all science needs a paradigm, and that each scientific field has an additional state called the "pre-paradigm" state. During this state, scientific work still happens, but it is not as organized. At some point during work, some striking piece of data appears that provides scientific insight about the world and supplies a model for further investigation, and evolves into the first paradigm of its field.

There are two main points that Kuhn (1962) makes in his book that address Popper's rigid response to progressing science. Firstly, Popper believed that science should have a rigid set of rules by being permanently open to criticism, even on fundamental theories (Godfrey-Smith, 2008). Kuhn disagreed on the permanent openness to the testing of fundamental ideas since science would not be efficient if scientists argued on the basics beliefs around science. Science is meant to be efficient in making substantial progress, and debating about fundamentals defeats science's purpose of having a coordinated structure. In an odd way, according to Kuhn, having a rigid way of doing science makes it too loose and open, and having more flexibility gives science more structure.

Secondly, Popper believes that all science proceeds in a single process of conjecture and refutation, and while there are still revolutionary periods, these are bigger and more dramatic conjectures and refutations compared to Kuhn's revolutionary science (Godfrey-Smith, 2008). Kuhn (1962) characterizes science into two distinct categories, and one transitional period called crisis science. Normal science is well-organized and can make clear progress, and scientists tend to agree on which problems are important and how to approach problems with possible solutions. Kuhn characterizes the work done in normal science as "puzzle-solving", where science uses the tools and concepts provided by the paradigm to describe, model, or create new phenomena. The "puzzle" is trying to get new cases and observations to fit smoothly into framework provided by the paradigm. Revolutionary science is when one paradigm replaces another, and it is hard to tell if progress has been made.

Crisis science is a special transitional period when an existing paradigm has lost the ability to inspire and guide scientists and no new paradigm has emerged to get the field back on track (Godfrey-Smith, 2008). At this point in crisis science, scientists tend to suddenly become interested in philosophy, which according to Kuhn, is a field quite useless for normal science. When Kuhn talks about changing from one paradigm to another, there is a gray area for when to abandon a paradigm. Theories can be refuted by observation by normal science, but completely abandoning a paradigm is much more difficult. Kuhn says that scientists can abandon a paradigm when a critical mass of anomalies has arisen and a rival paradigm has appeared. Kuhn's definition of an anomaly is a puzzle that has resisted a solution, which is called a "problem". All science will face anomalies, but as long as there are not too many of them, normal science can proceed as usual. Eventually, when there are enough anomalies, scientists lose faith in the paradigm and results in crisis science.

Kuhn (1962) argues that normal science is structured in a way that makes its own destruction inevitable, and the breakdown of paradigms is the "proper functioning" of science, though it does not feel that way to the scientists involved (Godfrey-Smith, 2008). However, paradigm breakdowns need to be in response to the correct stimulus. According to Kuhn's perspective on the destruction of paradigms, a paradigm acts similarly to a well-shielded and well-designed bomb. The bomb is meant to blow up at some point in time, but in very specific circumstances and not just at any old time.

After *The Structure of Scientific Revolutions* in 1962, Kuhn wrote a "Postscript" to *Structure* in 1970 and introduced the idea of incommensurability between paradigms (Godfrey-Smith, 2008). He expanded on the his previous book that when shifting from one paradigm to another, we should think of the shift like a "conversion" phenomenon, or a gestalt switch. The gestalt switch can be seen in illustrations that can be construed as either a rabbit or a duck, but not both at the same time. Relating this to paradigm shifts, Kuhn argues that revolutions are noncumulative in nature. When moving on to a new paradigm, it would feel like we feel like we've gained more than we have lost, but there is no unbiased way of measuring real progress. In other words, he thought that people occupying two different paradigms are incommensurable based on two reasons.

First, paradigms cannot communicate with one another because people from each paradigm will communicate in different ways and in a sense be speaking slightly different languages. Second, even when communication is possible, people in different paradigms will use different standards of evidence and argument and will not argue what a good theory is supposed to do. Though Kuhn thought he had a moderate view, philosophers of science have not found many examples of failed communication and are often adept at "scientific bilingualism". However, Kuhn raises a significant point: if paradigm shifts are not causal and are incommensurable, then are previous scientific revolutions, at least in part, based on irrational grounds?

THE LASTING EFFECTS OF KUHN: HEROIC OR VILLAINOUS?

The social sciences embraced Kuhn (1962) with enthusiasm. His depiction of science appeared to permit a more liberal conception of science and Kuhn's rejection of rules as determining scientific outcomes appealed to other factors outside of science in explaining why a scientific revolution took course that it did (Bird, 2018). The social scientists referenced Kuhn to use as a route to respectability and research funding by arguing that their field of expertise is in a pre-paradigm state, which eventually led to the emergence of scientific paradigms like economics (Bird, 2018; Naughton, 2012). His proposal that paradigm shifts are due to factors involving sociology and community agreement sparked a growth of a new academic discipline – the sociology of science-, in which researchers regarded science as not an "untouchable product of Enlightenment but as just another sub-culture" (Naughton, 2012).

As mentioned before, Kuhn revolutionized how to define scientific progress. The point that shook the sciences is that shifting between paradigms ensues when sociology, enthusiasm and scientific progress agree in unison, and is not a logical, determinate procedure. The irrationality of paradigm shifts caused a major uproar in reaction to his work because the way to progress science is not an empirical way to expand the field of knowledge (Godfrey-Smith, 2008). Though Kuhn made significant points on how to define scientific progress, he struggled to identify what progress was in the final pages of his book. He claimed that more recent paradigms have more problem solving power than earlier paradigms when he was asked about how to understand progress in science, but he was still vague on his answers. Also, with his follow up work on incommensurability, he raised the question that there are no linear, logical pathway for science and if science is moving from paradigm to paradigm with no logical foundation, then are scientists basing current work on irrational grounds? Though most scientists and philosophers agree that this is not the case, Kuhn brings a poignant point for scientists and the future of scientific progress.

Webster's definition of a hero is "a contempt of danger, not from ignorance or inconsiderate levity, but form a noble devotion to some great cause, and a just confidence of being able to meet danger in the spirit of such cause" (Franco, Blau, & Zimbardo, 2011). Depending on one's definition, Kuhn can be regarded as hero, villain, or both. Though there are many ways to define heroes and villains, Goethals and Allison (2012) proposed a social influence-based taxonomy with ten subtypes of heroes: trending, transitory, transitional, tragic, transposed, transparent, traditional, transfigured, transforming, and transcendent. Within the three taxonomies of heroes, Kuhn's contributions to the scientific and philosophical community fits the transforming and transposed hero in the social influence-based taxonomy (Allison, Beggan, & Efthimiou, 2019; Goethals & Allison, 2012). Transforming heroes transform entire societies, which in this case are the science, philosophy, and sociology communities and their attitudes towards scientific progress. Kuhn revolutionized the definition of scientific progress, made a notable and noble contribution in the pursuit of truth, and paved the way for new disciplines like economics and sociology.

Kuhn could also be seen as a transposed hero that rapidly changed from a hero to a villain. Kuhn shifted from working as an esteemed quantum physicist from Harvard University to writing a philosophy of science paper that changed the views of scientists and philosophers , making them question their own paradigm (Naughton, 2012). Ironically, Kuhn weakened the faith of some normal scientists, even though Kuhn wrote that they should have deep faith in their paradigms (Godfrey-Smith, 2008). However, the case for seeing Kuhn as a philosopher and a scientist who made significant contribution to the field of science can be arguably be seen as more heroic than villainous since he asked the necessary questions and thoughts to expand the field of knowledge.

THE STANFORD PRISON EXPERIMENT: EXPOSURE OF HUMAN MORALITY

Philip Zimbardo and his colleagues made a major breakthrough in the field of social psychology through the Stanford Prison experiment. The Stanford Prison experiment was a 1971 social psychology experiment which attempted to investigate the psychological effects of perceived power, focusing on the struggle between prisoners and prison officers (Haney, Banks, & Zimbardo, 1973). Zimbardo and colleagues were interested in "finding out whether the brutality reported among guards in American prisons was due to the sadistic personalities of the guards (ie. dispositional) or had more to do with the prison environment (i.e., situational)" (McLeod, 2018; Haney et al., 1973).

The study was conducted between August 14 and 20, 1971, with 24 male college students who were judged to be the most physically and mentally stable, the most mature, and the least involved in antisocial behaviors were randomly assigned to be either "guards" or "prisoners" in a mock prison, with Zimbardo serving as the superintendent (McLeod, 2018). Several prisoners left the mid-experiment, and the experiment ended early just after six days rather than the intended two weeks. The reports indicated that the subjects quickly assumed their assigned roles, with the guards enforcing authoritarian measures and subjecting prisoners to psychological torture, while most of the prisoners passively accepted psychological abuse and, by officer's request, actively harassed other prisoners who tried to stop it (Haney et al., 1973; McLeod, 2018).

Zimbardo designed the experiment with the goal of inducing disorientation, depersonalization, and deindividuation in the participants (McLeod, 2018). Prisoners were treated like criminals by being arrested at their own homes without warning for armed robbery or burglary and taken to the police station. The prisoners were strip searched, fingerprinted, took mug shots, given prison clothes and bedding, and given their new numerical identities (Zimbardo, 2019b). The numerical identities were meant to induce a sense of deindividuation, and the prisoners also had to wear stocking caps to minimize self-expression (McLeod, 2018). The basement of the psychology department at Stanford University was remodeled to be like a prison to invoke a sense of disorientation and depersonalization, with barred doors and windows, bare walls and small cells (McLeod, 2018; Zimbardo, 2019a).

The assigned prison guards dressed in identical khaki uniforms with a whistle around their neck and a Billy club borrowed from the police (Zimbardo, 2019c). Guards also wore reflective sunglasses to further invoke the sense of depersonalization between the guard and the prisoner (Zimbardo, 2019c). The guards were not given specific training, but were instructed to do whatever they thought was necessary to maintain law and order in the prison and to command the respect of prisoners without physical violence (Zimbardo, 2019c). Though the prisoners knew that no physical violence would be involved, they were warned in the consent form to expect harassment, invasion of privacy, minimal adequate food, and other civil rights infringement in the simulated prison.

To ingrain the identity of the prisoner and guard, prisoners were regularly rudely awakened at 2:30 a.m. by the guards to do counts, which involves prisoners doing roll call with their numerical identities (Zimbardo, 2019c). The counts served to familiarize the prisoners with the numbers and for the guards to regularly exercise authoritative control over the prisoners. The guards also used push-ups as a way to "punish infractions of the rules or displays of improper attitudes toward the guards or institution" (Zimbardo, 2019c). Though this was initially deemed as an inappropriate kind of punishment, it was later learned that it was a form of punishment in Nazi concentration camps. During the study, one of the guards stepped on the prisoners' backs or made other prisoners sit or step on the backs of fellow prisoners doing their push-ups (Zimbardo, 2019c).

The first day of the experiment was uneventful, but a rebellion broke out on the morning of the second day (Zimbardo, 2019d). The prisoners "removed their stocking caps, ripped off their numbers, barricaded themselves inside the cells by putting their beds against the door". The guards responded by shooting the prisoners with a stream of skin-chilling carbon dioxide from a fire extinguisher and forced the prisoners away from the doors (Zimbardo, 2019d). The guards realized that they cannot control the prison using physical tactics given the physical constraints of nine guards for nine prisoners, so they decided to resort to psychological tactics instead. "The guards broke into each cell, stripped the prisoners naked, took the beds out...and generally began to harass and intimidate the prisoners" (Zimbardo, 2019d). The prisoner's rebellion played an important role to produce greater solidarity among the guards.

The guards designated one of the three cells as a "privilege cell", where prisoners who were least involved in the rebellion were given special privileges such as getting their uniforms and beds back, were allowed to wash and brush their teeth, and were given special food. In an extra effort to break solidarity among prisoners, the "bad" and "good" prisoners switched cells after half a day of this treatment, and the prisoners became distrustful of each other. This tactic was used by real guards and prisons to promote aggression among inmates and to redirect the aggression from guard to prison mates (Zimbardo, 2019d).

The guards also implemented arbitrary control by granting or denying prisoners the toilet, and the prisoners were often forced to urinate in a bucket after 10 p.m., which the guards sometimes denied prisoners the ability to empty these buckets- further degrading the quality of their environment (Zimbardo, 2019d). Even Zimbardo was blinded by his role as a prison superintendent. When Zimbardo heard of a possible mass escape plot from a released prisoner, he moved the prisoners to the fifth floor storage room with bags over their heads while Zimbardo anxiously waited for the part participant to come (Zimbardo, 2019f). Instead, he was met with a former Yale graduate student roommate who wanted to see what the study was about and asked what the independent variable was. Zimbardo, to his surprise, got angry at him for asking such an unimportant question in amidst a potential prison break through, and that was when he realized that he was thinking like a prison superintendent rather than a research psychologist (Zimbardo, 2019f).

As the study progressed, the guards very noticeably escalated their level of harassment by having them do more push-ups, jumping jacks, and increasing the length of the counts to several hours each (Zimbardo, 2019g). At this point in the study, Zimbardo invited a Catholic priest who had been a prison chaplain to evaluate how realistic their prison situation was (Zimbardo, 2019g). The priest interviewed each prisoner individually, and the prisoners responded with their number instead of their names (Zimbardo, 2019g). With each interview, the priest asked each of them what are they doing to get out of the prison (Zimbardo, 2019g). When the prisoners responded in puzzlement, the priest explained that the only way to get out of the prison was with the help of the lawyer. The priest volunteered to contact their parents to get legal aid if they wanted him to, and some of the prisoners accepted his offer (Zimbardo, 2019g). The priest's role blurred the lines between role-playing and reality for the participants.

During the sessions with the priest, one prisoner in particular, #819, did not want to see a priest but rather wanted to see a doctor because he was feeling sick (Zimbardo, 2019g). He was eventually persuaded to see the priest and Zimbardo to determine what kind of help was needed. The participant broke down and started to cry hysterically, just as the two prisoners released earlier (Zimbardo, 2019g). Zimbardo then released him to a room adjacent to the prison yard and told him that he would get him some food then take him to see a doctor. While Zimbardo was doing this, the guards lined up the other prisoners and had them chant in unison in utter conformity "#819 is a bad prisoner. Because of what Prisoner #819 did, my cell is a mess, Mr. Correctional Officer" a dozen times. Zimbardo realized that #819 could hear them chanting and rushed to the room where he left the participant and found him sobbing uncontrollably (Zimbardo, 2019g).

Zimbardo suggested that he leave, but the prisoner refused because he said he could not exit because the others labeled him a bad prisoner. Even though he was sick, he wanted to go back and prove he was not a bad prisoner (Zimbardo, 2019g). Then Zimbardo finally said, "Listen, you are not #819. You are [his name], and my name is Dr. Zimbardo. I am a psychologist, not a prison superintendent, and this is not a real prison. This is just an experiment, and those are students, not prisoners, just like you. Let's go". The participant suddenly stopped crying, and agreed to leave with Zimbardo (Zimbardo, 2019g).

The study continued to escalate, and the guards and prisoners became more and more entrenched in their assigned roles. Eventually, it became evident to end the study when some visiting parents asked Zimbardo to contact a lawyer to get their son out of prison (Zimbardo, 2019g). Zimbardo and colleagues created an overwhelmingly powerful situation where prisoners withdrawing and behaving in pathological ways and guards were behaving sadistically (Zimbardo, 2019g). Zimbardo also learned that the guards were escalating the abuse of prisoners in the middle of the night when the experiment was "off" and thought no researchers were watching. Also, Christina Maslach, a recent Stanford Ph.D., saw the state of the study and spoke up in outrage by saying, " It's terrible what you are doing to these boys!", who was the first out of 50 outsiders who had seen the prison to question its morality. When the study ended, the guards, prisoners, and staff had a series of encounter sessions to reflect what they had exhibited and observed in the study and also made it a time for moral reeducation by discussing the conflicts posed by the simulation and their behavior (Zimbardo, 2019h).

Overall, the prison environment was an important factor in creating the guards' brutal behavior since none of the participants showed sadistic tendencies prior to the study. The findings support the situational explanation of behavior rather than the dispositional characteristics (McLeod, 2018).

PHILIP ZIMBARDO: THE CREATOR OF FRANKENSTEIN OR A HERO?

The Stanford prison experiment clearly breached ethical lines and tested the lengths of human morality. The study continued despite the fact that prisoners expressed their desire to withdraw, and the prisoners did not consent to being 'arrested' at home, which is a breach of ethics of Zimbardo's own contract that all their participants had signed (McLeod, 2018). Half of the prisoners were released early on in the study due to severe emotional or cognitive reactions (Zimbardo, 2019h).

The study was also funded by the Office of Naval Research, the Psychology Department and the University Committee of Human Experimentation to investigate the causes of difficulties between guards and prisoners (Zimbardo, 2019h; McLeod, 2018). Though the Committee did not anticipate the extreme results, alternative methodologies that caused less distress to the participants were looked at, but no other suitable alternative could be found that would give the desired information (McLeod, 2018). This funding could have indirectly pushed Zimbardo to progress the study the way he did.

Although the negative consequences seemed the most prominent after the study, Zimbardo argues that it provided insight about the current understanding of human behavior and society can improve to balance the distress caused by the study (McLeod, 2018). To Zimbardo's defense, he himself did not know the beast that he had created and has fallen into the trance of the study himself as a prison superintendent. After extensive group and individual debriefing questions and post-experimental questionnaires over several weeks, months, then years later, Zimbardo concluded that there were no lasting negative effects in the participants (McLeod, 2018; Zimbardo, 2019h).

However, decades after the study took place, "prison conditions and correctional policies in the United States have become even more punitive and destructive, with politicians vying for who is the toughest on crime along with the racialization of arrests and sentencing (Zimbardo, 2019g). The media contributes to the problem by generating heightened fear of violent crimes, even though statistics show that violent crimes have decreased. Now, the number of jailed Americans have doubled during the past decade. Another positive effect is that juveniles accused of federal crimes are no longer housed before trial with adult prisoners due to the risk of violence against them (McLeod, 2018).

Surprisingly, the American Psychological Association approved the experiment and concluded that all existing ethical guidelines had been followed (Zimbardo, 2019h). The experiment contributed to the creation of the institutional review board (IRB) for human studies and adhered to stricter guidelines for future human experimentation studies. The prison experiment propelled Zimbardo make positive contributions following the study. Zimbardo found a non-profit organization dedicated to promoting heroism in everyday life called the Heroic Imagination Project (HIP) in 2014 (Heroic Imagination Project). The prison experiment also motivated Zimbardo to write *The Lucifer Effect*, which he argues that humans cannot be defined as good or evil because humans have the potential to act both ways given the state of the situation (Zimbardo, 2007).

Zimbardo argues that good people can be "induced, seduced, and initiated into behaving in evil ways. They can also be led to act in irrational, stupid, self-destructive, antisocial, and mindless ways when they are immersed in 'total' situations that impact human nature in ways that challenge our sense of stability and consistency of individual personality, or character, and of morality." (Zimbardo, 2007). In his TED talk The psychology of evil, he says that are seven social processes that led people down the "slippery slope of evil": mindlessly taking the first small step, dehumanization of others, de-individuation of self, diffusion of personal responsibility, blind obedience to authority, uncritical conformity to group norms, and passive tolerance of evil through inaction or indifference (TED, 2008).

Using the Goethals and Allison's taxonomic structure of the different subtypes of heroes, Zimbardo can be argued to be three subtypes of heroes: transforming, tragic, transposed, transitory, and transparent (Goethals & Allison, 2012). Although one of the first major controversial social psychology studies was the Milgram experiment at Yale University, Zimbardo's prison experiment contributed to the growing social psychology field, made a big splash in popular media, and made the potential limits of human morality known to the public. Zimbardo not only contributed to the beginnings of social psychology, but he transformed how much people weighted dispositional factors rather than situational factors when viewing prison and criminal justice systems. Zimbardo also fits Franco and colleagues' scientific (or discovery) heroes under the twelve subtypes of heroes (Franco et al., 2011). Scientific heroes are individuals who explore unknown areas of science, use novel and unproven research methods, or discover new scientific information seen as valuable to humanity, all of which Zimbardo did in the Stanford prison experiment.

From a certain perspective, Zimbardo is also a tragic hero. He began as a respectable psychologist who graduated summa cum laude from Brooklyn College with a triple major in psychology, sociology, and anthropology, and eventually completed his Ph.D. from Yale University. In some ways, Zimbardo tarnished his reputation with the Stanford prison experiment by bending his own ethical rules from his contract, succumbing to his own role in the study, and handling the consequences and long-term effects of the study. Despite his potentially tarnished reputation from the study, Zimbardo moved on to other great works and projects, which the acts can be seen arguably be seen as a transposed hero recovering from the study. In 2012, Zimbardo received the American Psychological Foundation Gold Medal for Lifetime Achievement in the Science of Psychology (Award, n.d.). He went on the pursue other projects like publishing his book *The Lucifer Effect* and creating the non-profit The Heroic Imagination Project to increase awareness of the human potential to be evil and to instill good works in others.

Since Zimbardo was widely known for his Stanford prison experiment in the eyes of the public, he can also be argued to be transparent and transitory. He is widely known for the prison experiment, but his other future good works and projects seem to be less well known to the public. Richard Griggs (2014) looked at Stanford experiment coverage in textbooks, and 11 out of 13 discuss the Stanford Prison Experiment, 5 of which did not contain any criticism of the experiment and the other 6 provided very minimal discussions of the study's flaws. Some introductory textbooks are even starting to omit the experiment completely (Gray, 2013). Zimbardo can also be argued to be both heroic and villainous, but he has made long lasting contributions to the field of science, particularly social psychology, and his current works to improve society's morality has painted him as an overall hero.

CONCLUDING REMARKS

Thomas Kuhn and Philip Zimbardo have expanded their respective fields of scientific knowledge. Kuhn's questioning of the foundations of scientific disciplines and of the definition of scientific progress through the paradigm shifts served as a rippling effect for the proliferation of other fields. Zimbardo's Stanford prison experiment expanded the realm of social psychology and provided significant insight on human morality. Both examples made took risks to expand the field of scientific knowledge and exhibited heroic qualities using Goethals and Allison's social influence-based taxonomy of heroes and Franco and colleagues twelve subtypes that call forth heroic action (Allison, 2019; Goethals & Allison, 2012; Franco et al., 2011). I hope that this chapter contributes to the growing field of the psychology of heroism by shedding light on scientific heroes who either do not get enough attention or the appropriate attention for the significant works that have influenced contributions towards our collective understanding of science.

REFERENCES

Allison, S. T. (2019). Heroic consciousness. Heroism Science, 4, 1-43.
Allison, S. T., Beggan, J. K., & Efthimiou, O. (2019). The art and science of heroism and heroic leadership. Lausanne, Switzerland: Frontiers.

Allison, S. T., & Goethals, G. R. (2013). Heroic leadership: An influence taxonomy of 100 exceptional individuals. New York: Routledge.

Allison, S. T., & Green, J. D. (2021). Nostalgia and heroism: Theoretical convergence of memory, motivation, and function. Frontiers in Psychology.

Award: Phil Zimbardo to receive the APA's Gold Medal Award. (n.d.). Retrieved from https://web.archive.org/web/20130116021952/https://psychology.stanford.edu/node/2533

Bennett, D., Efthimiou, O., & Allison, S. T. (2020). The role of heroic creativity and leadership in creative work. In A. de Dios & L. Kong (Eds.), Handbook on the geographies of creativity. Cheltenham, UK: Edward Elgar.

Bird, A. (2018, October 31). Thomas Kuhn. Retrieved from https://plato.stanford.edu/entries/thomas-kuhn/#CritInfl

Britannica, T. E. (2018, July 14). Thomas S. Kuhn. Retrieved from https://www.britannica.com/biography/Thomas-S-Kuhn

Eylon, D., & Allison, S. T. (2005). The frozen in time effect in evaluations of the dead. Personality and Social Psychology Bulletin, 31, 1708-1717.

Franco, Z. E., Blau, K., & Zimbardo, P. G. (2011). Heroism: A conceptual analysis and differentiation Between heroic action and altruism. Review of General Psychology.

Godfrey-Smith, P. (2008). Theory and reality: An introduction to the philosophy of science. Chicago: Univ. of Chicago Press.

Goethals, G. R., & Allison, S. T. (2012). Making heroes: The construction of courage, competence and virtue. Advances in Experimental Social Psychology, 46, 183–235.

Gray, P. (2013, October 19). Why Zimbardo's Prison Experiment Isn't in My Textbook. Retrieved from https://www.psychologytoday.com/us/blog/freedom-learn/201310/why-zimbardo-s-prison-experiment-isn-t-in-my-textbook?page=1

Griggs, R. A. (2014). Coverage of the Stanford prison experiment in introductory psychology textbooks. Teaching of Psychology, 41(3), 195-203.

Haney, C., Banks, W. C., & Zimbardo, P. G. (1973). A study of prisoners and guards in a simulated prison. Naval Research Review, 30, 4-17.

Heroic Imagination Project. (n.d.). Retrieved from https://web.archive.org/web/20120425151645/http://heroicimagination.ning.com/

Kuhn, T. (1962). The Structure of Scientific Revolutions. Chicago: University of Chicago Press.

McLeod, S. A. (2018, September 16). Zimbardo - Stanford prison experiment. Retrieved from https://www.simplypsychology.org/zimbardo.html

Naughton, J. (2012, August 18). Thomas Kuhn: The man who changed the way the world looked at science. Retrieved from https://www.theguardian.com/science/2012/aug/19/thomas-kuhn-structure-scientific-revolutions

Rabbit-Duck Illusion. (n.d.). Retrieved from http://mathworld.wolfram.com/Rabbit-DuckIllusion.html

Merriam-Webster (2019a). Retrieved from https://www.merriam-webster.com/dictionary/science?utm_campaign=sd&utm_medium=serp&utm_source=jsonld

Merriam-Webster (2019b). Retrieved from https://www.merriam-webster.com/dictionary/scientific%20method

TED. (2008, September 23). The psychology of evil | Philip Zimbardo. Retrieved from https://www.youtube.com/watch?v=OsFEV35tWsg

Zimbardo, P. G. (2007). The Lucifer Effect: Understanding how good people turn evil. New York: Random House.

Zimbardo, P. G. (2019a). 2. Setting Up. Retrieved from http://www.prisonexp.org/setting-up

Zimbardo, P. G. (2019b). 3. Arrival. Retrieved from http://www.prisonexp.org/arrival

Zimbardo, P. G. (2019c). 4. Guards. Retrieved from http://www.prisonexp.org/guards

Zimbardo, P. G. (2019d). 5. Rebellion. Retrieved from http://www.prisonexp.org/rebellion

Zimbardo, P. G. (2019e). 6. Grievances. Retrieved from http://www.prisonexp.org/grievances

Zimbardo, P. G. (2019f). 7. Escape. Retrieved from http://www.prisonexp.org/escape

Zimbardo, P. G. (2019g). 8. Conclusion. Retrieved from http://www.prisonexp.org/conclusion

Zimbardo, P. G. (2019h). More Information. Retrieved from http://www.prisonexp.org/faq/

ABOUT THE AUTHORS

Tai Lea Ho is a graduate at the University of Richmond where she earned her B.A. in Psychology and Cognitive Science. She is a native New Yorker but still gets lost in the city from time to time. Born on Halloween, she is an enthusiast of the macabre and an appreciator of morbid art.

Esther (Heera) Ha graduated from the University of Richmond Class of 2019 with a B.S. degree in Psychology. Striving to be Rick in amidst a sea of Jerrys, she strives to be bold and different from the millennials, just like every other millennial. While she hopes to expand the current knowledge of moral psychology, she enjoys outdoor activities, particularly rock climbing (or pebble wrestling), chess, learning new skills, and smiling in her free time.

Jacob Roberson graduated from the University of Richmond in May of 2019. Born and raised in Richmond, Virginia, he played four years on the varsity football team while double majoring in psychology and sociology. He was Vice President of the UR Mentoring Network, an appointed member to the Dean's Student Advisory Board, and the President's Advisory Committee for Sexual Violence Prevention and Response, among other obligations. He enjoys relaxing with good company and listening to R&B and Soulful music as well as writing poetry. He plans to pursue a PhD in social psychology en route to becoming a professor.

Sharon H. Shin is a graduate of University of Richmond with a degree in Psychology. She loves to play Settlers of Catan, watch Disney movies, and quote vines. When she grows up, she hopes to go into the neuroscience field and learn about the relationship between the brain and mental illnesses.

Megan R. Wirtz is a graduate of the University of Richmond. A D.C. native, she graduated in 2019 with a B.A. in Theatre and Psychology, and a minor in Latin American, Latino, and Iberian Studies. She was the President of University Players, and was on the Kairos Leadership Team and Alpha Psi Omega executive board. After graduation, she hopes to continue her social psychology research while doing theatre on the side – she doesn't understand the concept of not being busy.

Lauren A. Lambert is a graduate of the University of Richmond, who earned her Bachelor of Arts in Psychology in May of 2019. Lauren was the student captain of the University Dancers and an active member of the Delta Delta Delta sorority. She is excited to move to Nashville, TN to teach elementary school in August of 2019. She has a deep passion for Mexican food, babies, and Reese's peanut butter cups.

Jamie L. Katz graduated from the University of Richmond with a double major in Leadership Studies and Psychology and a minor in Religious Studies. She works to add people to the national bone marrow registry through a company called Gift of Life in hopes of discovering new heroes. She hopes to live by the water one day and is happiest when totally immersed in nature.

Chloe L. Zaloom received her undergraduate degree from the University of Richmond. In 2019 she graduated with a B.A in Leadership Studies and Psychology. Originally from northern New Jersey, she plans on moving back to the New Jersey/New York area to start her new life chapter in life. Her dream is to one day retire to a New England state and live on a farm full of Golden Retrievers.

Jessica M. Stanfill graduated from the University of Richmond with a double major in Psychology and Journalism. Jess was also a varsity athlete on UR's soccer team for four years. Jess enjoys photography, dogs, coffee and spending time with her family and friends.

Natalie R. Schiano is a graduate of the University of Richmond with a major in Psychology and minors in both Elementary Education and Leadership Studies. She worked as a Psychology Teaching Fellow and at the Curriculum Materials Center as a librarian. She was a member of of Delta Delta Delta sorority and involved in Best Buddies during her time on campus. Her favorite food is cheese, which is quite unfortunate since she is allergic to dairy.

Alexa M. Bertrand is a graduate of the University of Richmond with a major in Business Administration with Concentrations in Marketing and Management, and a major in Psychology. She is very musically inclined, and plays guitar in her spare time. When she's not playing guitar, she enjoys looking at photos of cats. She hopes one day she will be able to sleep for more than 4 hours a night.

Smaragda P. Spyrou is a graduate of the University of Richmond with a B.S. in Psychology and a minor in Mathematics. Born and raised in the Mediterranean, she hopes to never have to live away from the beach again. Smaragda likes to keep herself very busy, with 3 jobs and several extracurriculars – or she just has a hard time saying no. Her personality motto is Espresso Patronum!

Other Books in the Palsgrove Series

Allison, S. T. (Ed.) (2020). *Core concepts in heroism science: Volume 1.* Richmond: Palsgrove.

Allison, S. T. (Ed.) (2020). *Core concepts in heroism science: Volume 2.* Richmond: Palsgrove.

Allison, S. T. (Ed.) (2019). *Heroic transformation: How heroes change themselves and the world.* Richmond: Palsgrove.

Allison, S. T. (Ed.) (2018). *Heroes and villains of the millennial generation.* Richmond: Palsgrove.

Allison, S. T. (Ed.) (2017). *Heroes of Richmond: Four centuries of courage, dignity, and virtue.* Richmond: Palsgrove.

THE SERIES EDITOR

Scott T. Allison is Professor of Psychology at the University of Richmond. He has published 15 books on heroism and heroic leadership and over 100 academic articles. His books include *The Romance of Heroism, Heroic Transformation, The Heroic Leadership Imperative, Heroism and Wellbeing in the 21st Century, Conceptions of Leadership, Frontiers in Spiritual Leadership, Heroic Humility,* and *the Handbook of Heroism and Heroic Leadership.* His work has appeared in USA Today, National Public Radio, the New York Times, the Los Angeles Times, Slate Magazine, MSNBC, CBS, Psychology Today, and the Christian Science Monitor. He has received Richmond's Distinguished Educator Award and the Virginia Council of Higher Education's Outstanding Faculty Award.